A Path through the Forest

A Path Through the Forest is a comprehensive and thought-provoking compilation of essays on subjects that have great relevance for Druidry today. With sections on Druid basics, environmentalism, metaphysics, history and ethics, this collection provides food for thought through the lens of one Druid seeker and is a valuable insight into a Druid's philosophical exploration of their path.

Philip Carr-Gomm, author of *Druid Mysteries*

A wide-ranging collection of essays written by an Irish Druid that pokes jabs at modern Pagan dogmas and leaders, and advocates for the re-learning of practical skills and a life path that respects nature. The articles are at times complaining and cranky but always thoughtful, and filled with warnings about the state of the world. If you ever wanted insight into the mind of a practicing contemporary Druid, this book should be a pleasing read.

Ellen Evert Hopman, Archdruid of Tribe of the Oak, author of the *Druid* trilogy of novels, *A Legacy of Druids: Conversations with Druid Leaders of Britain, the USA and Canada, Past and Present*, and other volumes on tree lore and Celtic Herbalism

Luke Eastwood's essays are thought-provoking. Like diving into any subject, you don't have to agree with everything, but only open your mind to hear what is being said, and use that knowledge to expand your own view. These essays do just that: they approach the subjects from a personal viewpoint, combined with academic research and years of practical experience and offer a perspective on Druidry that is interesting and heartfelt. Some of the essays are a snapshot in time, that still resonate

today, while others are more contemporary. All in all, this is a good collection for Druids who want to consider their own practice more deeply and who are looking for inspiration.
Joanna van der Hoeven, author of *The Book of Hedge Druidry* and *The Path of the Hedge Witch*

Luke Eastwood's eclectic and thought-provoking book touches on aspects of Celtic and Druid culture from history and ecology to ethics and metaphysics. Throughout, Eastwood applies a critical lens to the landscape of modern Druidry, challenging practitioners to reflect on their own behavior and make improvements where possible. This collection will leave those involved in Druid or Pagan communities with many hard questions to mull over, and that can only be a good thing.
Logan Albright, author of *Libertarian Paganism* and *Conform or Be Cast Out: The (Literal) Demonization of Nonconformists*

In this down to earth book, Luke offers no-nonsense Druidic history, wisdom and logic relevant for today's modern world. To learn how to live now and for future generations we need to understand our past, both sociopolitical and historical. This book offers guidance to do just that.
Emma Farrell, Plant Spirit Healer and author of *Journeys with Plant Spirits*

In *A Path through the Forest*, Eastwood invited us to join him on his life-long journey from his childhood to the present day. In this remarkable series of essays and articles, spanning a period of over a decade, Eastwood shares his experiences and learning as he continues along his personal path of learning. It is impossible to read this collection of works without admiring Eastwood's tenacity, the breadth of his interests and the depth of his knowledge. The variety of topics addressed is noteworthy and one can only be inspired by the fearless way Eastwood approaches a variety of contentious issues, refusing to submit to the pressures of convention, whilst forging his own path through what can often be a confusing and disheartening landscape. This book is a must for all those committed to following a similar journey of spiritual and practical growth. There is no doubt that a great deal may be garnered from Eastwood's insights and writings.

Jon G. Hughes, author of *A Druid's Handbook To The Spiritual Power of Plants* and *The Druidic Art Of Divination: Understanding The Past And Seeing Into The Future*

I always find Luke's books to be informative and engaging and this set of articles does not disappoint. As well as, on one level, these articles being well written, Luke has also done a lot of research on his topic — Druidry. On another level, Luke is sharing with us, his readers, his own personal journey and how he eventually became a horticulturalist / Earth Guardian. There are so many one-liners that stood out for me, making me stop and breathe that comment in. Two in particular stand out. 1. *Morality is clearly part of our Spirituality* & 2. *There was once a garden and that garden was the world.* Thank you, Luke for again reminding us of our own 'inner garden' of our Soul-Self and our responsibility to protect Great Mother.

Amantha Murphy, author of *The Way of The Seabhean: An Irish Shamanic Path*

A Path through the Forest

Collected Essays on Druidry

A Path through the Forest

Collected Essays on Druidry

Luke Eastwood

**MOON
BOOKS**

Winchester, UK
Washington, USA

JOHN HUNT PUBLISHING

First published by Moon Books, 2024
Moon Books is an imprint of John Hunt Publishing Ltd., No. 3 East Street, Alresford
Hampshire SO24 9EE, UK
office@jhpbooks.net
www.johnhuntpublishing.com
www.moon-books.net

For distributor details and how to order please visit the 'Ordering' section on our website.

ISBN: 978 1 80341 508 6
978 1 80341 512 3 (ebook)
Library of Congress Control Number: 2023932041

A CIP catalogue record for this book is available from the British Library.

Design: Lapiz Digital Services

UK: Printed and bound by CPI Group (UK) Ltd, Croydon, CR0 4YY
Printed in North America by CPI GPS partners

We operate a distinctive and ethical publishing philosophy in
all areas of our business, from our global network of authors to
production and worldwide distribution.

Contents

In memory of Diane Howe 1958–2023

Acknowledgements

Thank you to everyone who has supported my work over the years and in particular book publishers, the magazines and websites that published many of the essays and interviews within these pages. I am also very grateful for the help and input from friends and family who helped edit my typo-ridden work and also to Elena Danaan for her wonderful illustrations in several of my books. Thank you to supporters in the media and my fellow authors, Druids and other esoteric practitioners who have supported and promoted my writing over many years, a kindness that should never be forgotten. Thank you to David Sparenberg for his thoughtful preface, and general encouragement. Finally, a big thank you to Trevor Greenfield, Editor at Moon Books, for supporting my work, from my first book, right up until now and for his patience with a writer who can be pedantic and difficult at times!

Preface

Planetary conditions continue to worsen as the awareness of danger increases — awareness outpacing what urgently needs doing and as urgently needs changing to protect evolutionary diversity and keep Earth habitable. We live in a time and place beset by cumulative historical trauma to human identity and the diversified integrity of biomass and biosphere. The dangers are real, looming large in the reality before us and are in pressing need of global address. Here is reality and here is necessity in the 21st century. Our species, humanity, is both instrumental and swept up in emergency, ever more increasing swept away intensifying catastrophes.

Pragmatic, practical efforts and developments in the counter direction of sustainable solutions come to the forefront and resist denial with persistent and serious focus. Behind the practical signals and assertions are deeper questions that conditionally demand to be asked, thought through, searched, researched, experienced, and imagined. These are connected to the long-term necessities of appropriate and inappropriate modes of life, values, and re-evaluations of functioning human presence within the dynamic, immense and intimate intricacies of overall biotic wellbeing, eco-systems, and Earth's organic structures

This is not the place to delve into several of these profound and spiritually grounded inquires. Yet there is one such question that is at the heart of what I find to be Luke Eastwood's intention in assembling this thematically unified collection of essays. I am referring to an authentication of the human image, which is to say a vibrant perspective and sensitive content that rings true as an identity, and perhaps even one definition of what to be a human being is or can be, at home within a context of vital relationships, not as a dominating superiority but a dedicated participant — one among many, among all.

Framed within the urgent necessity for Ecosophy (Earth Wisdom), an affirmation of how being human is compatible with balance and maintenance of planetary animism, we see that as a world society and international culture we are ingrained with images of acceptability — adjustment and respectability versus socially tabooed or outlier status. We look at the increasing failure of the images of the politician, the corporate CEO, the military hero, and pop culture star, and can and should ask what are the relationships of such models to crisis solutions and how reliable are they to be role played and followed? Many of us, perhaps, when the surface is scratched, a majority already know the answer to this question and disillusionment and distrust are widespread. Gray is not a colour native to the spectrum vitality, experiential playfulness, and value narrating extensions of our humanity. There is a spectrum of options outside of contemporary norms.

If we give credit to our intelligence capacity, we are left to wonder then, are dimensional limitations all that are possible, or only what is available in service to a set of values antagonistic to the natural functions of Earth? Is human truth found exclusively within the given "images" or is there actually a more fulfilling "and yet," potentially accessible through experiments in a back-to-the future immersion? Are we evolved for intimate wisdom along with enchantment? Or are we no more than functionary automatons, eaters of the planet, shallow rooted by industrial displacement and without identifications outside of technology and the market pushing of gargets? Is the fossilizing ideology and false imagery of what is given the extent of our developmental possibilities?

The seeker in the role of retriever and pathfinder searches into the past to gain vision and perspective on what can be possible as an authenticating future. From that vantage, we should dare to ask, what of the Shaman, the bard, the storyteller and troubadour, who contain and continues the cosmology linked to an intimate sensuality of place, and a cultural heritage of intergenerational people? What of the Earth Keeper as an authentic image of grounded and integral human being, being consciousness and a presence in the encompassing all aliveness of this life giving and life affirming planetary home? Indeed, to come directly to author Eastwood's essays, What about the Druid? Is this a compelling, trustworthy image and model to base our future human identity, species direction, and collective destiny on?

From the transpersonal perspective, there are sports teams, many with massive followings, and social clubs, why then can there not be clans, why not again tribes and such intentional communities as eco villages? These and the other questions asked here are not idle, rhetorical, superficial, or daydreams of groundless make-believe and escape from both boredom and desperation but emerge rather from a mutuality between various persons and the Living Earth. And yes, we are truly, at survival and spiritual levels alike, in urgent need of viable differences into Earth-appropriate identities (images) and eco-founded communities of Earth Wisdom.

Is it therefore foolishness to think, coalesce and plan small, or is small seeding an unfolding of profound instinct and intuition, pointedly considered since the disasters around and compounding against us are so immense, so apparently bigger than ordinary capacities to cope? Life is what it is on this planet of trauma and trouble, and the earnest search for alternatives is on. Luke Eastwood's *A Path through the Forest* is one such search.

This book of essays is an author's journey, spanning more than a decade of seeking and gathering. It is as such a vision quest, an interweaving exploration backward and forward in describing a path. No steps in the journey, no altars of insight along the way are passed over or left out. Like all such undertakings, the research within these pages is adventure for the mind, pioneering for the forlorn and craving modern soul. There is knowledge herein, framed in honesty, looking for something more, of more substance, perhaps of an unpretentious nobility of existence, that the author like all true questers understands is a back-and-forth process, sifting ancestry into the alchemic potentials of responsibility and connectiveness for the far and near workings of life. Which is to say, what was has been and recurs and in recurring is better than what was before.

Worth asking: Is it not within the human complex, the oft denied enigma of human life, that while facing into the dire and darkest doom some will show the grit and spirit to dream of renaissance? Then why not a rebirth of an education in enchantment? Of the audacity of re-enchantment at a time and in a place when an entire planet needs strong measures of courage, humility, noninvasive confidence, and nature invested magic? Magic, not a mind trip, not a floating world fantasy or angry wish for dark revenge, but magic of relationships with the miracles of what is given, circles and returns, encompasses, and penetrates the belonging sentience of existence.

As I approached this preface, I found myself recalling something learned decades ago from Ludwig Binswanger. Binswanger was one of the major founders of existential analysis and he identified a category of individual and social behavior he named "extravagance." By extravagance Binswanger meant a condition, not only of mind, but the entire gestalt of the driving dynamic of a unit, which had concentrated its total external and internal resources into a single direction. And then when trouble came, and alarms sounded, life was out on a limb, as he put it, hanging over the abyss of disaster if not oblivion, because there was nothing remaining within the parameters of normalcy, the normalcy of exhausting and bankrupting extravagance to summons up, to reverse and undergo the transformations demanded for survival. Extravagance so understood provides a perspective on suicide, commitment to daydreams of holocaust, of apocalypse, and the final resignation of extinction.

But are we finding before this grim prospect that now and then, here and there, arise visions, emerge resources carrying potentials for alternatives? And if the pathfinding toward the alternatives is clarified through the touchstone of honesty, then the way that is pointed out may well deserve focused and inclusive attention.

That characteristic of honesty, for me, comes through powerfully in a middle essay — 'Becoming the Person You Meant to Be' — when Luke Eastwood writes of his vulnerability, his struggles and the tenacity required to maintain the quest. After all, he is in search of the legitimacy and authenticity of a specific human endeavor under the titles of Druid and Druid culture. It is there where he lays out the price in suffering and of recovering (and the work of and with and for spiritual advancement in this world of obstructions, enervating resistance, and hard stuff, is never without a toll). It is in this middle essay that the why and the "what for" of Eastwood's seeking shine most humanly through.

In the essay which follows, titled 'Druidry: a Force for Positive Change' is a single quotation that epitomizes the core of Eastwood's commitment. He writes, *"Like author Thom Hartman, I believe that we are all connected in a cosmic consciousness and that great shifts in the way that human society acts have been achieved from small beginnings."* The remark is radiant, a touchstone of purpose, and it sheds light throughout *A Path through the Forest*.

A key characteristic at the core of a sentient human being is that of conscious-mortality. On this, I have a strong conviction that a vital component in an individual's maturity is recognizing and embracing the spiritual desire of person-as-person's need to connect with an entity or intimation of a greater, vaster other or otherness than the perishing small self. This awareness (inclination) and embrace is not merely a bulwark against anxiety, anguish, despair, but an innate generosity of liberation in the soul's disposition to connect, to offer praise, wonder, and contribute to the endurance and empowerment of that specific, personally relatable other — a god, a goddess, sacred grove, holy river, a blessed island.

To read the words, engage thoughts and the aspirations of Luke Eastwood's *A Path through the Forest: Collected Essays on Druidry* is not only to travel with the author among trees and tree lore, but it is also to walk a path through time and through the mist of time, and into the inspirational dreaming — the giving garden — of the human heart.

David Sparenberg author of *Earth Spirit: Confronting the Crisis*

Introduction

I've been interested in writing since I was young — at 15 I began writing (rather poor) poetry and by the time I was at university, in London, I had progressed to writing articles and reviews for the university magazine. It was the mid-1990s when I became seriously interested in Druidry/Druidism but I spent the next decade or more learning about the esoteric arts and Druidism in particular. By the early 2000s I had developed the confidence to write a few articles on the subject, meanwhile I was already writing on social and political subjects and on environmentalism from an entirely secular viewpoint.

For some time, I had been considering gathering the bulk of my Druidic writings into one place, but as with many projects, it ended up being put on 'the long finger', an Irish slang term that means it was put off indefinitely. Finally in 2022 I began the process of collating and sifting through what I had been writing over the last twenty odd years and putting it into some kind of sensible order.

This is not an exhaustive collection, I have chosen to leave some pieces out, for a variety of reasons that remain personal, but it does represent much of my thoughts on the subject. One thing that particularly concerned me immensely is the subject of ethics in magic, and within Druidry in particular. This is a subject I feel many writers are loath to tackle, perhaps because it is a minefield of disagreements and diverse opinions. Nevertheless, it is something that deeply interests me and so I have written extensively on this subject both in relation to Druidry and in a more secular vein, which, of course, is not included in this collection.

Another area of deep interest is environmentalism. I first got involved in conservation at second level college, as part of a conservation group attempting to control the Rhododendrons that were crowding the native species in the college grounds. In London I got involved in Greenpeace, Shell to Sea and McLibel, becoming a member of Friends of the Earth and, more recently, of Extinction Rebellion. Changing our interactions with this planet is an important goal and if anything I've done over the course of my life was worth-while I'd say this has to be the main one.

Of course, this is not a guide book, a teaching aid, or anything of that sort, but it is a kind of story, a story of one person's path into Druidry and many of the things that have caught my attention or concerned me during that time. This is very particular to me, but I hope my words may be of interest or even of some use to those who are looking to take, or already are on, a similar path through the forest.

Luke Eastwood, April 2023

The Basics of Druidry

What Does It Mean to Be a Druid Today?

First published in Touchstone *magazine, July 2006*

From my observation those who describe themselves as Druids appear to often fall into one of two categories; these two categories I would describe as 'Reconstructionist' and 'Revivalist'. These two categories appear to be at odds with each other but I believe the reality of modern Druidry is that elements of both are valid and indeed necessary for a viable and living spiritual path.

Taking the 'Reconstructionist' approach first — there are those who in the name of truth, purity and other lofty ideals reject anything that cannot be traced back to ancient Celtic society, this may also include exclusion of all information not originally in a Celtic language and people of non-Celtic ancestry. Whilst one must respect the ideals and single-mindedness of such an approach, I believe that it is somewhat impractical attitude and also not really true to the spirit of Druidry. For a start the ancient druids worked in their own tongue which at the time was a Celtic language; over time these languages have been unfortunately supplanted leaving English as the most common first language. It is documented that the Irish medieval bards spoke and wrote a dialect which had long since ceased to be in common use, hence providing a common tongue which all could work with is difficult. In this current age how many of us are able to comfortably converse in Irish, Scotts Gaelic, Welsh or Breton yet alone conduct a ceremony or compose a poem in an ancient dialect? Sad as the demise of Celtic languages may be, English is the common tongue for most Druids today and it would seem wise to use it, perhaps in conjunction with the native language where possible.

Looking at what we know of the Druidic system of learning, how many of us are in a position to take 12 or 19 years' full-time to study as did our predecessors? In our current society such a thing is only possible for those who have no financial burdens to carry. Unfortunately for us patronage of poets by kings and nobility is no longer practiced; Druidic medical practitioners have long been superceded by Hippocratic medicine and eastern alternative methods and as a true sign of the times, various oracular/divination services are now available to the public at the end of a telephone line.

As for ritual and ceremony as practiced by the ancients, there are some clues given in ancient sagas (e.g. selection of the *Ard-Rí*) and classical accounts, however, these are only outlines and there are no known exact details of procedures as practiced by any of the Celts in the pre-Christian era. All of the ritual and ceremony that is currently practiced appears to be based on residuals from the Druidic era and extrapolations from medieval works, but at best they are like jigsaws where half of the pieces have been made to replace those which were missing. As far as my investigations have led me, I am as yet unaware of one verifiable unbroken link to the ancient form of Druidry either via literature or by a continuous verbal tradition.

With regard to the spirit in which Druidry should be undertaken, it is well known that the Druids were familiar with the Greek language in both written and spoken form. There would also have been considerable trading interaction between the Celts and non-Celtic neighbours and also occasional military alliances down through the ages (e.g. Dermot MacMurrough's unfortunate alliance with the Normans). The Celtic peoples obviously attempted to rebuff destruction of their culture by aggressors but I can find no evidence of the ancient Celts adopting a totally isolationist stance, hence I feel that such an approach in modern times would not be in the Celtic or Druidic spirit. Most modern Druid orders encourage an attitude of respect and tolerance of other religions and variations within Druidry itself, surely if we are confident in our own beliefs such an attitude should not present a problem?

So far this all paints a very bleak picture for the 'Reconstructionists' however, although there are huge problems in trying to accurately recreate Druidry in its former likeness, taking this approach does encourage a 'return to the source' and reveals a vast treasure trove of literature which if not useful as a methodology throws considerable light on the history, mindset and culture of the ancient Celtic peoples. For that purpose alone I would consider serious study of the ancient literature an invaluable tool simply because it puts our modern practices into context.

Moving on to the 'Revivalist' approach, much of what is currently practiced is based upon medieval or later works. The Celtic revival of the 1700s onwards led to many translations of Celtic works into English and German, some of note and others highly suspect. Many translations of that era are Christianised or heavily edited — 'awkward' passages were altered for the social mores of the time or worse still, omitted altogether. The creation of Druidic orders inspired by the likes of John Toland, William Stukeley and Iolo Morganwg (Edward Williams) it could be argued were based on romantic notions of the time about Druids rather than actual historical facts and accurate translations.

I fear that for many who take the 'Revivalist' approach this is as far back as they will look, that is if they have made it beyond the myriad works on Druidry produced in the last thirty years. I am not trying to rubbish modern works but I think that in order to make a clear judgment about what Druidry actually is it is necessary to delve into 'source' material rather than blindly accepting second or third hand interpretations and opinions.

A common thread in modern Druidry is a 'mix and match' technique in following the spiritual path. Some Druids happily combine Tarot with Kabbalah, Yogic meditation, Ogham and

Wiccan ceremonial methods and indeed some may also be Buddhist or Christian in addition to Druids.

I would not like to pass judgment on such people as wrong or misguided, but I would ask 'is what you do really Druidry?' After all, one cannot be both a Jew and a Christian or both Muslim and Taoist; to resolve this problem one must ask the question 'is Druidry a religion or just a philosophy?' Personally I regard Druidry as a religion, and although I have an interest in other religions and magical techniques, I am wary of diluting the Druidic path to the extent that it becomes a meaningless hotchpotch of other cultural values. In the end this is a personal choice and it would be intolerant and narrow-minded to condemn other Druids for incorporating non-Druidic practices into their work.

Although use of 'authentic' Druidic practices may be desirable it is obvious that various aspects of ancient Druidry are not viable in the modern world. For instance inducing the three blemishes on enemies, aiding tribes in war, imposing a *geis* on someone, sacrificial and divinatory use of animals/people, collection of dead enemies' heads etc. poses difficulties in a modern context and hence such behaviours need to be either eliminated or altered for the world in which we live. Adjustments must be made but they should be made from a position of knowledge and understanding of the past and not a position of ignorance.

There is a definitely a tendency to 'go with the flow' or adopt any technique or method that 'feels right', which is not surprising given the increased interaction between different cultures in the last century. Whilst I can see the value of diversity, I think that this must be tempered with a respect for the ancient Celtic traditions and culture, underpinned by a genuine understanding of what this means. After all, if an ancient Druid had to sacrifice years of his or her life to the study of poetry, genealogy, divination, healing arts and Brehon law then surely simply donning a cloak and staff does not give one the right to confer the title of *Baird, Fili* or *Drui* upon oneself!

Druidry should be a serious business and if we wish to be taken seriously as a religious community it is necessary to maintain genuine continuity between the past and the present. I think that the extremist view of both the 'Reconstructionist' and the 'Revivalist' as I have described is flawed and those who take either path cannot be reconciled with those of the opposite path. I believe that the way forward is the combination of an experiential approach with continued exploration of the ancient roots of Druidry, only through sensitive application of both approaches can we maintain a spiritual path that is progressive and alive whilst remaining true to the traditions and culture of the ancient Celtic peoples.

The Druid Revival in Ireland

First published in Touchstone *magazine, July 2007*

Over the last twenty years there has been a slow and steady increase in Paganism in Ireland which has gathered pace in the last few years. This article is an examination of that re-emergence of Paganism and a look at what direction it might take in the future.

The seeds of the Pagan revival in Ireland were sown not here but in the UK after the repeal of the Witchcraft act in 1951. Following this repeal two strands of esoteric thought emerged into the mainstream via two men who have become very well known in magical circles.

The first person was Gerald Gardner, author of several books, most notably *Witchcraft Today* which blew the lid off what had until then been a religion practiced in total secrecy. It was Gardner who coined the term 'Wicca' and almost single-handedly created a new form of the ancient Pagan religion that existed throughout Europe up until the middle ages. It is from Gardner's foundation that the Wiccan religion has grown, evolved and spread throughout the western world.

The second person, who led the other main strand in neo-Paganism, was Ross Nichols. Nichols was a contemporary of Gardner, the two men knew each other and some say that they were in fact good friends. What is definite is that Ross Nichols was chairman of the Ancient Druid Order (a Freemason like Druid order) however, he left the order and established the Order of Bards, Ovates and Druids (OBOD) which was set up as a vehicle for returning to Celtic spirituality.

OBOD fell into chaos for some time following Ross's death, however, his successor Philip Carr-Gomm eventually took up the reins again in 1988 and has continued the process of exploring Celtic spirituality in a modernized form of Druidry, gradually moving away from Kabbalistic and Masonic forms of ritual.

This re-emergence that took hold in Britain transferred to Ireland to some extent, although this process was to some degree hampered by the much later repeal of the Witchcraft Act (1983) in the Republic. Subsequent to the British Pagan revival, which is largely focused on British traditions, the Irish revival has gathered pace but seems to have taken place in a slightly different way to in Britain.

Wicca has become very popular in Ireland, but as elsewhere it has subdivided into several strands such as Faerie and Celtic Wicca. As with the original Wicca these are primarily based on a combination of Kabbalah based magical systems (originating from Jacobs Ladder, Key of Solomon etc.) with elements of Celtic and Neolithic goddess worship. The Celtic/Faerie Wicca strands would tend to incorporate somewhat more of the native Celtic elements than Gardnerian/Alexandrian Wicca, however, they still operate within the basic semitic magical tradition.

The Druid revival in Britain could be described as pan-Celtic — it draws on the traditions of Wales, Scotland, Cornwall, Northern England, Brittany and Ireland. England itself, where the revival seems to be strongest is the country, which is least Celticised, due largely to the influence of the Romans and later on the Saxons and the Normans. Ireland, in contrast to England, despite conquest and many attempts at cultural genocide has retained the bulk of its Celtic cultural heritage and still retains the native language in pockets round the country (*an Gaeltacht*).

As a result of the strong cultural heritage in this country the Druidic revival in Ireland seems to be split to some degree. There are those who take a nationalistic or purist approach to Druidry and those who are somewhat more eclectic in their approach.

The main ideological difference it seems would centre around the magical systems employed. Most of western esoteric tradition has its roots in Kabbalistic magic, which originates in the middle east, however, this is not the case with Celtic magic. The Druids and Shamans of the pre-Christian period had a system that shares some of the concepts found in Kabbalistic magic, Alchemy and Witchcraft and also in Hellenic and Vedic culture. However, the expression and practice of these concepts is often quite different from what we know of Druidic culture. A basic example of this would the elements, kabalistic magic has four, Chinese has five and Celtic magic had three — sky, sea and land.

The divide between the pan-Celtic and eclectic Druid is not clear cut, it is more of a continuum with Druids appearing at any point between the two extremes and in fact peoples' ideas and beliefs are prone to change over time as their knowledge and experience changes.

At one end, the purist is hell-bent on preservation of Celtic practice to the exclusion of all else, those who take this approach often have extreme political beliefs as well, which is clearly demonstrated in the alliance between Celtic purists and those on the political far right. At the other end there is the 'anything goes' Druid who like a magpie will absorb or assimilate anything that they find useful, even if it flies in the face of the tradition that they have chosen to follow.

Fortunately the bulk of Druids in Ireland seem to fall somewhere in the middle, they have a respect and reverence for the ancient traditions of the Irish Druids and a genuine desire to rediscover Celtic wisdom, however, they realize that in the modern world respect and tolerance for other spiritual paths is essential.

There is at present some conflict between the two camps, with derision being heaped on 'eclectics', foreign traditions and those who follow non-Celtic paths by a small but extremely vocal and politically motivated minority. The bulk of Irish Druids it would seem do not wish to be involved in this conflict and wish to just practice their beliefs as they see fit. It may be the case that their practices are a synthesis of several different traditions, but at the end of the day we have to ask ourselves if intention is of lesser importance than technique? I personally would have more time for those of pure intention who lack skill and knowledge than I would for the erudite but arrogant bigot!

The world has become a very small place, no-one can live in total isolation any more. While I value and wish to protect Celtic culture from being overrun by other cultural values, I think that it is essential that we remain tolerant and open minded, as I believe that failure to adapt and partake in exchange with other cultures eventually leads to cultural death.

Druidry — The Union of the Spiritual and Practical

Originally published in Touchstone *magazine,*
February 2007

Like most Druids (so I believe) I see Druidry as a spiritual path, a belief system that guides my actions in each world. In truth it is as much for me a practical path as it is spiritual; in fact the two are as inseparable as the two strands in DNA, or put another way, they are like yin and yang — perfectly complementing each other to make the whole.

As a typical Aquarian some people see me as "away with the fairies" or "not quite the full shilling". I am aware of this ability to be ungrounded in myself and to become lost in dreams and thoughts — this is where the practical path comes into its own! Practical actions and skills act as an anchor, they give manifestation to thought and help focus the mind; they can also be meditative as well.

If we take a brief look at the skills our grandparents began forgetting, our parents forgot and that we are largely or completely ignorant of — these skills might well nowadays be considered to be Druidic. For instance, when out walking if you become lost but you know that to your west is a road, by day or night how do you find it without a compass? If you're in a woodland and have a sudden headache, could you find something that might give you some relief? Suppose you found some juicy plums but had no pockets and no bag with which to carry them, could you devise something to carry them home? The answers to these and countless other questions were common knowledge not so long ago — not just among Druids or cunning folk but to almost everyone. Sadly in today's de-skilled world even country people often lack this basic knowledge of how to interact with the natural world.

These skills and knowledge are immensely practical but mankind has obtained it through millennia of experience and a bygone perspective of the world that was in far greater spiritual harmony with the land. This is where the practical path meets the spiritual — the practical actions and knowledge being an outward manifestation of the inner spiritual attitude to life. I would see the practical and spiritual paths of Druidry as synergistic — they benefit each other and the sum is greater than the constituent parts.

An example from my own life is the creation of my stone circle and grove of trees that surrounds it (in my garden, Co. Wexford Ireland). This grove is practical in that it provides food and habitat for wildlife, reduction in air pollution etc., but I also find it a valuable aid in my spiritual work — it is a place where I can find peace, connect with nature and occasionally share with my friends too.

As I've worked more and more directly with the land it has led me to begin studying horticulture so that I can eventually change profession. I find the subject fascinating, but as well as gaining a deeper understanding of the plant kingdom, in working outside I gain exercise, stress relief, mental space, fresh air and a healthier and more productive garden. Working with the natural environment has many lessons to teach us about life on many different levels.

More than anything I find that practical action brings form, structure and greater understanding to ideas, feelings and urges that I've gained on my spiritual journey but which may have remained internalized. This can be summed up by the Chinese proverb "To see is to know, to do is to understand" or by the Celtic triad "The first three parts of understanding: to see what is, a heart to feel what is and a boldness that dares to follow them."

As well as bringing things into focus, a truly practical approach has the added benefit of manifesting our spiritual work on the physical plane. Surely, there is nothing more encouraging that to see the seed of an idea take root and sprout in the world around us — it serves as a reminder of what we can do with belief and also serves as a great example (and hopefully inspiration) to others. Given the present state of our beautiful world such an outcome can only be a good thing!

Exploring a Spirituality of the Past, for a Better Future

First published in Watkins' Mind Body Spirit *magazine,*
May 2012

Most of us are aware of the Druids, even if the image in our minds is somewhat obscured and our perception is that of a religion shrouded in mystery. Most people would regard Druidism/Druidry as a long dead, primitive spirituality that met its demise as Christianity spread across Europe. However, the truth is hugely different and far more complicated than most people expect.

I became seriously interested in Celtic culture and more specifically Druidry, nearly twenty years ago. At that time my understanding of what Druids did was very limited and I was not aware that they still existed in any serious sense. I have long had an interest in religion, stemming from my Catholic upbringing and my introduction to Buddhism as a teenager, plus a fascination with mythology.

As I looked more deeply into the roots of Christianity, I became increasingly aware of the legacy of Celtic Paganism that has been absorbed into Christianity to a surprisingly large extent. Having also developed a great interest in ecology, social/ political issues and creativity, I was pleased to find that these areas are of no small significance within Druidry — hence this path seemed an obvious choice for me.

After some years, studying the Druids of old, encountering many stumbling blocks, I eventually joined a Druid grove in Ireland and also joined the international Druid order the Order of Bards, Ovates and Druids (OBOD). Of course, the modern path has dispensed with the more violent and undesirable aspects of the ancient path, nonetheless modern orders I have encountered generally aspire to the principles and spiritual wisdom, of what is perceived as the original form.

Through the course of my own study and study with OBOD it was clear to me that much of the original source material that has inspired the modern Druid movement has fallen into obscurity and what exists is widely scattered among the literature and lore of the past. I have also become increasingly aware that almost all of the modern texts on Druidry focus on the Welsh traditions, with other Celtic nations remaining in the background.

I felt that I could perhaps throw some light on the obscured roots of the modern Druid path, particularly many of the beautiful and extensive traditions of Ireland and Scotland. I also wished to demonstrate that Druidry is a highly practical and relevant spiritual path for today's world — uniting our heady spiritual aspirations with a deep love and respect for the natural world.

The book (*The Druid's Primer*) starts with a brief history of Celtic culture, a chapter defining what Druids do and a compendium of the major deities. I felt it important to lay an honest and detailed foundation before moving onto more complex ideas such as cosmology or the annual seasonal observances.

I've structured my book so that each chapter stands alone but builds on the content of previous chapters. In all cases I've drawn from verifiable sources from Wales such as *The Black Book of Carmarthen* and *The Mabinogion*, Irish texts such as *The Scholar's Primer* and *The Book of Invasions* and more recent Scottish texts such as *Carmina Gadelica*. I've also consulted the works of most of the major writers on Druidry from the 18th century revival onwards.

I've blended my own personal insights from experience with the core aspects of Druidic thought and practice with the intention of giving a more picture of what Druidry is. I hope that this proves useful to the would-be Druid, but in truth I wrote it as much for myself as anyone else.

In compiling this distillation of Druidic knowledge the process of writing crystallized my own understanding and conception of what it really means to be a Druid in the modern world. As I understand it, Druidry is not really about magic, creativity or being an environmentalist; indeed it may incorporate all of these things, but primarily it is about forging a connection to the divine in a very direct way. Having much in common with Taoism, Druidry is about becoming more in touch with the world, with the rest of humanity and in doing so, discovering your true self and the spark of divinity within us all that exists throughout all creation.

The Re-emergence of Celtic Druidry

First published in The Cauldron *magazine,*
May 2012

Druidry or Druidism no longer exists in its original form; unlike some forms of Paganism or other religions, the continuity through successive generations was broken. However, this happened in some countries at a much later date than one might expect. In Gaul and most of Britain the Druids were obliterated by the Romans: in Gaul Druidry and the native language were lost by the 5th century AD, in England and Wales it may have survived a little longer, although rapidly declining with the supplanting of the Celtic church by the Roman Catholic church in the early 7th century.

In Ireland there was a gradual transition after the arrival of Patrick in approximately 432CE. Far from being an instantaneous conversion, archeological evidence from burials proves that Celtic Paganism and Christianity co-existed for at least two hundred years. In Scotland, Christianity made inroads after Colm Cille (Columba) was exiled to there in the mid-6th century, from Ireland.

Despite a formal switch of allegiance to Christianity the royalty and nobility retained most of the structure of Celtic and Druidic culture, largely unchanged. Apart from the religious functions, Bards, and (O)Vates in Ireland, Scotland, Wales, Armorica (Brittany) and Cornwall continued to perform secular functions with many of the Druid class becoming Christian monks or priests, although some may have continued their own religious practices informally.

This situation continued unbroken until the arrival of the Normans in what is now England in 1066. The Normans quickly consolidated their initial success by invading Wales, northern

England and then Ireland. Attempts to conquer Scotland met with occasional success but they were unable to retain control for significant time periods. The Normans saw the indigenous cultures of the British Isles as a threat and so did their utmost to Romanize their new colonies, hence as well as military and political domination they imposed cultural domination on all of their territories.

The result of this cultural domination was a gradual erosion of Celtic culture in first England, Wales and eventually Ireland. In Ireland it took several centuries to colonize the majority of the country, however, in 1607 the 'Flight of the Earls' dealt a hammer blow to Gaelic culture, in particular the Bardic schools that received patronage from nobility until this time. In Scotland a similar system with Bardic schools existed, but after Scotland lost its independence in 1707 the Gaelic culture collapsed.

So from this potted history, one can see that Druidry and Celtic culture in general declined gradually, but going into free-fall from the baroque period onwards. Strange as it may seem, it was in England that the seeds of the modern Celtic revival were sown. Irish born philosopher John Toland is credited with beginning the first Neo-Druid order in England. *An Druidh Uileach Braithreachas* or The Druid Circle of the Universal Bond, later becoming the Ancient Druid Order, is claimed to have begun in 1717.

This order, and other subsequent orders were heavily influenced by Freemasonry and were often run by Freemasons whose ideas were of the Romanticist Movement, which tended to idealize and romanticize the ancient Celts. In the early 18th century, most of the early Gaelic and Welsh texts had not been translated into English, archaeology was in its infancy and the remnants of oral Druidic culture remained solely with the downtrodden and poverty-stricken Celtic speaking peoples of the British Isles. So one can easily believe that the early revivalists based their ideas on fantasy mostly and otherwise on the writings of the Greeks and Romans. After the publication of the mostly forged *Barddas* by Iolo Morganwg in 1862, a Welsh element to the revival developed, although originally part of the anti-monarchy Welsh nationalist movement.

It is only really from the second half of the twentieth century that any serious attempts have been made to reintroduce genuine Celtic culture into the centre of the Druid movement. This process began in earnest with the departure of Ross Nichols from the Ancient Druid Order and his formation of the Order of Bards, Ovates and Druids in 1964.

Since then, various other orders around the world e.g. in Britain, France, North America and Ireland have continued Ross's work of re-Celticizing Druidry. It is indeed unfortunate that the last of the genuine Celtic Pagan remnants in Scotland and Ireland seem to have vanished with the demise of the Irish Triads (three members) and the *Gáidhlig* bards in the Scottish Isles, given the renewed interest in Celtic survivals. What has been happening though, is a re-invigoration of the Celtic languages amongst the Druid communities, a re-discovery of the Gaelic literature and a renewal of the traditional knowledge in music, art, herbalism, mysticism and religious observances.

Sadly, due to a huge loss of Druidic lore and wisdom this process remains difficult. However, widely reduced and scattered as it is, there is still a considerable amount of genuine Celtic remnants in both the early literature, folklore and cultural survivals. Neo-Druidry is finally re-establishing itself as a genuine Celtic spiritual path and moving away from its somewhat misguided and romantic beginnings. This process is far from complete as various groups and orders differ in ethos from strict reconstructionist to pan-theological revivalists, meaning that there is no unified approach to the evolution of Druidry.

However, regardless of these differences, the general trend seems to be towards an honest re-evaluation of the roots of Druidry in an attempt to give it the continuity and credibility to take a distinct role within the more general Pagan revival. Whilst it is important to remain open and respectful of all other spiritual paths, I see it as an enlivening and necessary step for the future of Druidry that it continues to redefine itself in terms of its ancient Celtic past.

My Journey with OBOD

First published in The Golden Seed
(Slippery Jacks Press), 2015

I was interested in history and mythology from an early age, something that my father also had a great interest in and easily transferred to myself. This interest didn't translate into anything concrete until my late teens — I regarded all of those as fascinating curiosities of an ancient past.

It was from my mid-teens that I really began to question modern western values — the vast inequality, constant expansion, devouring of the natural landscape and the elevation of financial success to a godlike status (very evident in the Thatcher years of my youth).

Indirectly, via Indian, Chinese and Native American spirituality, mythology and history I gradually became aware that Europe had once had a more holistic (albeit still violent) way of life that was centred in the sacred earth rather than the detached pursuit of wealth and reward in the afterlife.

The more I read about Norse and Celtic culture, the more fascinated I became, leading me to start my own reading on early Christian and late Pagan culture of the British Isles. In my early 20's my involvement in the underground electronic music scene brought me into contact with Shamanism which had lose connections with the drug and hippy culture emerging out of that scene, but I had still yet to meet anyone who I could describe as a genuine Druid or Shaman.

I carried on reading and hoping I would someday meet people that had a real understanding of what Celtic culture is about, but mostly I met other interested people with similar or less understanding than I had myself. Contact with the

Glastonbury Order of Druids, visits to Stonehenge, Silbury Hill and Avebury helped confirm my desires but still left me no wiser in terms of embarking on the journey of becoming a Druid. Mostly what I found was an increasingly visible and growing Wiccan community, which although interesting, was not quite what I was looking for.

Then, in 1996, I was walking past a bookshop window in Swiss Cottage, London, en route to the publisher I was working for. In the window was a paperback copy of *The Book of Druidry* by Ross Nichols, which caught my eye enough for me to return at lunch-time.

I had a flick through and immediately knew that this was unlike any other book I'd seen on Druids. Mostly what I found were varyingly detailed historical accounts of the Druids, with nothing of any practical value in terms of a working spirituality. This book was the revelation I had been searching for — despite the hefty price tag of £15, I bought it (it was the only copy they had) and I devoured it over the coming weeks.

Much of Nichol's wisdom was lost on me, being unfamiliar with many of his terms of reference and finding his style rather dry and the content very dense. However, it was a book I would return to with greater appreciation, but even on the first reading it awakened me to the knowledge that Druidry/Druidism was revived, and quietly alive and well in Britain.

Work, musical endeavours, marriage and children took precedence in my life for a time, as is the natural way of things, but I found my attention drawn back towards Celtic mysticism, particularly after moving to Ireland in 1999.

After a painful and acrimonious marriage breakup, I was severely depressed and found myself wallowing in self-destruction. However, after hitting rock-bottom, I realised that the spiritual life was key to my recovery, together with taking better care of my physical self. During this process of self-healing I began yoga, acupuncture and meditation, long walks in the woods and by the sea, using sunlight and St. John's Wort as a natural cure.

After tentative attempts to reach the esoteric community in Ireland I met several people with Druidic connections in 2003 via an introductory course on Wicca, run by well-known High Priestess Barbara Lee. Although I learnt much from her course, I knew that Wicca was not for me and I pursued these connections that enabled me to join a small grove in Wexford and meet OBOD members.

Somehow, I had missed the connection between the revitalised OBOD and Ross Nichols, and besides, I had been looking for an individual teacher rather than a correspondence training course. However, it did not take much convincing for me to sign up and begin my Bardic studies. I soon realised that this one all-knowing individual who I sought probably did not exist, but I did realise that the many kind and helpful people I was meeting were collectively fulfilling this role.

Membership of this grove (*Uath Nemed* or hawthorn grove) ended many years of isolation and solitary learning, giving me the chance to learn and grow within a reliable framework and share my experiences with my tutor and other grove members.

Much of what I'd learned over the preceding years suddenly took on new meaning in the light of first-hand practical experience and the courage that no longer being alone can give. Although much of my study has been firmly rooted in the past, being within the OBOD fold gave me a sense of what being a Druid in a modern context could or should be.

One aspect of OBOD I have found particularly appealing is the sense of purpose and the inclination to be of service. Knowledge is a wonderful thing, but it is of little use if it cannot be of any benefit — clearly something that OBOD is well aware of. If we are going to be Druids in this modern age, then surely, we should use our knowledge and gifts to help steer our teetering human society in a better direction?

Practical and positive change is paramount in my own vision of the future — within OBOD that same vision is apparent, along with all the support, encouragement and non-judgmental assistance that any would-be Druid could hope for. My only regret perhaps is that I did not join OBOD sooner.

The Growing Pains of the Irish Pagan Community

First published in Aontacht *magazine, March 2016*

Unlike the UK and other modern countries, Ireland did not make Paganism legal until 1983 with the repeal of the witchcraft laws, something that has happened much earlier elsewhere — e.g. 1951 in Britain. Many Pagans may not consider themselves to be practitioners of witchcraft, but as far as the Irish government was concerned, to follow the ancient gods amounted to the same thing.

As a result of a two faith religious system (Catholic or Protestant), with little provision for, or consideration of, other religions, it was practically impossible to openly practice any form of Paganism in this country until after 1983. However, even long after, being Pagan still often involved being shunned and derided by mainstream society.

In fact until 2006, some remnants of anti-witchcraft still remained, although no longer in use:

Any person who shall pretend or exercise to use any type of witchcraft, sorcery, enchantment, or pretend knowledge in any occult or craft or science shall for any such offense suffer imprisonment at the time of one whole year and also shall be obliged to obscursion for his/her good behaviour.

Technically anyone performing a ritual or pretending to do so (such as an actor) could have been imprisoned for a year and also been 'bound over to keep the peace'.

In 2009 the Blasphemy Law in Ireland offered protection to all religions, including Paganism, with possible fines of up to

€25,000 for blasphemous publication or speech. Although this seems somewhat excessive (considering you could be fined far less for running someone over whilst drunk driving) however, it does offer Pagans and other minority religions a level of protection that was formerly completely absent.

The last few years have seen some dramatic changes for Pagans across Europe — since early 2015 Iceland has the first Pagan (Asatru) temple, in any Nordic country, for close to 1000 years. In 2010 Druidry/Druidism was officially recognised as a religion in the UK due to the efforts of Druid Network. Here in Ireland Celtic Druid Temple was recently (2015) recognised as a religious charitable organisation by the government.

Unlike other parts of Europe and USA, Ireland is still only beginning to achieve full legal and moral status for Pagan religion. Thanks to the work of Pagan Federation Ireland (PFI) legal marriages for Pagans have been able to take place since 2009, however, with a large number of restrictions imposed. Now in 2015 Pagan Life Rites (PLR) is attempting to gain Legal Solemniser status for its clergy. PLR is the first solely Irish Pagan organisation (the Irish Order of Thelema is part of OTO) that is not run by an individual or a couple and hence marks a significant change for Paganism in this country.

Since Paganism re-emerged in Ireland it has been dominated by the cult of personality — small organisations, covens, groves, schools, colleges, lyceums etc. run by a charismatic individual or couples. Although this has its strengths on a personal level, such a structure has great weakness in that the organisation usually dies when the key people involved either move, retire or die. The history of modern Paganism in Ireland is littered with defunct groups and dead small organisations, simply because they could not survive the loss of a key person(s). It is important to acknowledge the work of individuals and couples, many of whom have worked tirelessly for decades for the benefit of the

Pagan community in Ireland. Without the hard work of these people there would have been no fledgling Pagan Community, from which to develop a more mature community.

However, times are changing and Paganism in Ireland is necessarily beginning to adapt to being part of the wider world. Elsewhere in the world Pagan organisations have a proper structure that does not rely entirely on one or two charismatic leaders — a much healthier and generally a far more democratic and transparent situation, that needs to be emulated in Ireland. I for one am glad to see a more mature structure beginning to establish itself in this country, as it is deeply unhealthy for only a few individuals to have power over the direction and development of the Pagan movement. A few individuals usually contribute massively to Paganism here, while most people sit back and watch, but now is the time for that to change — a real community needs the willingness for widespread involvement and also opportunity and structure that allows for everyone to contribute and get involved.

I hope that we will see schools, orders etc. of Wicca, Druidry, Asatru, Shamanism and all forms of Paganism established that are run by a board, collective or a committee, and that are accountable to their members, students etc. Obviously too much bureaucracy is not good for any religious organisation, least of all Paganism, however, it is high time that Irish Paganism matured. Ireland needs to join the rest of the Pagan world in organising itself in a way that offers the public a service and facilities that are transparent, fair, responsible and free of the nepotism, secrecy, infighting and competitiveness that has mired Irish Paganism in the past.

It is with great anticipation and excitement that I await Pagan Ireland moving beyond its teen-like growing pains and emerging as a fully-fledged adult in the greater world of religious multiplicity!

Magic: The Inconvenient Truth

First published in Pagan Dawn *magazine,*
February 2020

Those who have an interest in magic, be it Wicca, Druidry or other esoteric arts are most likely to be aware of the persecution of Witches, Alchemists etc., the horrors of the Inquisition and many other events in the 'history' of magic and witchcraft. I use the quotes around the word history simply because what many of us believe (myself previously included) to be fairly accurate historical fact is in truth often urban myth and supposition.

The mythology that has grown around the subject is immense and has been so often quoted by esoteric practitioners, teachers and authors that it is generally not questioned at all. I cannot possibly hope to debunk all of the misinformation commonly quoted as fact in a short article such as this, I will, however, reveal some of the most common and shocking 'facts', that are either grossly exaggerated or not true at all.

Witch trials – It is commonly understood that thousands, if not millions of witches, wise women, cunning men etc. were tortured, put on trial and then executed by being burned alive at the stake. The majority of people put on trial were acquitted and in almost all cases if those found guilty were executed, they were hanged. In England there were laws against Witches since the time of king Canute, however, it was a fairly minor misdemeanor attracting only penance and fines, becoming a common felony in 1542. It was not until 1601 that an Act was passed prescribing more severe punishment. In all cases it was necessary to prove that injury to property or person or gain at the expense of the person had been caused or attempted (the only exception being love philtres).

A fairly accurate guess for the number of executions in Europe in the 300 years from 1450 onwards is 50,000, the most occurring during the 1600s. In England there are only 200 confirmed cases of execution resulting from allegations of witchcraft. Almost all executions were hangings and in the cases where burning occurred (it was more common in France) it was usual to strangle the victim at the stake prior to burning. In total up to 1650 there were only three recorded cases of burning at the stake in the British Isles, which would seem to indicate that it was not a common practice. Those found guilty were often heavily fined, pilloried or given some punishment other than death.

Records indicate that approximately 75% of trials ended in acquittal, given such accusations are rather hard to prove. In Britain the Church was not directly involved in any of these trials after the mid-1500s as these were secular trials by jury; even in Catholic Europe, ecclesiastical courts often failed to convict suspects. Witch hunting was generally unpopular and conducting trials was expensive. For example, in the case of Isabel Cockie, who was burned in 1596, her execution expenses totaled over 100 shillings (more than 750 euro in today's money).

The wide-spread misconception surrounding witch burnings may well be linked to the executions, often by burning, of religious heretics during the Protestant/Catholic strife that plagued Europe during the same period, which led to huge numbers of people being executed, particularly by the Catholic Inquisition of the counter-reformation.

Benevolent magicians – It is often stated that Witches & Druids were not in any way evil, that they were all victims of Christian propaganda and that they generally did no harm to anyone — it is often suggested that they were just as likely to do the opposite. It is true that in rural communities healers existed who used their knowledge of herbs to help members of their village, in many cases these people were practicing Christians and few of them would have described themselves as Witches. Pre-Christian mythology of the Greeks, Persians, Celts etc. portrays the witch as an often solitary person who is willing to perform magical acts in exchange for some form of compensation, most often money; the services provided may have been anything from a curse to a love spell. Many examples exist of Sorcerers, Witches, Wizards, Druids etc. using magic to harm others, in battles, against their enemies, the enemies of their patrons and compatriots and even random strangers. One such famous example is the sorceress Circe, in *The Odyssey*, who turns men into swine and other creatures, she shows her charming side to Odysseus, who is immune to her magic, but otherwise she is cruel and unmerciful. In the Story of *Deirdre and the Sons of Usna*, King Connor treacherously implores his Druid Cathbad to trap the Sons of Usna so that they may be murdered, Cathbad duly obliges by creating a lake of slime/tar in which they become stuck and unable to defend themselves. It is also well known that Druids were believed to be able to cause illness or even death by the use of satirical verse, a course of action that can hardly be described as benevolent.

It would be wrong to claim that all magical practitioners were evil, and it is equally wrong to claim that all magical practitioners were virtuous, the same being just as true today. Early mythology and honest historical accounts portray the Witch or Sorcerer as impartial if anything, an occultist for hire with a portfolio of benign and malevolent skills available.

In order to prove the ambivalent nature of many magicians really is the case, one need only look at the array of spell books available which include curses as well as beneficial spells. From antiquity to modern times, a number of grimoires exist from the late medieval period (note: Book of Shadows is a modern invention), which contain instructions for both malevolent and benevolent activities.

Black magic does not exist – It is true that the Church has previously portrayed the magician as an instrument of Satan — a claim that is somewhat illogical as the notion of Satan would have been foreign to pre-Christian European religion, from which witchcraft evolved. The 'Good Witch' myth appears to me to be a belated counter-propaganda move aimed at destroying the equally ridiculous 'Servant of Satan' dogma still emanating from the Catholic Church. The reality is that since the Church began linking the occult with Satan (a practice that has its roots in Athanasius's borrowing of Egyptian ideas in the late 4th century CE) that a certain element of society has been attracted to the more reprehensible end of magical practice. Numerous trials in modern times have taken place in which crimes have been committed in which Satanic rituals have been used. Books on magic that refer to Satan (and/or demons) exist from the middle ages; some grimoires, in particular those referencing 'The Key of Solomon' make use of both angelic and demonic forces, others are clearly 'Black magic', for example, *Grimorium Verum* published in 1517 and 'The Grimoire of Honorius' published in 1629. As early as the 1400s Black Masses occurred, the practice being a bizarre inversion and sexualisation of the Catholic Mass. Gilles de Rais was executed in 1440 after he was caught with other French nobility conducting a mass to raise Lucifer by means of offering body parts of children they had murdered.

Black magic may well have come into existence as a distinct genre of magic as a result of hysteria generated by the Church, it is indeed a hotchpotch of ceremonial magic and pure sadistic inventiveness, however, over time all manner of crack-pots have been attracted to it and become its practitioners. Black magic is often the work of the third rate and the insane, but to pretend that it is non-existent or never existed is pure foolishness. Esoteric Satanic orders such as The Order of The Nine Angles do exist, which to the ignorant might appear to be cut from the same cloth as Pagan organizations. By definition real Pagans cannot be Satanists as they do not acknowledge Satan or Yahweh, something that non-Pagans generally fail to comprehend. Satanic covens also exist – I personally know a young man who was briefly a member of a Satanic group, he became extremely ill during this time after receiving a ring that he was told to wear at all times. He gave back the ring but was fortunate enough to be ejected from the group without further harm and went on to live life outside of esoteric circles.

Wicca and Druidry are ancient religions – Wicca was invented by Gerald Gardner, who recreated 'The Old Religion' in a new form, in part using the ideas of Margaret Murray and Aleister Crowley (who initiated Gardener into OTO). He published several books after the repeal of the Witchcraft act in 1951 in the UK, this was the launch pad from which Wicca has grown into a world-wide religion. Druidry is a reinvention of Celtic Paganism created in the early 18th century. In pre-Christian times Druidry or Druidism is not a term that existed, according to O'Curry and Joyce the Irish term translating as 'Druidical' refers to all magic in the ancient mythology. It appears that even the word 'Celtic' is an invention of the late 17th century and it was Edward Lloyd who first linked the 'Celtic' nations – based on linguistic similarities. In the ancient world the people of Ireland, Britain, France, Spain, Switzerland etc. where the 'Celts' existed were not a coherent group or race and were all referred to by their own tribal names, even the Romans regarded the 'Celts' as distinct groups. Modern Druidry is linked to the revivalists of the 1710s onwards (John Toland, John Aubrey and

William Stukeley) via the Ancient Druid Order and the Order of Bards, Ovates and Druids, but there is absolutely no discernable link to ancient Druids or even the Bardic schools of Ireland and Scotland, that died out by the end of the 1600s. One might expect all modern Pagans to be aware of the relatively recent origins of the Pagan revival, however, it appears that a great many people are entirely ignorant of the truth in this respect.

All of the above 'insights' might give you the impression that I have something against Wicca or Druidry, which is entirely untrue. The purpose of this exercise is to demonstrate how little we can trust what is commonly regarded as fact, which leads me to quote the often-used cliché 'a little knowledge is a dangerous thing'. I am an unashamed Pagan, but one thing that I abhor in all people, religious or otherwise, is prejudice and opinion based on ignorance. I think that we owe it to ourselves to understand what we believe and why we believe it. If you don't believe what you've just read then please feel free to go and find the answers for yourself!

Bibliography

New Illustrated Everyman Encylopaedia
Wikipedia (various articles on Satanism, Celts, Witchcraft, Druids etc.)
Dictionary of the Occult – Andre Nataf
Witchfinders – Malcolm Gaskill
The Wordsworth Book of Spells – Arthur Edward Waite
Celtic Myths & Legends – T W Rolleston
Ancient Celtic Romances – P W Joyce
Witchcraft Today – Gerald Gardner
The Golden Bough – Sir James Frazer
The Book of Druidry – Ross Nichols
Manners and Customs of the Ancient Irish – Eugene O'Curry
The Bardic Source Book – John Matthews
Dark Initiatory Witchcraft – Thomas Karlsson (Hidden Spirit 1:1)

Growing Sacred Food in a Small Space

First published in Weathering the Storm *(Moon Books),*
April 2020

Organic growing, permaculture and biodynamics might seem like a luxury — for those with a farm or a huge garden, but this is not really the case. Even in a tiny garden or an apartment it can be possible to grow food, although it must be conceded that it is somewhat more challenging.

As Pagans we are supposed to care about the Earth, to respect nature and the gods of the Earth, perhaps the Earth Goddesses most of all — Gaia, Danu or whoever you choose. In reality many Pagans fall short in practical application of their good intentions — I have visited the abodes of many Pagans and found both house/apartment and garden sadly bereft of plants, and any sign of a living connection with nature. Perhaps the current COVID-19 crisis is not only a wake-up call, but an opportunity to get closer to nature and become more self-sufficient? Getting into a natural space, especially a wild space, is the easiest and most obvious way to connect physically with the elements and the natural world, but this is not always practical for those in cities and large towns.

The other alternative, in this situation, is to bring nature to your home, with an abundance of plant life, that will oxygenate your home, provide food and also provide a direct and practical means to connect with the natural world. Of course, we are already part of the natural world, but in our technological age, it is very easy to forget that fact, and for many, the connection to nature is weak or almost non-existent.

Where to start — small gardens

You may have a really tiny garden, but there are creative ways to make good use of what space you have. If you have no ground because of paving or tarmac you can do one of two things — dig it all up (time consuming and difficult) or create raised beds on top of it. Even if you have flower beds or a lawn, you might have terrible soil or a thin layer of soil on top of rubbish/rubble. If this is the case you are probably better off to use raised beds.

Assuming your soil is ok, you can dig over the lawn and turn it into a vegetable patch and patios can be repurposed, by using the slabs to make a walkway across your vegetable patch. If you are still short of space then you can work vertically — a series of troughs or cloth bags fixed to a south-facing wall can serve as a growing medium, when filled up with soil and compost. Hanging baskets can be put up on wires as well as on brackets, again making 3-dimensional use of your space.

A raised bed can be made out of railway sleepers, fake sleepers or planks. Ideally planks should be 5–10cm thick and of pressure-treated wood or larch/elm/alder for durability when wet. Three sleepers/planks are needed per bed, with one cut in half to make the ends of the rectangle. The bed should be no wider than twice the length of your arm, so that you can reach the middle!

Once constructed the raised bed(s), which are hopefully south-facing (for maximum sunlight) can be filled with soil and/or compost. If your soil is heavy clay you may wish to add some non-salty sand and some lime to make it more workable and improve drainage. If your soil is sandy you will need to add organic matter such as well-rotted manure or good quality (preferably organic) compost. You can make your own compost from food scraps, even in a tiny garden, by using a dustbin or wheelybin, with air holes or you can try creating one out of wood.

A space saving trick to grow spuds is to use a tower of old tyres or a collapsible garden bag. The bottom tyre (or the bottom of the collapsed bag) is filled with soil and 2 or 3 potatoes, hopefully with eyes already, can be planted 3–6cm below the surface. Once the plants are about 10–15cm tall you can bank up more earth around them, leaving just a few leaves sticking out of the new, higher ground level. Once the plants have again reached 10–15cm tall again you repeat and repeat — adding more tyres or raising the bag as necessary. Once you reach the top, leave the plants to grow, keep well-watered and fertilize, if needed (tomato feed should do). Harvest the spuds when the plants start to die off. This technique can be used on a balcony as well as in a small garden.

Where to start — apartments

This is more challenging I have to admit, but not impossible! If you have a balcony this will be your primary growing area, if you don't have one then south, east and west facing windows will be your growing areas. In an apartment you will have to use containers but on a balcony, you can also use grow bags.

Pots, window boxes and hanging baskets are all possible inside, as well as on a balcony. With hanging baskets, they can hang off the balcony banister or inside they can hang off of hooks from the ceiling or walls. It is quite surprising how many containers can be fitted into an apartment, within reach of daylight. Of course, you will need to buy in soil and compost, unless you have friends or family that can help out with that (difficult during a lockdown).

Seeds & seedlings

Getting plants started will require either buying 'plugs' from a supermarket or garden centre or buying packets of seeds. Plugs are far more expensive but save the job of germinating seed, which might be helpful if this is your very first attempt at gardening. Seeds can be germinated in the airing cupboard, and then brought into the light, otherwise you can buy a cheap electric propagator in certain budget German supermarkets! There is tonnes of online advice on growing from seed, so avail of that for each specific crop that you intend to grow.

Sacred gardening

You can take a very technical approach to gardening — weedkillers, pesticides, highly ordered and logical or you can be more holistic. However, organic gardening methods work with nature and are more suited to the spiritually minded. Biodynamics is an approach that involves working with nature but also involves a more esoteric element. Even if you decide not to get into more advanced methods, one can take a spiritual and sacred approach. Using eco-friendly and natural techniques is a good starting point, but you may wish to take it further with blessings, prayers and meditations with your plants, or even just talking to them.

Watching plants grow is quite an enlivening and inspiring process — to nurture them into life from an embryo (seed) or baby and bring them through their full life cycle is a very direct and powerful connection to the Earth and the life force that inhabits all living things.

Having nurtured plants and experienced their life and death, their sacrifice for our benefit, one cannot help but feel enormous gratitude for our food. Growing your own food puts you directly in touch with the knowledge that all life is sacred and the fact that living beings must die, in order for us to live.

Staying positive

Growing plants will keep you busy, it can also be great fun and highly rewarding. It is also something that can be done as a family, with even small children taking part. Growing your own food will provide you with food that is fresh, nutritious and full of life energy. Good food is important for both physical and mental health. Gardening requires both mental and physical effort and this in itself is beneficial, especially in times when normal activities are suspended. Gardening is a skill that can augment your life during difficult times but it is also a skill that is useful for all of your life, and may even become a new hobby for some. Even if it does not appeal as a hobby, it will certainly help you to connect with the Earth on a physical level, if not on a spiritual and emotional level.

In these times, change is becoming the new constant — it is likely that life will not be quite the same when this crisis finally draws to an end. We are all having to adapt to difficulties, just as previous generations had to do, although they did so with greater regularity. We cannot rely on everything going back to normal — now is the time to rely on ourselves and communities we are part of. With ingenuity, faith, hard work and sharing of knowledge, skills and resources we can hopefully all get through this in good shape. Perhaps cooperation, spiritual awareness and resourcefulness are qualities not just for an emergency, but for a better and more humane way of living in the future? The future has not been written yet, so we now have a chance to play our part in how our collective future will unfold — we are not powerless, it is up to us whether we see this as something to be fearful of, or as an opportunity.

Rebirth of the Druidic Path

First published in MePagan *(Moon Books), 2021*

Druidry or Druidism is an ancient religion or spiritual path that has been re-discovered, re-interpreted and re-invented since the 18th century. The last remnants of the original Celtic Druids died out in the previous century with the last of the Bardic Schools in Ireland and Scotland, following the demise of the native culture due to the Elizabethan conquest in Ireland and the joining of the English and Scottish crowns under James I.

Ironically it was in England that the Druid revival began — under the influence of a former Irish Catholic, scholar and historian from Donegal, named John Toland. According to historian Ronald Hutton, Toland combined several Druid groves in Britain to create a Druid order in 1717, which became known as The Ancient Druid Order (ADO), *An Druidh Uileach Braithreachas* or just The Druid Order. However, in the republished edition of Toland's *History of The Druid's* from 1814 (nearly 100 years after his death), there is no mention of this event in the biography of him given by R.T. Huddleston. There are no mentions of this event in any online encyclopedias I could find, so I am left wondering why this rather important event is largely un-noted.

Out of these mainly romantic origins, other Druid organisations such as The Ancient Order of Druids began in 1781 and others appeared, mostly in the 20th century onwards. One of the most successful of these is the Order of Bards, Ovates and Druids (OBOD), which I myself am a member of. It began in 1964 with the departure of the ADO Scribe, Ross Nichols, to start his own Druid organisation. Following his death there was a hiatus until it was revived by the former 'Chosen Chief' Philip Carr-Gomm who was asked to take on the position by Nichols.

Many other organisations now exist such as ADF or GOD, in Britain, Ireland, North America, throughout Europe and Australasia, again all of which were created at some stage during the 20th century or are offshoots of earlier organisations. Despite the quite obvious lack of continuity between the original Celtic Druids and Bards and the organisations that sprang up after 1717, there are those who claim descent from the original Irish or British Druids.

In my research there is little evidence to corroborate any stories pertaining to ancient lineages. Some people may have a genuine link to the revival Druidry of the seventeen hundreds, but any further links are not only suspicious, but very hard to confirm. I have been fortunate to have had second-hand contact with two Druids who claimed to be members of Irish Triads (two separate ones). Many of the people who knew these two men are alive today and I've had the opportunity to quiz them extensively about the genuineness of their claims. An Irish Triad was basically a group of three people (often men) who performed the three tasks of Bard, Ovate and Druid, or more properly — *File*, *Fáith* and *Ollamh (Draoi/Drui)*.

These two men had already been dead for a number of years when I first became aware of them and I was most fortunate to befriend a few people who had known them. Most of this exclusive group are thankfully still alive themselves, at the time of writing, and were able to discuss these men with me. One of the Triad Druids, Ben MacBrady, was quite well known in esoteric circles and was also a member of Druid Clan of Dana (*An Clann Draoidheachta Danann*) which I am myself a member of. DCD was started in 1992 by Lady Olivia Robertson, the co-founder of the Fellowship of Isis, which is based at Huntington

Castle, Clonegal, Ireland, which was built in 1625 on a site owned by the Esmonde family, who arrived in Ireland in 1192.

In the grounds of the castle is an ancient *bulluan* stone, which is linked with the Druids of old, that can be used for both cursing and healing by those who possess the knowledge of how to use it. Those of us who know how to use such an item guard this information carefully as such a stone can just as easily be used for evil as for good. And so, the knowledge has to be passed only to those who will use it in a responsible manner.

From my investigations I cannot confirm or deny MacBrady's claims — his order (The Order) may or may not have genuine Druidic origins or it might equally be a creation of the romantic revival — at this stage we will never know for sure. What we can be sure of is that MacBrady was the last of a group of three Druids who claimed to have an ancient pedigree, even though MacBrady was also a member of a very recently created Neo-Druidic order (DCD).

The other man who I know of, who shall remain nameless, was the acquaintance of a good friend and mentor of mine, who is himself now of advanced years. When he met this Irish Triad Druid, the man was close to 90 years old and the last remaining of a group of three. My friend had enough time with this gentleman to ascertain that he was probably the 'real McCoy' and not an egotistical imposter. However, what knowledge he did possess died with him, and what snippets and nuggets of information he passed on remain with my friend who is himself in the closing decades of his life.

From my understanding of it, both MacBrady and Druid X (for want of a better name) were of the opinion that their time was over and that what they had to say was no longer relevant or valued by Irish society. Unfortunately, whatever they did have to pass on to future generations is now lost, with the exception of the few bits and pieces that they told to their friends and acquaintances. I spent some time mulling this over, somewhat amazed and devastated by my discoveries. I had come so close to contact with perhaps the last living links with a Druidry that possibly reached back into the pre-Christian, genuine Druidic culture of Ireland.

After some time, I came to the realisation that, for whatever reason, this was how it was meant to be — that their knowledge was not meant to be retained and perhaps it actually didn't matter after all. Modern Druidry is not the same as its ancient predecessor and we should regard that as a good thing. There is no place in the modern world for the worst excesses of ancient Druidism — war, cursing, human and animal sacrifice, rigid hierarchy, slavery etc.

The modern or Neo-Druidic movement is based on ancient foundations, albeit rediscovered via an ignorant and romantic period from the seventeen hundreds onwards. Modern Druidry continues to evolve and has gradually moved away from Masonic and Classical antecedents. The modern movement continues to explore and unearth the remnants of genuine Celtic culture and integrate what is appropriate for these times into current ideas and practice. That does not mean that the unpalatable aspects of ancient Druidism are ignored, they are noted and recorded for posterity, but they are not included in our practice because they are no longer of value in a society that is attempting to rid itself of the worst aspects of human behaviour.

Whichever Druid path or order one might wish to follow, solitary or as part of a large group or organisation, there is a general recognition that we have still much to learn about the original Druidic religion and that the Druidic spirituality of today will continue to evolve. This is a natural progression as our understanding of the past changes and so too our values and perception of the time we live in now also changes.

One should beware of anyone who makes grandiose claims with regard to Druidic knowledge, lineages or other such unlikely connections with the original Druids of western Europe.

In almost all cases, such claims are fraudulent and are based in ego and self-promotion, rather than any genuine desire to pass on proven ancient Druidic wisdom. At the end of the day, we all have to follow our own path and our own judgment. For me this is a very Gnostic path, informed by my understanding of both the ancient Druidic tradition and the Neo-Druidic tradition of the last three centuries. If following the Druidic path helps one to achieve genuine wisdom and be of service to humanity and the world then whether it is ancient or modern becomes largely irrelevant.

The Ever-changing Faces of the Gods

First published in iPagan *(Moon Books), 2019*

Over the last thousand years or so there have been huge changes in religion — most notably the one god coming to replace the many — the Judeo-Christian god Yahweh, who has swept through the world at the end of a conquering sword or a gun. However, as with all things in life, change eventually comes and now we see a resurgence of multi-religious as well as secular life, as a result of the fact that the iron grip of enforced religiosity has begun to loosen.

Just as the Spanish, Portuguese and the British brought their Christianity to most of their conquered domains, I suspect that ancient conquerors did much the same in early and pre-recorded history. Certainly the Romans brought their own brand of Hellenic Paganism to their conquered territories such as Gaul and Britain. Archaeological evidence shows that Romano-Celtic gods were worshipped in the time before Christianity became the official religion of the empire.

It's also clear that the earlier Greek forays eastwards had a significant effect on Middle-Eastern culture, which strangely lasted into the early renaissance period, long after Europe has lost and forgotten the religious and philosophical writings of the Greeks. Strange as it may be, the Greek corpus retained by the Persians made its way back into Europe via people from this region who had long since become monotheists (Islam) and who once again worship the same god as the Jews and Christians, albeit called by a different name — Allah.

Probably there has been ebb and flow throughout known and unknown history with lone gods supplanting pantheons and vice versa along with military achievements or mass migrations of peoples. A good example of this is the reforming of Babylonian polytheism by Zoroaster (Zarathustra) to become monotheism with various classes of lower spiritual beings (both good and bad). Zoroastrian religion was incredibly powerful in the Middle East for at least 1000 years and influenced both Judaism and Christianity. However, it was gradually marginalised by Greek and Roman influence before being almost eliminated by the spread of Islam. Ironically, it has survived in India and also Iran, largely due to the protection afforded it by moderate Islam as 'people of the book', along with other scripture-based monotheism.

From a Celtic perspective, there have clearly been a multitude of changes over time, as is evidenced by the different layers of gods that exist. Unfortunately there is no exact timeline, like we'd find with the Egyptians. Their foray into monotheism under Akhenaten is well known and recorded, despite the fact that his religion and his great city barely survived a decade after his death in 1336BCE.

The early history of western Europe was not written down, it was passed orally, despite the fact that the Druids were well able to write. In the territories of the Romans the old religions and the histories (or mythologies) were largely wiped out or absorbed by the Roman culture, with what little remained being further degraded with the arrival of the Roman church.

So with a few notable exceptions, there is little known of the indigenous gods of western Europe and not much more known of the gods that the Celts most probably brought with them. The two notable exceptions, as sources of the largely lost religious culture of western Europe, are Ireland and Scandinavia. Neither of these places were conquered by the Romans and both were rather late in coming under the influence of the Roman church (approx. 1000CE in Scandinavia).

The Viking's religion, (now called Asatru or Heathenry), is of unknown age and is most probably the indigenous religion of northern Europe, which was also to be found in what is now Germany and Russia and in Britain (by introduction). Like the Celts they had an oral culture even though they had the ability to write (Runes). Unlike the Celts, they had a clearly defined pantheon (the Aesir), which appears to have remained largely unchanged, most probably due to their isolation.

Unlike Scandinavia, Ireland was a warm and inviting area, excellent for cultivation and full of mineral resources, which obviously made it an inviting place to try and colonise. From the medieval book *Lebor Gabála Érenn* (The Book of The Taking of Ireland), which is believed to have been orally transmitted in earlier times, we discover that Ireland was subject to several waves of invasions by different races, over an unknown time period.

Because of these waves of invaders the culture of Ireland that has been recorded can to some extent be separated or compartmentalised. The mythology that has survived is quite clearly related to different races and times. The people of Dana, or *Tuatha Dé Danann*, as the name implies were followers of the Goddess Dana, otherwise known as Danu or Anu and the pantheon of gods associated with her as descendants. This group of gods comprises just a dozen or two of the Irish gods. The goddess Tailtiu, the foster mother of Lugh is remembered in the name of the town Teltown, but she was in fact *Firbolg*, not *Tuatha Dé Danann*. Lugh himself, to complicate matters further is descended from both the *Tuatha Dé Danann* and the *Fomhoire* (grandson of Balor).

The pantheon of the *Tuatha Dé Danann* is clearly defined by the genealogies and admittedly imported into Ireland, which is corroborated by the existence of *Tuatha Dé Danann* deities in lands other than Ireland — such as Britain and France, where one can find, for example, both Brigid and Lugh. Other Irish gods may or may not be traceable to earlier peoples but many of them are still known to us — such as Bilé (Beli), Crom

Cruach, Ériu, Tlachtga or Bel (Belanos). These gods may have belonged to the Milesians, Fomorians (Fomhoire) Firbolgs, the Nemedians, or Partholans, but it is thought that they are not of the *Tuatha Dé Danann*.

At this stage it is nigh impossible to tell at what point many of these gods arrived in Ireland if indeed they are not actually indigenous. Amergin (famed Druid of the Milesians) gained victory over their *Tuatha Dé Danann* opponents by agreeing to name Ireland after the three goddesses Ériu, Banba and Fódla. In a few cases (e.g. Geoffrey Keating, 1634) they are linked to Ernmas of the *Tuatha Dé Danann*, but it is likely that they are a much older triad than say the Morrigu (Badb, Macha, Nemain/Anand) which is found in the *Tuatha Dé Danann* and later mythology.

In addition to the various layers of pantheons or remnants of earlier pantheons there is also a plethora of localised gods that relate to places, some of these are simply linked to a river or hill, many of which are forgotten or forgotten in all but name. The Irish *Metrical Dindshenchas*, codified in the Middle Ages, demonstrates that many place names are derived from gods or mythical heroes. Some deities such as the goddess of the river Boyne, Boann are clearly localised but were appropriated by the dominant culture (*Tuatha Dé Danann*). In some of the mythology Boann is also linked to Brú Na Boinne, also known as Síd in Broga (now called Newgrange), which is situated very close to the Boyne itself.

Although Boann and other *Tuatha Dé Danann* gods such as Aengus Mac Og and Dagda are linked to this site, it is clearly a much older location than this bronze age mythical supernatural race. Newgrange has been estimated to have been built around, 3000BCE, during the Neolithic period, yet Boann is clearly linked to both the river and the site; in fact, she is credited with creating the river and losing her life in the process.

Although accepted as part of the *Tuatha Dé Danann*, she does not appear outside Ireland like Ogma, Lugh, Brigid, Nuada and various others of this pantheon that can be found in Britain or France. My belief is that she is much older than the *Tuatha Dé Danann* gods but was assimilated by invading peoples in much the same way that Christianity assimilated some of the Pagan beliefs (e.g. transforming Brigid from a goddess into a saint).

Boann has survived through the writings of the medieval scholars into modern Pagan consciousness, but one can only guess wildly at how many other river gods and goddesses have not survived. Significant finds such as the Battersea shield, and many others like it in river beds are generally accepted as votive offerings to the gods, perhaps even specifically the god of the river the article was thrown into. Likewise, there were probably gods of hills, mountains, lakes, forests etc. that have simply disappeared from history.

Often people think of the transition of religious belief and practice as discrete — e.g., a sudden conversion from Paganism to Christianity, however, it is rarely that simple. Taking Ireland as an example — despite what the monks wrote, we can be sure that all Ireland did not convert to Christianity with the triumph of St. Patrick. The evidence of graves is undeniable — a period of transfer from Pagan style to Christian style burial took approximately 300 years to be completed. One must consider also that given the enormous amount of Pagan survivals in both folk belief and practice that became reluctantly absorbed into the new religion — the Christianity that developed in Ireland was most likely much more a fusion of old and new than Patrick may have hoped for.

Given that such a fusion did in fact occur (although largely dismissed by the Christian church), it's also quite likely that similar fusions took place in earlier eras with the arrival of each new race into Ireland. I could imagine that by the time that

St. Patrick arrived, the seemingly homogenous Paganism of the Druids was a mishmash of popular deities and practices from various races, survived, fused, recycled or added to over a huge time period.

Even now, long after Paganism was supposed to have died out in Europe there are survivals of Pagan folk practice, particularly in the remaining Celtic world and parts of Eastern Europe. Even now, after around 1500 years of Christianity there are still people in Britain and Ireland who claim to have inherited Pagan beliefs in secret and carried on their religion in isolation.

Up until the second half of the last century it was still unsafe to identify oneself as a Pagan. If not likely to suffer actual physical danger, any overt Pagan would have been liable to perhaps lose their job or be ostracised by their neighbours. Since the 1950's with the emergence of neo-Paganism it has gradually become safer for secret Pagans to reveal their beliefs.

The vast majority of Pagans today are not hereditary Pagans; they have gained an interest in Paganism only because of the fortunate survival of Paganism in literature, folk practices and the anthropological sciences. Of course, in previous centuries there were always people who had Pagan leanings but unlike today, such people would not have been free to express it without suffering some form of retribution.

As a neo-Pagan Druid myself, I first experienced Paganism as a child, through the mythology of the Greeks, Romans, Vikings, Egyptians and Celts. I did not choose to become a Pagan until I was already an adult; being free to explore a number of different religions over time. Eventually I settled on Celtic Polytheism, not because I was born into it, but simply because it suits my beliefs.

Modern people, to a large extent, have the luxury of picking their own religious beliefs or converting to another religion if the religion of their birth does not suit them. Much the same as the known world was before Christianity swept across it, there are now a multitude of religions to choose from, both monotheist and polytheist. In the pre-Christian era there was certainly co-existence of vastly different religions, but whether it was as easy to move from one belief system to another, like it is today, is hard to say.

As now, where collective religious life is in flux, I imagine that various religions and cults rose and fell like the tide, perhaps increasing in one region and declining in another. We can see clearly from history that religion, like culture, is not static, that extent and popularity of religions shifts, as do the practices and belief within individual religions.

In recent years, I was able to attend a Lughnasadh ritual with a varied group of other Pagans, mostly from the west of Ireland. The bulk of those in attendance were neo-Pagans like myself, but there were a small number of secret hereditary Pagans too. It was fascinating to hear one of these hereditary Pagans recite a prayer that I have never heard spoken and that bore great similarity to a prayer attributed to St. Patrick.

I suspect the St. Patrick's prayer I speak of is itself a modified version of a prayer used by the Pagans of the time. The imagery used in St. Patrick's Breastplate, to me, has more in common with Druidic incantations than it does with the more familiar Christian prayers and may well be a case of recycling by early Christians in Ireland.

Of course, my understanding of what it is to be a Druid, to be a Pagan and to be a human being is probably vastly different from the understanding of people of Europe who were Pagan in pre-Christian or early Christian times. Today there are Celtic Druids, Christian Druids, Buddhist Druids and even secular Druids, not to mention the vast array of different types of other Pagans that exist. One can only speculate whether or not the original Pagans would approve of the re-emergence of their gods and the resurrection or re-imagining of many of their beliefs and practices.

Either in secret, through many generations, or through a personal Gnostic journey of choice one can find oneself praying to these same gods of our ancient ancestors. How one arrives at a particular belief system may be very different and the understanding of that belief system might be quite different. In a dogmatic religion there is little or no room for interpretation and where differences occur it most often leads to conflict. In Pagan spirituality, at least in its current form, there are as many gods as there are colours and there is apparent freedom to express our own experiences of them.

The gods may be defined by history but they are also ethereal inhabitants of our world, not of some far-off heaven separated by an impassable chasm. Our relationship with the gods is for us to choose, it is not mapped out for us and the face of the divine we see now may change in the future, just as it has always changed throughout human history.

The Celts were said to have laughed as they destroyed the statuary at the Oracle of Delphi in their 3rd century BCE attempted sacking of the town. The Celts supposedly understood that these were not gods, but merely laughable human representations of what deity is. Both the Celts and the Norse of the time were highly skilled in art, yet their representations of the gods were rudimentary, crude and barely humanoid, while their Greek counterparts produced life-like 'human' statues to represent their own pantheon. In truth, whether we are Christians, Pagans, Hindus, Buddhists or whatever, the images of deity we might choose to use are not real. At best they are tools that enable us to conceptualise and imagine the qualities of the divine that we wish to connect to. At worst they are abominable idols that give a false and childish representation of a power that is beyond human understanding.

Just as every dandelion leaf is unique, the face of the gods is unique to each and every one of us. Perhaps it is not the divine that has changed at all, it is us, humanity, that has undergone immense changes over thousands of years. As we change so does our ability to see, feel and understand what the divine actually is and what our relationship with the Creation is, or should be.

Perhaps after endless generations of being trapped by our beliefs, trapped by dogma we are arriving at a time in which we can be free to choose the gods and spiritualities that most enable us to connect with the divine as we understand it. Each of us has to live our own life, no-one else can live it for us. Perhaps it's time to accept responsibility for our own personal Gnostic journey — to begin understanding both ourselves and the divine. If we all took responsibility just for ourselves only and bringing the sacred into our own lives, this might bear more fruit than endless religious debate and conflict. Surely, when our lives come to an end, how we, ourselves, have chosen to live is all that really matters? What everyone else chooses to do is not our responsibility.

Re-finding Our Balance in the World

First published in Pagan Ireland *magazine,*
March 2021

Here we are again, at another balance point — the point of equality between day and night, at the entry point into Spring 'proper'. In Ireland it is traditional to begin sowing plants and venturing into the garden from St. Patrick's Day onwards. This is because of the doubtful weather, that has a tendency to swing backwards and forwards erratically until about now.

The battle between winter and summer is symbolized by the demise of *An Cailleach,* vanquished by the strengthening sun and replaced by the youthful Brigid, a goddess (or saint) who finds herself officially recognised in Irish culture and government for the first time in well over a millennium. With the creation of the St. Brigid's Day bank holiday, Ireland now recognises this mythological/semi-historical character or archetype as culturally important, not just for women but as a symbol of the re-emergence of the divine feminine into public consciousness.

It is rare to find something that Christians and Pagans can agree on, but in this case, there seems to be universal welcome of this new bank holiday and the acknowledgement of Brigid. Strangely, the Roman Catholic Church never canonized Brigid as an official saint, and, of course, many might question the existence of an actual person called Brigid, perhaps this being a title afforded to the priestess or (later on) nun who was responsible for maintaining her rites?

As we emerge into the Spring, a time of action, it is good to see the symbolic and actual progress of women in Irish society. Now as this is a time of balance, for a healthy society some kind of equilibrium is necessary. One can only hope that some kind of balance between the sexes can be maintained, for the good of human society — with neither misogyny or misandry being acceptable behaviour from anyone.

In Pagan religion or spirituality there is room and even necessity for a significant role for both men and women, in particular as they represent the duality of nature, the fertility cycle of all life, both in humanity and in the life of this planet. Of course, there is room for other models and inclusivity, but we should not lose sight of the basic building blocks of life — usually propagated through the dynamic between female and male counterparts.

The rise of feminism and a shift towards favouring women is a necessary process to redress the balance that has favoured men for perhaps three or four thousand years in most societies or cultures, but does that mean we should swing the other way, and for how long?

One can already see a massive rise in male suicides across the world as many men feel they have no purpose or have total confusion about what their role in life should be. One can argue that this is not the fault of women, but of the seismic shifts and inevitable upheaval and the failure of men to cope with change. However, if society ends up revolving solely around either just men or women it is not a healthy state of affairs. A vibrant, fair and viable future human society should enable men and women to live in true equality, with the strengths and weaknesses of both sexes being acknowledged and understood. This surely is the way forward for a more happy, hopeful, inclusive and evenly balanced humanity?

Forgotten Treasures of the Plant Kingdom
5 Druidic Herbs No Longer in Popular Use

First published in Pagan Ireland *magazine,*
September 2022

Today most people know very little about plants — not only having a general lack of understanding of gardening and care of plants, but of the many uses of plants — mostly due to our modern urban lifestyles.

During the early 20th century, before modern medicine, hospitals and general practices were widespread, many people in Ireland retained some or much of the traditional knowledge of plants that would have been passed on by the *Bean Feasa* or *Fear Feasa* (wise women/men) down generations of families or to those interested to learn these skills.

Sadly, with the rise of modern knowledge, modern ways and the use of traditional ways falling out of fashion, many of these traditional teachers and healers died with no-one to pass their treasure on to.

With its desire to become a successful modern country, many Irish people discarded that which they associated with the old Ireland and ways that they had come to regard as backward, or redundant. However, this knowledge has not been lost, even if the average person has little or no understanding of it. In fact, now we are seeing something of a renaissance in this area — particularly in the area of magic, Witchcraft, Shamanism and Druidry.

In Irish tradition there were seven main Druidic herbs, but opinions vary as to what they were. I'll not go down that road here, but I want to discuss five woody and herbaceous plants that were once considered valuable, useful and important and that are largely disregarded by the average person today. as simply a weed, a flowering plant, or as a herb for cooking.

Yarrow (Achillea millefolium/ Athair Thalún)

Now often found in cultivated form in garden centres, the wild form (white flowers) is increasingly rare in Ireland.

It was once commonly used in divination (love related particularly) as well as a magical aid for women to make the wearer more attractive to men. It is one of the traditional seven Druidic herbs and often call 'the herb of 7 cures', as it has extensive healing properties. It was particularly useful to staunch wounds and was valued by warriors for that purpose as well as relieving headaches, toothache, colds, fever, rheumatism and boils.

Yarrow is also edible, both raw and cooked, but is somewhat bitter and it can also be used as a flavouring in beer. Aromatic oil from the flowers can be used to make a pleasant drink, or a tea can be made from the whole flowers. The plant itself deters ants, beetles and mosquitoes (when dried) but it is a valuable plant for bees.

Although not very tasty, Yarrow is a very nutritious food and also makes an excellent plant food if pulverized into a liquid plant feed.

Nettle (Urtica genus / Neantóg)

A well-known plant famous for its sting, although not all nettles do so. The stinging nettle was used against rheumatism, inflammation and as a blood thinner.

In hard times it was eaten as it is highly nutritious although not tasty. A tonic made from the leaves is great for recuperation from illness or for someone who is 'run-down'. Nettle juice makes a great general fertilizer and also makes a decent green dye.

Medicinally it has many uses — dermatitis, circulatory problems, measles, swelling and dog bites as well as the uses already mentioned, so it is really an essential plant for the herbalist. The stems are suitable for making clothing and string and the biomass can also be used in making alcohol and starch. Today it is often regarded as a nuisance but it is one of the most versatile and useful plant we have!

Common Horsetail (Equisetum telmateia / Eireaball capaill)

One of the world's most ancient plants, which first appeared during the Jurassic period. This ancient fern is regarded as a pernicious weed as it pops up everywhere including through stone and tarmac.

It has been used as a medicinal herb to treat osteoporosis, tuberculosis and kidney problems. It is also thought to help relieve fluid retention (it is a diuretic), stop bleeding, and heal wounds. Ingested it is said to enhance skin, nail, hair, and bone health and it contains a large amount of antioxidants.

Horsetail can be easily consumed in the form of tea, which is made by steeping the dried herb in hot water. It is anti-inflammatory, antimicrobial against bacteria and fungi — including Staphylococcus aureus, Escherichia coli, Aspergillus niger, and Candida albicans. It also has an anti-diabetic effect. Horsetail extract may help lower blood sugar levels and regenerate damaged pancreatic tissue. Lastly, like nettle, it makes an excellent liquid feed for your plants by macerating into a bucket of water and steeping, or as manure if dried.

Thyme (Thymus vulgaris / Tim, Lus na Brat)

Is a well-known culinary herb generally from the Mediterranean region, but is also native to Ireland and grows well here, despite the dampness of the climate.

Today it is used mainly in cooking but it was once used to prevent bad dreams, as an inhalation or an infusion to drink. The infusion also helps with digestive problems and internal infections. It is also effective for respiratory problems such as bronchitis, as well as menstrual pain and for alcoholism detox or as a general antiseptic. Its oil makes a great disinfectant and antifungal. In the garden it makes a good companion plant for cabbage to deter root fly. The leaves are small but can be eaten raw as well as in cooking.

Saint John's Wort (Hyperican perforatum / Beathnua)
Once a highly valued and sacred herb of the Druids and Ireland generally, it is now rare in the wild. Today it is mostly used as an alternative therapy for treating depression or Seasonal Affective Disorder.

Until the 20th century it was regarded as a holy plant, used in sacred rituals, even in Christianity, particularly linked with the summer solstice and the feast of St. John.

Although it has many medicinal uses it was commonly regarded as a powerful magical plant, linked with the sun. It is believed to protect against evil, to bring abundance and expel demonic forces/entities. It is a general protection and was also used in love divination, love charms and for prophecy.

Its medicinal uses include jaundice, lung and bladder problems, diarrhoea, dysentery, minor cuts/wounds and sore eyes. It was used for mental health problems in ancient times, as today, but also for more mundane uses such as dye and flavouring mead. It is illegal to buy it in Ireland, except via a doctor's prescription.

Environmentalism

Making a Difference

First published in Crann, *Ireland's tree Magazine, 2009*

For those of us who are fortunate to own large amounts of land or those who work in positions of influence within the forestry and horticulture professions our ability to make a difference in the future development of our environment is quite significant.

So, what about everyone else? All of you reading this article have an obvious interest in the preservation and improvement of the natural world; otherwise you would not be holding this magazine in your hands right now. Perhaps you are already doing your bit to change things, but I am sure many of you would like to do more.

Like many other people, I've felt tremendous frustration in the past due to my lack of ability to make a significant and tangible difference 'on the ground' despite my good intentions. At times that frustration can be stultifying and lead people to give up their efforts altogether, something that I experienced myself. However, eventually despite these feelings of being ineffectual I decided I would persevere no matter how small my contribution happened to be.

I realized that even though I did not own any land or have any specialist knowledge I could still make a difference, for my own satisfaction and also for the future generations that will inherit our beleaguered environment. I believe that we all have a contribution to make if we are willing to try and not be disheartened by difficulties or failure to create a huge impact.

I started out very simply by planting trees one at a time in the drive and garden of my rented house in Camolin, Co. Wexford. At the time I had little spare cash and very little knowledge, but despite this, when I eventually moved to my first bought property, I had made more progress than I expected. I had saved a dozen mature trees from being choked by ivy plus I had managed to plant over 30 trees, plus I also had the pleasure of seeing many of them grow from puny saplings to the size of standards and half standards that stood a fair chance of survival.

Four years later I am still at the house I bought, which sits on a mere half acre near Carnew, Co. Wicklow. I made a decision to buy native trees when I moved in and gave over approximately half of the garden to a woodland area. I was lucky enough to buy 300 bare-root saplings from Coillte for a knockdown price, which I have used to create the woodland area and hedgerow on three sides of the garden. I initially planted around 250 trees — Sorbus accuparia (Rowan), Betula alba (Birch), Fraxinus excelsior (Ash), Acer platinoides (Sycamore), Prunus spinosa (Blackthorn) and Salix caprea (Willow) and rehabilitated the few existing trees that were chocked by brambles. I gave the remaining 50 trees to two friends who planted them in their own gardens.

I will eventually be harvesting most of the Sycamore and some of the Ash for firewood to run my heating system and the remainder of the trees will eventually form a beautiful native woodland. Since planting four years ago not only have I had the pleasure of seeing my efforts bear fruit but I have been inspired to retrain as a horticulturist, which has enabled me to transform what was a hobby into my work. I now have a much better understanding of trees and have seen what was just a pipe dream become a reality.

When I planted the first tree in Camolin several years ago I was not even sure what kind of tree it was! Who would have thought that I would be where I am now? I currently look after 180 acres of amenity lawns, gardens and woodland surrounding a hotel and golf course where I am able to have a direct influence on how the land is managed and I am currently involved in evaluating the viability of a tree planting programme together with a switch to woodchip heating.

Obviously not everyone is going to be as fortunate as I have been, however, from small beginnings we can all grow to eventually make a significant difference. If you don't have ten hectares to plant up, consider a small area in your own garden, perhaps join a local group that is involved in conservation, help plant at your school or workplace, or get involved as a volunteer in Friends of the Earth or Crann.

Recent news of environmental cutbacks at government level is depressing but when you think of the huge number of private gardens, local schools, parks etc. that could be improved there is tremendous scope for redressing the balance. You don't need to be a big landowner, farmer or an environmentalist to improve the situation — many small individual contributions will make a significant difference, and who knows you might inspire others to do the same!

Reclaiming Our Tree Heritage

First published in Crann, *Ireland's tree magazine,*
Winter 2009

Many foreigners come to Ireland expecting a green and pleasant isle full of welcoming faces, stone walls, trees in abundance and sheep everywhere, of course, the reality is far from the marketed image of rural Ireland. I am sure that many visitors are shocked to see how materialistic we have become — what with every other person driving a huge SUV and families living in palatial houses that have more bathrooms than people to occupy them.

It was not always this way, as anyone who remembers life prior to the nineties will know, however, going much further back, Ireland was a very different place again. In ancient Ireland it was said that a squirrel (red that is) could travel from one end of the country to the other without ever having to touch the ground. Of course, over the course of time (like the rest of Europe), the situation changed to make way for agriculture and more people. In Ireland the ship building ambitions of Henry VIII and Elizabeth I made an enormous dent in the nation's tree cover, further exacerbated by population rises and increasing sheep farming that decreased the natural replacement from new seedlings. At the beginning of this century a mere 1% of Ireland was forested, fortunately this has improved to over 9% in recent years but we are still a long way behind the rest of Europe, in fact so far as our modern attitude to trees is concerned, we could be viewed as Philistines by our more progressive neighbours.

So what happened? We all know that Ireland was once a country where trees were held as sacred. It is well known that the Druids revered trees and that well into the Christian era there were harsh punishments for abuse of trees. In the eighth century legal tract *Bretha Comaithchesa* four classes of trees were defined — nobles, commoners and lower divisions of the wood and finally bushes. Each class had its value based on the quality and quantity of wood or another attribute such as its food or resin yield. The fine or *eric* for destroying a noble tree without good reason was the value of 2.5 milk cows, which at the time was a considerable sum of money.

Trees appeared greatly in Irish folklore and in herbal medicine, originating in the pre-Christian era, much of the lore relating to trees continued to be known and passed down until relatively recent times. The significance of trees is highlighted by the appearance of trees in Irish place names to the day, perhaps the best-known example being Kildare or *Cill Dara* meaning 'church of the oak'. Trees also played a part in early Irish poetry, a prime example being Sweeney's Lay which is attributed to the 7th century King *Suibhne Geilt* (Mad Sweeney) who was cursed by St. Ronan. The opening verse is shown below:

A dhair dhosach dhuilledhach	Thou oak, bushy, leafy (note can these have a gap?)
At ard os cionn crainn.	Thou art high beyond trees.
A chollàin, a chraobhachàin,	O hazlet, little branching one,
A chomhra cnó cuill.	O fragrance of hazel nuts.

In addition, the Gaelic alphabet, known as Ogham, is widely regarded as a tree alphabet. Although only half the letter names are actually trees names the letters collectively were known as *feda* and singularly as *fid*, which respectively means 'wood' or 'tree'. Consonants were called *táebomnai* which means 'the side of a tree-trunk', and the individual lines of each letter were called *flesc*, meaning 'twig'. So when taken in the context of the words describing the alphabet and the information from the medieval *Ogham Tract* and *Scholar's Primer* it is easy to see that this alphabet is clearly linked with the native trees of Ireland.

The Ogham alphabet had twenty letters, split into four groups of five, a supplementary group of a further five being added at a later date, this being for the purpose of rendering Greek and Roman words into Irish. The letters were cut or carved onto a vertical line from the bottom upwards, many examples of which can be seen on standing stones around Ireland, particularly in Cork, as well as in Scotland and Wales. Early Irish literature states that Ogham writings were carved onto pieces of wood and Julius Caesar claimed that the Druids of Gaul wrote in Ogham, also on wooden staves. Of course, wood being prone to decomposition, there are no known examples of Ogham on wood, which has led many to assume it was only used for stone boundary markers etc., however, I suspect that it was widely used on a day-to-day basis until the Romanised alphabet was adopted in the early Christian period. It's interesting to observe that the full Roman alphabet of 26 letters with the modern letter shapes was not adopted until the 1960s; prior to this the alphabet had only twenty letters and letter shapes that were uniquely Irish. It is still possible to see this alphabet today, in use on the occasional old blue and white road name sign that has somehow not been updated.

The lore relating to the trees of the Ogham alphabet confirms the important status of trees in the earlier Irish psyche: Hazel, Oak, Yew, Rowan and Hawthorn being particularly useful or revered in past times. Even today we see echoes of past importance, illustrated by the lone hawthorn tree in a field that a superstitious old farmer refuses to cut down. This was considered a fairy tree and also unlucky: bringing it into the house was to invite death into your home. This might seem a strange superstition, but when one considers that the smell of the blossoms is very similar to that of a few-days-old corpse, one can begin to understand where this tradition arose from!

The Oak is well known to be a significant tree, it was used to kindle the *Bealtine* fires here and also in Scotland. The ancient

Tuatha Dé Danann god *Dagda* possessed a magical harp made of oak, which demonstrates its cultural as well as economic importance far back in history. The oak is also linked with many place names and also with Irish saints such as Colmcille and Brigid.

The hazel is widely known to be linked with wisdom in Irish folklore, and many of us today are familiar with the story of the Salmon of Knowledge who fed on nuts from the nine hazels surrounding the well of *Segais* at the source of the Boyne river. There are many more examples easily found and it doesn't take very much digging to see that trees were a vital part of Irish culture until the dawn of the modern era.

Somehow, in our headlong rush to be modern citizens of the world, we have jettisoned much of former cultural importance, as well as making a giant building site of large sections of the country. Perhaps now that the Celtic Tiger is well and truly dead it is time to take stock of our impoverished cultural situation as well as the poor state of our wallets?

As people who are interested in trees and their re-emergence in this country, perhaps it is time for us to put a greater value on trees — not just as economic and ecological benefits — but as a living and breathing part of Irish heritage and culture? The native trees are every bit as culturally important historically as the GAA or Irish dancing and traditional music, I think that this should not be allowed to be forgotten. In fact the body of beautiful folklore and tradition surrounding our trees could well be used educationally as a means of helping us to fall in love with trees all over again, so that they once more become a vibrant part of the Irish landscape and culture.

Biodiversity Begins at Home

First published in Crann, *Ireland's tree magazine,*
Summer 2010

Most of us like the idea of biodiversity, eco-friendliness and boosting the environment but for many that does not extend beyond buying fairtrade coffee or going to the garden centre for a few bedding plants.

What many people fail to realize is that all of us as individuals can make a huge impact on biodiversity and the quality of our environment simply by using our own homes in a creative way.

For those who live in the country, land is not generally a problem — the average house might have half an acre of land, often much more. In such cases it's easy enough to set aside land as a woodland, a wilderness or wildlife area. Other options could be specific areas of interest such as a native garden, Japanese garden, a rockery, vegetable garden, composting area or a pond, all of which encourage bird and insect life, and in the case of ponds — much needed places for frogs, newts and toads to live in.

All such areas are generally complemented by thoughtful selection and sighting of trees. It is, of course, possible (and helpful) to pick these based on the number of species that they might support in addition to their attractiveness of potential size.

Unfortunately, as one drives through the Irish countryside, all too often houses are surrounded purely by large expanses of lawn with fences used to mark the boundary. Such sites fail to qualify as gardens to my mind, a grass monoculture is effectively useless to the environment, providing nothing for wildlife and producing only very low levels of oxygen.

Worse still is the neglect of country hedgerows and in some cases their replacement with either block walls or fences. The old-fashioned stone ditches were walls in essence but allowed plants (if not deliberately planted) such as hawthorn, blackthorn, ash, gorse and fuchsia etc. to develop within them until they formed a hedge.

In order to counteract this lack of awareness of the need for biodiversity, and the lack of effort that goes with it, it is really up to individual householders to make efforts to reintroduce diversity into the landscape. There are a large number of books that offer excellent advice and ideas on developing such gardens which are widely available in bookshops and garden centres. Also courses, such as those offered by The Organic Centre, in Leitrim or maybe evening classes at your local school/college might be useful in collecting ideas and find the inspiration to get started.

For those that live in the city, a greater level of imagination and creativity is often required, as generally space is at a premium. However, if you only have a roof terrace, yard, balconies or a very small garden it is still possible to make a valuable contribution to biodiversity.

For instance, if there is no soil area it is possible to grow shrubs and small trees in containers such as the butterfly bush (Buddleja davidii) which as the name suggests is frequented by butterflies. In the wild these can grow to about 15ft in height but in a large pot they will remain a manageable size. Even if you are only able to have a couple of trees in pots this still makes a valuable contribution to air quality and may also provide food for birds and insects. Small individual contributions add up to a large contribution if the whole street or whole neighbourhood joins in!

Inventive use of space and taking into account shelter and where the sun travels in relation to the space available can enable the biodiversity enthusiast to grow a variety of plants in a small area. I personally have seen a small urban garden of just 20ft wide by 30ft long absolutely crammed with trees, plants and even a small pond that the local frogs took full advantage of. In a few short years this became a haven for all manner of insects as well as birds, frogs and hedgehogs. In addition to looking very attractive (which adds value to the house) and providing a habitat this garden traps carbon dioxide within the plants (trees especially) whilst also producing many times more oxygen than the lawn and gravel garden next door.

One does not need to be a creative genius or have to spend a fortune to make such a Sylvan paradise a reality Again there are books that cater specifically for the small garden or urban dwelling and there is also plenty of useful information on the internet that will help one to make the best use of limited space.

With major cutbacks in woodland and cuts in more general environmental funding, largely as a result of the banking crisis, it is now more vital than ever before that individuals and local communities who have an interest in biodiversity and sustaining the natural world get involved on a practical level. We cannot rely on government or semi-state bodies to ensure that suitable environments for endangered or diminishing species continue to exist. It really is necessary for us to take the initiative in protecting and preserving the rich mixture of native, naturalized and foreign plants and animals that inhabit this island if it is still going to be intact for future generations to enjoy.

Survival Is Simple

First published on inteldaily.com, August 2011

At this, still early, point in the twenty first century only the sensory deprived or those living in brainwashed denial can escape from the fact that the modern Western way of life is doomed. Of course, as I write this millions of people still living a non-Western life of relative poverty are aspiring to our decadent foolishness of self-indulgence, consumerism, environmental, social and self-destruction.

The obvious truth is that our current mode of existence is propped up mostly by hubris at this late stage. The most cursory of investigations will uncover a wealth of evidence that our financial system is close to collapse, our ecosystem and its resources are becoming exhausted, our social structure is becoming degenerate and our public infrastructure is disintegrating.

One could say this is the cost of human progress or our intellectual evolution, part of a process of growing up that we will 'grow out of'. It would be nice to believe that this is true and that we can evolve into a culture with modern benefits whilst regaining the holism of other more naturalistic cultures that now barely exist. I fear that what is more likely is that our technological development will never provide this 'holy grail' of sustainable living or some kind of equilibrium with our environment. Personally, I am not willing to wait around and see if this approach will actually deliver anything concrete, it is my belief that the only way forward is to go backwards.

The level of degradation caused by Western lifestyles is hard to fathom due to many unseen or intangible results. We are all many stages removed from the sweat factories where our useless crap is manufactured and the resulting effects on these far-away people and lands. What is clear though is that even if fully understanding that the negative effects of the modern lifestyle are hard to grasp (not least because it is too horrifying for many to fully conceive), a major change is required if we are to make it to or beyond the end of this century.

We could sit around and wait for our governments and institutions to wake up and begin a programme of social and economic change, a peaceful revolution if you will. However, at the moment virtually every government in the world seems to be running full-pelt in the wrong direction — increasing depletion of resources, papering over the cracks of broken financial and social institutions, protecting vested interests, oppressing decent and failing to take any concrete actions that might solve our long-term problems.

So we could wait for the government fire truck to arrive while the new Rome burns, but if it ever does show up, it is likely to arrive far too late to have any effect. So why wait? Perhaps it is better to forge ahead and create and enact our own personal goals to create a more sustainable life, ones that might just enable us and our families to survive if the systems around us continue to collapse?

First of all it's necessary to realize that much of our infrastructure that we take for granted such as electricity, motor vehicles, gas, oil, plastics, consumer products, easily available and convenient food could possibly be largely unavailable within a decade from now. If this is the case, then one needs a realistic plan for survival in a downscaled world, a world where simplicity is going to be key to any viable and sustainable mode of existence.

Our ancestors possessed a wealth of relatively simple but practical skills as well as practical hand/animal operated tools that allowed a still fairly complex society to exist. Obviously, a non-mechanised, non-electronic existence would be significantly harder than what almost all of us are used to, but it can still provide a successful and fulfilling way of life. Unfortunately most of us lack both the skills and the tools required to live this very practical lifestyle — which means our number one goal has to be acquisition of both the practical knowledge and the means to put it into practice.

Within my own life I have begun 're-skilling', a slow and difficult process that I am some way from completing. However, I am progressing towards becoming self-sufficient in terms of food, water, energy, DIY skills etc. I am also in the process of collecting what I consider to be useful tools that I will still be able to avail of if there is no petrol or electricity available to someone of no great status, such as myself.

Assuming I manage to learn all of the necessary life skills to survive independently of our social system and I have also acquired the necessary tools and resources to begin doing so before an economic and social collapse, I think that I have a fair chance of making a decent life for myself and my family. Through networking and building a community of likeminded people within a short distance of where I live, I could further increase our chances of survival and perhaps provide greater security for all involved.

What is most frightening is the prospect of those who are preparing or are already prepared for the 'doomsday' scenario being overwhelmed by a tidal wave of hungry, violent and desperate people who have continued to sleepwalk through the decay of modern society. Some survivalists/preparedness aficionados may wish to keep all these ideas to themselves in the hope that everyone else will just 'die out' leaving a much smaller number of like-minded people to carry on into a rosy future.

I believe a saner view of reality is that all of us need to begin making these changes now and encourage all our neighbours, family and friends to do the same. If a critical mass of people in each country can voluntarily simplify and begin disconnecting from the decaying systems then there is hope of a peaceful, orderly and empowering transition to a simpler but sustainable future that will also carry most of the remaining somnambulists along with us. There are just too many people in the world to go and hide on a mountain top and wait for the coming chaos to end — a huge mass of helpless and desperate people will annihilate the very people who can help save them if a mad scramble ensues.

Spreading knowledge like a virus through the human population, changing consciousness, acquiring the spaces and tools for a renewal of our agrarian past is our best and only chance for human society. If we can make this transition voluntarily while there is still time then, perhaps, we might not have to lose all of the positive gains of the last two hundred years — in areas such as medicine, engineering, art, agriculture, social/religious tolerance, philosophy etc. Time is running out for all of us, don't wait for the government or the TV to tell you when it's already too late — think it through now, today! Make a plan and begin changing while there is still time.

Forgotten Legacy: Fifty Years after
Silent Spring

First published on globalresearch.ca,
December 2012

This year (2012) is the fiftieth anniversary of the publication of Rachel Carson's seminal work *Silent Spring*, published first in the USA in 1962. This was the first book of its kind — an outspoken, powerfully argued and well researched condemnation of the reckless use of pesticides in modern agriculture, in urban and rural pest control and in and around the home.

At the time of its publication there was virtually no environmental movement. Conservation, its precursor was a minority interest and not taken seriously by governments or the public. However, the publication of *Silent Spring* changed both public and government awareness of one of the most serious threats to both man and the environment that we rely on.

Initially, the book and its author were ridiculed by the press at the behest of the chemical manufacturers and the book's findings were largely ignored or derided by government and major institutions such as the American Medical Association. Despite initial setbacks, the book sold incredibly well all over the world, so much so that it eventually gained huge media attention. By the time Carson died from breast cancer, in 1964, the book had created a legacy that would endure long after her death.

A former American vice president described *Silent Spring* as 'the beginning of the modern environmental movement' and no doubt she would have been delighted to see the impact of her work leading to the banning in USA and Europe of well-known carcinogenic pesticides such as DDT. However, one must wonder if she would be so pleased by the progress that has been made in the decades following the publication of what might be regarded as the most powerful indictment of misuse and negligence in the use and regulation of modern technology.

The orthodoxy of the time was based on adoption of 'chemical control' as a means of controlling the natural world and solving any perceived problems arising from its failure to behave in the desired way. Since the 1940's when chemical controls derived from the military became fashionable, alternatives such as 'biological control' were largely abandoned, at least until the effect of 'Silent Spring' began to be felt.

Thanks to Carson's work and subsequent research and regulation, chemical manufacturers have been forced to remove highly toxic pesticides from sale and replace them with safer broad-spectrum chemicals and selective chemicals. Although progress has been made it appears, from even a cursory investigation, that the world is still beset with a dangerous and worldwide problem relating to the use of pesticides. It would be nice to believe that her job was done, mission complete, and that there is no longer cause for concern or outrage. The sad truth could not be more different.

It is true that in Europe and North America standards for pollution of the environment from insecticides, herbicides, fungicides, rodenticides and other sources have been greatly improved in the last fifty years, however, according to official figures (such as given by the EPA in America) billions of pounds of such products are used each year. Individually, these may not be specified as particularly dangerous, however, evidence shows that when multiple products are applied or products combine in the soil, water table or water courses, the toxicity can be increased by many multiples. One such example is the organophosphate Malathion, which has been used for decades and alone can be dealt with by the human liver. Unfortunately when combined with other chemicals, either deliberately, or by chance, it can become extremely dangerous, it is also potentially dangerous if ingested by those with an impaired liver. Despite these proven problems, in excess of 20 million pounds has been used in the USA annually over the last decade.

The combined effect of multiple products on insects, mammals, fish and indeed humans can be catastrophic — potentially causing cancer, nerve damage and even death. This in itself is rather worrying given that large quantities of pesticides enter the food chain every year, ultimately ending up on our dinner plates or in drinking water.

What is more worrying still is the situation in the so called 'developing world'. In Africa there is a chronic problem of poorly stored or poorly disposed of chemicals that are obsolete. Chemicals such as DDT, banned in Europe and America since the 60s, were sold in Africa (and other places) for a much longer period of time but after they were banned, they continued to be used, were stored in unsuitable conditions that allowed seepage or were disposed of in ways that allowed soil and water to be contaminated.

Belatedly, in 2005 a programme was begun to clean up these obsolete pesticides from Africa, which is expected to take 15 years and cost about 250 million US dollars. Meanwhile this dangerous stockpile continues to poison land and water, having a hidden but terrible effect on both wildlife and humans alike.

Even where more modern chemicals are used, there is an appalling lack of understanding of safety procedures with workers using incorrect dosages, handling undiluted products, failing to use personal protection equipment (PPE) when applying products, due to either ignorance or lack of money. The consequence of the stockpile of old products and the reckless use of current products is an enormous cost to the African continent, in both financial and health terms, which has been highlighted by the Pesticide Action Network.

Moving on to India, the situation there in the last decade has been equally dire — researchers at the Centre for Science and Environment have found huge levels of dangerous pesticides present in the blood samples of not just agricultural workers but the general rural population in areas where pesticides are heavily used. For example, in Punjab state, which is famous for its agriculture, massive levels of organochlorine pesticides in humans is accompanied by worryingly high cancer rates among those exposed. Not only is this taking its toll on the human population, other organisms (fish and mammals especially) are vulnerable to damage or death at the hands of pesticides, which is devastating for the environment and local economies.

In China there have been ongoing problems with safety in agricultural products, leading to new regulations being drafted in 2011 to deal with the effects of chemical misuse. Previous regulations, issued in 1997, have proven to be insufficient to prevent public safety scandals due to dangerous levels of pesticides in food. This problem has a direct effect on the Chinese environment, its animal and human population with serious poisoning or even deaths.

In 2011 approximately 1.3 million tons of pesticides were used annually, many of which are proven highly toxic throughout the food chain, however, ten of the most dangerous have now been banned. In 2009 Greenpeace tested 50 fruit and vegetable samples in an independent laboratory and found that only 5 samples did not contain pesticides, multiple types were found in the rest.

As with both India and Africa, China has a catastrophic problem brought about by poor regulation, misuse and general ignorance. This problem, in developing countries all over the world, is exacerbated by the global economy — a blind eye often being turned while cheap, but sub-standard, food products are sold all over the world.

It would be understandable for a European or American to say that pollution in Africa, South America, Asia etc. is not our problem. However, when some or much of most countries' food arriving from abroad is laced with a hidden cocktail of poisons this becomes everyone's problem.

What is more frightening still is the tendency of chlorinated hydrocarbons to accumulate over time in the fatty tissues of animals, humans included. This means that over a long period of time dangerous levels of pesticides and other related chemicals can build up in the body, possibly eventually leading to infertility, poisoning or cancer. Often illness will not manifest itself for years, but once a critical level has built up in the body of a human (or animal) it can lead to a total collapse of the immune system, nervous system or raging cancer that kills with great speed.

It is well known that levels of cancer, nervous disease and infertility have increased dramatically over the last century, in the latter half especially. Is this just co-incidence or is there a correlation between poor health and the prevalence of chemical controls in modern agriculture?

Far from disappearing, the use of pesticides and the appearance of their side-effects has now become a world-wide problem. Rachel Carson's dire warning fifty years ago set alarm bells ringing in the 'western' economies but profiteering and negligence has enabled these problems to be transferred to the rest of the world to such an extent that the entire planet is now becoming poisoned by our stupidity and greed.

Furthermore, chemical control has proven to be only effective in the short term, requiring greater quantities over time or new variants in order to overcome the development of genetic resistance, particularly in insects. Biological controls, apart from being much safer, have been proven to be effective in pest control both in the short and long term. Given this indisputable fact, it makes no sense to allow widespread and careless use of chemical controls when the cost to humanity and all life far outweighs the benefits, especially when viable alternatives are available.

A marine biologist and painstaking researcher, Carson provided a stark warning of where we are headed — she believed that the road we are on is the deceptively easy road to destruction and that our only chance for the preservation of our planet is to "take the road less traveled by" which although harder, is the right and only sensible path to take.

Her impassioned plea was not rooted in hysteria or emotion but arose from her understanding of biological science and the fragile relationship of the ecosystem that we and all other living things rely on. Despite well over fifty years of evidence regarding the catastrophic effect of polluting the natural world that feeds and sustains us; for political, economic and social reasons humanity continues to poison the world and itself at an alarming rate.

Surely, if it was not already time to end this madness fifty years ago, it is now a seriously pressing matter, if we are to avoid poisoning ourselves and many of the earth's organisms into extinction

Note: This is arguably not a Druidic article at all, but given the momentous effect that pesticides have had on the world, I felt it was important to include this reminder of Rachel Carson's seminal work and her contribution to humanity and the ecological movement. Rachel Carson's 'Silent Spring' is available in various editions, published by Houghton Mifflin.

Druidry and Environmentalism

Originally published in Touchstone *magazine,*
September 2019

Events in the last decade or so have seen a huge rise in Druid activism all over the world, most notably The Warrior's Call (which is pan-Pagan) and more recently Extinction Rebellion (there is an OBOD group for this). As Druids, it is blatantly obvious that we should all be concerned about the state of the planet and protecting our environment generally. However, theory does not always translate into action very well, with many people (from my experience) failing to act out their love of the Earth in their everyday lives.

I don't want to be sanctimonious, I can do better just like everyone else, but I feel there is no harm in some gentle encouragement of my fellow Druids to get more involved. It is startling clear that our governments are not really interested in making large scale changes, their main interest continues to be protecting the corporate sector and their tax revenue. Given that fact, it really is up to all individuals to help and help each other to make a real change in how our society functions.

For this reason I have personally got involved in Extinction Rebellion in Dingle on the west coast of Ireland. Oil and gas exploratory drilling are happening 200km away but it is also happening off the coast of Cork and south Dublin. Fracking may be permitted in county Fermanagh despite government assurances that it would never happen in the Republic of Ireland. Plans for a giant molybdenum-copper open cast mine in beautiful Connemara would allow almost 7,000 km of land to be wrecked forever if this goes ahead. A huge oil and gas depot is planned for county Clare on the banks of the Shannon river.

Ireland has enough environmental problems already, what with the lowest tree cover in Europe, excessive use of glyphosate and irresponsible farming practices. The latest round of threats shows how little our government cares, despite the hand wringing and idle promises of our top politicians. From where I stand, the situation is not much better in Britain, Australia, USA, Canada or France, where corporate interests also trump public/ecosystem interests every time.

My latest book is an attempt to convince people that we can make a difference and that we don't have time to waste on waiting for our governments to wake up and actually do something real and constructive. As Druids, I feel that it is vitally important that we be ambassadors for the environment but without being off-putting evangelical types. Getting the balance right is tough, it's very easy to lose people with over-zealous righteousness! But, of course, the first place to start is with our own lives and our own immediate circle of family and friends. This battle to save our beautiful world must be won, but it will be a grass-roots movement, not the politicians that will make it an unstoppable force.

Not Waiting for the World to Change

First published on beforeitsnews.com,
April 2013

A couple of my friends commented recently on the negative content of much of my writing; one of them in particular found it all rather depressing. I'd have to agree with them that much of what I write about is bad news and it is indeed depressing at times.

However, this negativity is not without reason. The purpose of all this negativity is to facilitate the 'scales falling from my eyes' moment in the vast majority of people who are sleep walking through life. Yes, you could accuse me of being arrogant in thinking that I can wake people up to the realities of human existence. I would not be so bold as to suggest that I have the answers, although I think (like many other writers), that I must try to highlight the facts that we are frequently lied to, and also that in so many areas of life the truth is hidden from us.

Deception and manipulation of the truth to control people's lives is hardly a new thing — the well-known expression 'bread and circuses' aptly describes the manipulation game played by the rulers of ancient Rome some two thousand or so years ago. In the late Middle Ages Niccolo Machiavelli's dark and cynical masterpiece on achieving and maintaining power, *The Prince*, became a great and perennial success. It remains a widely read book to this day — a dastardly instruction manual, if you will, for the political and financial elites of any era!

Such cynical underhandedness amongst our governments and social institutions is hard to accept, it's so horrific that it is in fact much easier to turn one's face away from it in disbelief. Unfortunately, such actions do not change the fact that the very bedrock of Western society is rife with corruption — so much so that often there is not even a cursory attempt to hide it.

The average person appears to be so stupefied by the sugar-coated drivel that the public is constantly bombarded with that there is little need for more than the most superficial deceit in most cases. People are too lazy to look under the surface, or they just do not want to look — preferring to believe the mind-numbing illusions that are conjured up for their enjoyment.

That is why in the same breath people complaining about the war in Afghanistan take a sip of cola and move on to wondering who their favourite celeb is sleeping with this week. Gosh, I sound so cynical myself, and yes, I am! However, I don't blame the ordinary individual for being unable to withstand the ceaseless barrage of nonsense that ends up dominating their thoughts. That is the fault of the system — a system of control that has been refined and improved over many, many centuries.

So then, what is the answer? Where am I going with all this? To my mind, Mohandas Gandhi had the right ideas, nearly a century ago — don't wait for change, make it happen!

You must be the change you want to see in the world.
I have nothing new to teach the world. Truth and Non-violence are as old as the hills. All I have done is to try experiments in both on as vast a scale as I could.
First they ignore you, then they laugh at you, then they fight you, then you win.

Gandhi's seemingly novel, non-violent form of non-compliance inspired his countrymen and sowed the seeds of the destruction of the world's largest empire. Shocking as his achievements are, it is even more shocking that in a few short decades most of us seem to have forgotten the lessons of his life and work.

However, an awakening is in progress, recognition of the state we are in has increased, as has both violent and non-violent resistance. Non-compliance is a tide that is rising once again across the globe, although the simple clarity of vision that Gandhi achieved appears to be missing. Gandhi did not live in an age of instant mass communication, person-to-person, he relied on the press and his followers to a large extent, yet he managed to achieve an astounding change in a few years.

In the current climate there appears to be almost open hostilities between 'the system' and those that are greatly dissatisfied with living in it. We have long since passed the 'laughing' stage that Gandhi spoke of and moved into the early stages of 'fighting'. However, like so many previous attempts to ferment change, it will fail unless a massive proportion of the public is prepared to make its disapproval known and begin taking concrete steps to resist.

Most of us are critical of the society we live in, not least of all our governments, but until we wake up to the need to be pro-active there is no possibility of things changing for the better.

So, if I come across as somewhat negative, in my attempts to stimulate a reaction in the aspartame-addled brain cells of the somnambulists out there, I offer no apology. I will though, offer another brief quotation for consideration, from the 18th century Irish philosopher and politician Edmund Burke:

All that is necessary for evil to triumph is for good men to do nothing.

How true that statement still is — one that our rulers rely on remaining true, and while that inertia remains the status quo will remain also.

Autumnal Equinox

First published on johnhuntpublishing.com,
September 2013

As we approach the autumnal equinox, I am aware of the richness of this year's harvest. This summer in Ireland has been exceptionally sunny and warm, with record-breaking temperatures and dry spells of the like that have not been seen in decades.

In my own garden it has been a bumper year for fruit, strawberries especially and virtually everything, that doesn't need constant watering, has done well. This dry spell was much needed, not just for farmers who will have good grain yields this year, but as a general morale boost for a population depressed by cold and windy winters, continuous poor summers and the depravations of political austerity that has hit most of us, even the ultra-rich in some cases.

Much as this has been a spiritual uplift for many, it has brought to mind some more serious issues. In Ireland the good weather is welcome but I am aware that elsewhere others are suffering drought, wild-fires and devastation as a result of one or the other, or even both.

This reminds me just how lucky we are to live in a temperate and stable part of the world, that does not suffer extremes, almost everyone here is well fed, clothed and in most cases housed, even if they could be described as poor. We take our abundant water supply and abundant food so much for granted that we annually waste huge amounts; in fact, in the case of water, over a third of it is lost in broken pipes before it even reaches people's homes.

This year, like all years, I am grateful for the amazing harvest from the Earth, that we rely on throughout each year. However, I am also aware of how fragile the balance is that gives us all that we need to live and also, I am aware how careless human beings have become with regard to this eternal balance of life and death. Right now Fukushima Dai-Ichi nuclear plant continues to contaminate both Japan and the Pacific Ocean, more than two years after the initial disaster. GM corporates continue to bully farmers around the world and lobby governments to inflict their toxic ideology on populations, when farmers and ordinary people are already under pressure from extreme weather and food insecurity.

My awareness of the bounty of my own personal harvest and its impact physically and psychologically is made all the more powerful by an understanding that while I receive the fruits of my work and the generosity of the land, others are blighted, starved, harassed or even killed on the other side of the globe.

It's so easy to see ourselves as islands, and in my own case I live on one! In reality none of us are islands — everything is connected. Our own apathy or ingratitude here has repercussions elsewhere, just as the gratitude, the efforts to facilitate positive attitudes and real-world changes also reverberates far beyond our own home, town or country.

There is a very real need to accelerate changes in how we live on this planet and I personally think the best way to inspire others is not just to talk about it but to live by example and actually show people that we really need far less that we think we do.

Our desire for far more than we need is disastrous, a subject I feel passionate about. A poem I wrote some time ago on this issue had sunk to the back of my mind but thinking about this time of year and recent reading material (such as *The Moneyless Man* by Mark Boyle) reminded me of it and how blasé most us have become — so here it is! I hope you all enjoy this wonderful time of year and I hope you'll also find the time to reflect on how blessed we truly are.

What I Need

I need a fast car, with plenty of electronics
I need expensive clothes, made in an Asian sweatshop
I need cosmetics and spa treatments, 'cause I'm worth it
I need cappuccinos, ciabattas, couscous and curries,
Since I can no longer remember what my own culture eats
I need an i-Toy and 24 /7 TV so I don't have to be alone with myself
I need internet friends since my real friends don't have time
I need to feel relevant, cool, sophisticated and successful
I need more stuff, more me-time, more
I need self-fulfilment, as simply being happy is not enough
I need a holiday, above all from myself!

I need a kick in the hole,
I need to take responsibility for this world,
And my part in its fading beauty
I need to wake up...
I need to LIVE.

Manifesting Your Connection to the Earth

First published in Indie Shaman *magazine,*
April 2021

I became interested in the environment before I became interested in Earth-based spirituality. When I joined a conservation group, removing invasive rhododendrons, at age 16 in college, I was still a practising Catholic. A few years later I lived close to the Greenpeace headquarters (in Islington, London) and I volunteered for their campaigns and actions. By this time in my life I was a university student and I had developed an interest in both Celtic and Indian spirituality, having realised that I could no longer be a Roman Catholic.

As a child, I had experienced raw nature, woods, fields, mud, running wild with my friends and disappearing all day, just making it home just in time for 6 o'clock dinner on many occasions. I also found myself doing forced labour in the garden, as was common enough for kids in the 1970s. I even had my own vegetable patch — 2m x 2m which I horribly neglected, until it was reclaimed by my dismayed father.

In my student days, I had little interest in returning to the garden, bad memories of seemingly endless pea shelling put me off, not to mention the call of the endless supply of books on spirituality, science, culture etc in the university library. This, however, changed when I started work and shared a flat in old Georgian house with a friend from uni. The house had a walled back garden, that was sadly abandoned but which must have been a total delight at one time. Not one of the other three households were remotely interested in it, so I decided I would begin restoring it as a project, to relax after a boring day stuck in a noisy office.

I soon realised that the garden not only cleared my mind and offered subtle relief from the stress of modern life, but it was a place where spiritual connection and revelation could happen. One thing led to another, and I soon found myself spending more time in the garden, growing new plants, including a huge marijuana bush, and when I finished the work, spending time just watching the birds and enjoying the peace and stillness. To my chagrin, those same birds ate all of the ripe cherries on the ancient cherry tree in the centre of the garden, all in one day, but I was also able to see the funny side of the disappointment caused by my inexperience.

I began to explore the Druid path and the slow process of learning what that really was (to me at least). It seemed to me to be the perfect fit for someone with a deep interest in nature, environmentalism, history and with a thirst for a direct relationship with spirit, deity or whatever you may call it. I look back fondly on that time — I really didn't know a lot about plants or how to look after them, and even less about how to be a Druid, but I did have an instinctive feel for it — I guess I had natural 'green fingers'.

More than 25 years later, I see the culmination of that path in the release of my latest book, *The Druid Garden*. While it is not an exhaustive tome on how to be a good gardener, it expresses my understanding of the natural world, the history of how we (as a species) got into such a terrible mess, and a fair portion of the botanical, herbalist and folklore knowledge that Druidism has gleaned from nature.

It has often struck me that many Earth-based Pagans have good intentions but often fail to 'walk the talk' in a meaningful way. I've visited the houses of Wiccans, Shamans, Druids etc that were bereft of any visible signs of a tactile connection with nature — none or sad looking house plants, empty back gardens, with nothing growing other than weeds! Don't get me wrong,

I am not perfect and do not expect all Pagans to be budding protégés of Alan Titchmarsh, but it occurred to me that a lot of people could do with a helping hand in this area.

So, in a nutshell, this book is a guide on how to take our interest in nature, in spirituality, our love for the Earth and turn that into concrete action in the physical world. Making this happen is easier than one might think, and as is the case with many areas of life, a little bit of learning and preparation beforehand can make all the difference.

I've studied horticulture and worked as a professional in that area for many years, but I have also spent many years prior to that as a novice gardener, falling into of the mistakes and pitfalls that are common. I've also been ignorant of the effects of pesticides, large-scale industrial horticulture and agriculture and lacked understanding of the non-spiritual attitude that regards the plant world as little more than objects.

We are all aware of the desperate state of the planet and the need for us to play our part in changing the situation. Lifestyle changes, including lower consumption are obviously essential in that process, but this can also go hand in hand with a spiritual awareness and practice that brings us out of the house and into the garden. Our ability to change government, corporations is there, but as individuals it is somewhat limited. However, we can make a real and immediate difference within our own living spaces, public parks, common land and abandoned spaces.

Making a sacred space to work, in the garden, is the most obvious interface of spirituality and horticulture, but this can extend far beyond that — by creating a paradise for bees and other wild life and also by growing your own food. For me, growing food is a very powerful way of connecting with the land, and creating a direct awareness of not just the cycle of the seasons, but of the cycle of life and death and rebirth. Essentially, the Earth is one giant recycling machine, all the living matter and consciousness on this planet has always been here, in one form or another. The seedlings I grow become my food eventually, which I excrete to become compost, indeed my own body may become compost eventually and out of my death new life will prosper, and so it goes on.

On a deeper level, if we accept that all life is connected, not just physically but on a meta-physical level, then we begin to see the animal and plant kingdom as our friends as well as our competitors. Modern science has proven what animists, such as Druids, have long believed — that consciousness and spirit extend far beyond the realm of human existence, everything is connected on this Earth, as one giant ecosphere that has intangible links, necessary for its prosperity and continued existence.

So, perhaps more than ever before, it is time to take up our love of Earth and carry it out of the mind and the realm of belief and ideas and into the garden. If ever there was a time when we need to manifest our love for the Earth in the physical world, then surely that is now. If ever there is a time when we need to make a difference and take up the trowel, the bag of seeds, the sapling and do sacred work in service of the Earth, then it is now.

Getting Back to the Garden

First published in Watkins' Mind, Body, Spirit *magazine,*
March 2021

We are all familiar with the allegorical tale of the Garden of Eden, which most esoteric practitioners would interpret in that way, rather than as a literal tale of humanity's infancy in a primordial garden.

Perhaps given the times we are in, a fresh look at this concept brings us full circle, not to a simplistic view of the Garden of Eden as a literal garden created as an enclosed Sylvanian paradise for unconscious humanity, but as an unspoiled and overflowing place that the Earth once was. In a short time, after the last ice age ended, plants repopulated the planet, covering vast areas in forest, and savannah. For our ancestors, some ten thousand or more years ago, the Earth was a paradise of abundance, partly because there were so few people and partly because humans had not had much opportunity to exploit, deplete and wreck the natural environment.

Here we are, in the early stages of the third millennium CE, finding ourselves on the precipice — in an overcrowded world, damaged and degraded by our own actions, one can clearly see how far we have strayed from the Garden. Visions of the future, often of a spiritual nature have become divergent — one offering a transhumanist world of high technology, in synergy or even merger with the human experience, where technology overcomes our problems on this planet and prepares us to venture out into the stars.

The other vision is entirely human, perhaps retrospective in its ideology — looking into our own past for the answers to today's problems. My own vision for a better world is very firmly in this camp, whilst seeking to move forward, combining the best of our past and present, rather than taking a reconstructionist approach to our future. History is full of examples of failed civilizations, dead spiritualities and doomed ideologies, but it is also full of shining examples, often isolated from colonial influences, that worked and could work again given half a chance.

Our great challenge as humans seems to be learning to not keep repeating our mistakes. Being cognisant of our past and its failings is key to making a better future — if we could only learn what not to do, that would help us a long way towards learning what *to* do. History is littered with lessons of both aspects of this knowledge — both what we should embrace and what we should avoid, but not enough of us are prepared to delve into this treasure trove with any real commitment or appreciation for the lessons held there.

One of the reasons that I wrote *The Druid Garden* is that I had become aware that the solutions to much of modern human lifestyles have been around for a long time. Fixing the future may be not so much a process of learning something new, but of remembering that which has been forgotten. On the most basic of levels — the fundamentals of life depend on the food that we eat. The daily alchemy of turning stored sunlight (plants and animals as food) into the energy to live is so taken for granted that most people don't even think about what it actually is or represents.

On the most simplistic level — 'rubbish in equals rubbish out' sums up the net effect of having so little care for the quality of our food, how it is produced, the life and death of living beings that constitute our food and how it is prepared and consumed. For many people there is nothing sacred at all throughout the process — from the birth of a seedling or an animal, through to the eating of the end 'product'. On a deeper level, when we consider the total absence of the sacred in our food then it is hardly a surprise that we are in such bad shape, as individuals, as communities and as a species, with the knock-on effects reverberating throughout the entire planet.

Food is just one aspect of our relationship with spirit and with nature — but this alone should ring alarm bells, as it is so fundamental to our existence. If we can begin to change in our relationship to food and its true value, rediscover the sacredness of the entire act, from intention, through to consumption, then there is some hope that we might be able to tackle more complex issues in a sacred and holistic manner.

In the book, I describe how we arrived at this sorry state of affairs, a process that took many thousands of years and a gradual shift in perception and attitudes. More importantly, I have tried to share real-world practical solutions to our immediate environmental problems, on our own doorsteps. It is all very well being 'spiritual' in our heads — but that counts for very little if we cannot implement our love for the Earth in a meaningful and practical way.

Time is running short, the time for procrastination was over a century ago, but it is still not too late to turn away from a horrible and dystopian fate. I believe that the decisions that humans collectively make now could have an impact on the future of humanity and this planet for hundreds or even thousands of years to come. So many areas of human life are currently being re-evaluated, so much of what we have done or are doing is being questioned, as we face into a very uncertain future.

There is little point in me, or anyone else, lecturing others about what to do — those who are not interested will not listen and those who are already aware do not need to be told what to do. So, what I have done, as best I can, is share what knowledge, experience and understanding that I think will be useful to those who wish to join me in trying to return to the Garden.

Joni Mitchell sang about this 50 years ago on the album *Ladies of The Canyon*, but perhaps we are further from the Garden now than we were then. This planet has amazing regenerative power, given a little assistance by us and the absence of destructive behaviour, it can return to being the paradise it once was.

Reclaiming the Garden for the Earth

First published in Elephant Journal *website,*
March 2021

Gardening has become trendy again, to a large extent because of lockdown boredom, but it has always been a good idea. There are so many benefits to gardening — fresh air, exercise, helping the environment and biodiversity by planting stuff, helping the bees by planting flowering plants, providing healthy food for yourself (and others), plus it's often a good community or social activity that people can enjoy together.

The most obvious benefit is to health and also to the wallet. With inflation looming on the horizon, food is going to become increasingly expensive and good, clean food more so, especially organic food. By growing food yourself you help to reduce your food bills and, of course, you know exactly what went into producing it. You have the choice to avoid using Roundup and other chemicals, use organic fertilizer etc., to produce an entirely natural supply of fruit and vegetables if you want to.

Apart from the benefits of non-GMO, non-sprayed food, food that is really fresh is better for you because of higher nutrient retention and it tastes better too, as well as you having the pleasing sense of pride from knowing that it is the fruit of your own labour (excuse the pun). There are multiple benefits, as I mentioned — one being the sense of activity from spending time on this instead of loafing about or watching Netflix caused by a lockdown excess of free time.

Another way of looking at this is the opportunity to reclaim your sovereignty in controlling your own life to some extent, from the corporate hordes that we buy our stuff from. Throughout most of human history, people have had to grow their own food if they were not rich. Until the 20th century, most people in the world had to grow their own food, barter for other products or sell produce in order to buy essentials such as salt, candles, medicines, shoes etc. Subsistence farming and/or hunting has been the predominant way of life for most people around the world for millennia — we tend to forget that this was the case and that it is still the case for billions of people today.

Gardening on your own patch (owned or rented) gives you agency over your own life — if you don't have to give most of it away to a feudal landlord! In history there were only two types of gardening — agriculture for food (which the rich did not participate in) and gardening for pleasure, which was the sole reserve of the wealthy. Even in ancient Sumer and Egypt the wealthy had gardens or sacred temples with gardens dedicated to the gods. As time progressed, the garden has been a symbol of wealth and power, perhaps most powerfully expressed by the royal gardens at the Palace of Versailles in France or the semi-mythical Hanging Gardens of Babylon.

Up until the mid-twentieth century, only the wealthy could garden for pleasure. Most people had practical gardens full of fruit, vegetables and herbs, with only a few ornamental plants that had no culinary function. Now, most of us in the 'West' at least, do not have to grow our own food at all. Peasant plots have disappeared pretty much, but colonial gardening has left its mark on the world with opulent gardens still here, both private and public. However, at least now many of us ordinary people have the option of creating gardens for pleasure instead of out of necessity.

Even so, times are getting harder and more uncertain. Like the 'victory gardens' of World War II, we may see a comeback of the practical garden. This is great for our own food security and all the other benefits I mentioned at the beginning of this article, but it is also great for the planet too. Biodiversity loss is a serious problem and monoculture farming has had a terrible effect on bees, our primary pollinator and wildlife in general. So, by getting out into the garden and planting a large variety of plants (even if it is selfishly feeding your belly), it will be of benefit to bees and a whole host of other creatures.

Attitudes to the garden, and nature in general are beginning to change, thank goodness. It was part of speeding up this sea change that I wrote *The Druid Garden*, intended as a practical guide to a more enlightened approach to the garden and how best to make it work for us and the Earth too. Whether you're interested in that or not, getting into your garden is a good idea — we all need fresh air, exercise, sunlight (in moderation) and it is also a good place to socialize, weather permitting. So why not get away from the couch, the laptop, phone or whatever and go out into glorious nature? Grow your own free food, which is also a chance to stick it to the corporate food vendors, you'll be helping both yourself and the environment!

Gardening with the Ancestors

First published in Kindred Spirit magazine,
April 2021

Gardening is something that has been with us for thousands of years — from the moment that we moved beyond simply gathering plants and their fruit or seeds. To begin with it was what we call agriculture — the intentional growing of plants for food and for medicinal purposes, the notion of growing for pleasure didn't really exist, so it seems.

It did not take that long for things to change — as we became 'civilised' we can see signs of gardening for pleasure and for sacred purposes in the Sumerian and Egyptian cultures. Temples often had gardens and one can presume that palaces of rulers were probably the first places in which gardens for pleasure emerged. Not that long after west Asian and north Africa, we see evidence of gardens in India and China, with the concept of the garden taking a very long time to reach Europe — via Persia.

For most people, the concept of gardening as we now know it didn't really exist until perhaps a century or two in the past — as most people simply were too poor to consider such a self-indulgent thing as creating a garden to delight the senses. Only wealthy people could afford a garden that was not practical in nature. Up until at least the industrial revolution the average person, across the globe, relied on either hunting, animal husbandry, growing food or a combination of two or three of these, unless they had a profession that paid well enough for them to be free of such requirements.

My personal interest is in Celtic culture in particular, although in my research it became clear that western Europe was not one of the first places to develop advanced techniques in respect to agriculture. It is clear that farming spread across Europe from the east and different methods then developed in situ in different cultures and areas. Much of modern gardening is derived from the Roman inheritance, which itself was passed to them by the Greeks, who in turn received it from the Persians. The Persians were incredibly advanced, having inherited the vast body of experience of the Sumerians, whose descendants were responsible for the famous hanging gardens of Babylon.

Where I live (Ireland), has been very much influenced by British culture but also by its own unique indigenous past — the image of the Druid is still very much alive as a cultural icon of wisdom, mystery and esoteric knowledge. The same can be said, to an extent, of parts of Britain, France and even northern Spain. However, the legacy of that past has been largely lost or merged with the Romano-Greek medieval knowledge that is the basis of modern understanding in gardening and many other subjects as well. It is to Ireland that we have to turn for most of the knowledge of the Celtic peoples with regard to attitudes to nature and the wisdom associated with it.

In Ireland particularly, trees were of great importance and great value. Herbalism, like in all cultures, was also a valuable resource for maintaining health and healing the sick and in both cases some of what the ancients knew has been recorded in Irish language texts on Brehon Law and Ogham. Without a time machine we can only guess what their exact techniques and practices were, as gardeners, but we do know that they differed somewhat from the Roman and Norman approaches to agriculture and the concept of land in general.

From my understanding, and generally accepted perceptions, the Celtic peoples were more holistic and in tune with their environment than the Romans and those that inherited their attitudes. The Romans were very efficient, but they clearly had begun to see the land as something to be exploited rather than something that was sacred in itself. One can lay the blame for our current ecological crisis at the feet of the Romans in some respects — as it is their attitudes that has been the foundation of the modern way of life, which prioritises wealth generation, commerce and economic expansion above all else.

So, in looking for spiritual solutions, as well as practical methods to change our way of interacting with the natural world, it makes sense that we look to other cultures than those heavily influenced by the Romans. The Druidic/Celtic way of life is one such culture, with many similarities in attitude to Native American, African, Taoist Chinese and other indigenous cultures, that we can look to for inspiration. That does not mean that we need to throw out all knowledge that came from Rome, Greece or Persia, but in terms of a holistic approach they now appear somewhat lacking.

In these times, it is clear that we cannot go on polluting the Earth, creating monoculture deserts, poisoning the planet with pesticides without catastrophic consequences. If like me, you believe that it is from our thoughts and intentions that our actions are derived, then a major sea change is required in our thinking if we are going achieve the necessary rapid change in direction. Everything we need to know is already there — buried in our own history and the knowledge of our ancestors.

With a little bit of consideration, time put into reflection and understanding the natural world, we can create a completely different and vibrant world around us — starting with our own spaces in the garden. The knowledge and understanding of ancient cultures may be hidden but it is still there, and combined with the best of modern technology and modern practices such as biodynamics and permaculture we have all that we need to make a major transformation that can turn dead land back into a Sylvanian paradise.

We are not just flesh and blood, we are spirit as well, and as we are rediscovering, the rest of creation is no different. Time is running out to undo the damage humans have done to the world, but it is still entirely possible and achievable. Nature has great strength and an amazing capacity to recover if only we work with it, instead of against it. If ever there was a time to recover the wisdom of our ancestors, then surely, we need it now more than ever before.

The Garden

First published in The Journey *(Moon Books), 2012*

Once there was a garden and that garden was the world. Mankind lived in that garden in happy ignorance, until one day, people ate of the tree of knowledge. As they ate the fruit of the tree of knowledge, the tree of life vanished before them, never to be seen again, and the garden became just an ordinary place...

A place to be divided into parcels, bought and sold, built upon and fought over until every wilderness was swallowed up. Those of men who had not eaten the fruit either yielded to the others or perished at their hands — and thus gradually mankind swept through the world, ever increasing in both knowledge and number. As men's knowledge grew so too did their desire until all was refashioned by it and the world shone nightly with the lights of vast cities, the forests gave way to endless fields and every creature of land and sea was allowed live only to serve man's insatiable needs.

The gods looked down upon their children and said of us "What have you done to your home?" Their sighs became the howling whirlwinds that uproot both tree and dwelling. Their bitter tears swelled the rivers and oceans until they broke upon the land leaving disaster in their wake. The heat of their fury baked the earth so that lakes emptied and rich pasture turned to desert sand.

But even in their fury, the gods still took pity upon mankind, as it is easy to forgive the foolishness of children. And so, in their mercy, they allowed men for one last time, the chance to amend their ways... and that time is NOW.

Druidic History

Healing the Celtic Lands

First published in Touchstone *magazine,*
March 2009

As someone of mixed heritage I have become well aware of the dark and painful history of the British Isles. Fortunately, after over a thousand years of conflict between these nations it seems that long lasting peace has finally broken out at last! Perhaps now after almost an eternity of war and oppression we have an opportunity to lay to rest the ghosts that still haunt us and begin, in earnest, the process of reconciliation and healing.

Like millions of people who live or have lived in England I feel somehow not entirely at home there. I was born and spent my early childhood in Scotland, however, I grew up in England but have spent the last 10 years in Ireland where my Irish ex-wife and my daughter also live. My ancestry is half English with a smattering of Irish, German/Danish, Scottish and Norse in the mix; so when I think about who I am I often think to myself "I'm not entirely sure". Am I English, Scottish, Norse or Irish or none of these?

Thinking about this, I realize that there are literally millions of people in England and its former colonies (e.g. New Zealand and Canada), who are in the same boat, who known or unknown to themselves have an ancestral and cultural link to the Celtic lands. I have grown up aware that I did not entirely fit with the predominant culture — spiritually and emotionally I've felt drawn to Scotland and Ireland much more so than to England. However, I must stress I have no antipathy for England (which is often not the case of many Scots, Welsh and Irish people and their descendants scattered around the world). I like England but I find I often feel like a dispassionate observer of the country that I've spent roughly half my life in, and in which I have many relatives.

For many English people I think there is a total or partial lack of awareness of the tragic history and deep divides that exist between them and the rest of the UK and Ireland. To a huge extent this is the fault of political propaganda and a view of history inherited from colonial times, through the education system. My knowledge of Scottish history comes from my father, my knowledge of Ireland from my wife and my own reading and conversations as an adult. What I learnt at school was almost exclusively English history and where history touched on other countries it was heavily slanted in favour of the official point of view.

Without getting into a big English bashing session (which is the last thing I want to do) I feel that it is very important to get to the bottom of this issue if there is to be any genuine forging of links between countries and substantive healing of the damage done over centuries. The growing interest in Druidry in the last few decades is now truly international, however, it is still predominately in the Celtic lands and their diaspora that people are reconnecting with their ancient Celtic cultures. This is great news all round, but in truth there is still a seething mass of pain, hatred, bigotry and sorrow lying under the surface of the lands and hearts of the modern Celts, which in many cases has passed down through generations.

As part of moving forward into better times in our personal lives it is necessary to heal our own hurts, confront painful issues in our past and deal with them for healing to take place. I believe that the land itself and peoples as a whole can be damaged in the same way as individuals and hence it strikes me as of crucial importance that the near demise of the Celtic culture of these islands be examined and laid to rest, as we move into a new era of Celtic resurgence in greater understanding and peace.

The history of these islands and its peoples is now so interwoven that hardly a person does not have an English, Scottish, Irish or Welsh relative somewhere and I think that we all owe it to ourselves to deal with the guilt, blame, anger and sorrow of all that has taken place since the Romans invaded England two thousand years ago. I feel that this is not just important for disgruntled Irish, Scots and Welsh but also for the English who are blamed for all evils in many cases and some of whom feel disproportionately the weight of guilt for the deeds of their forefathers.

While difficult issues remain buried, they cannot be resolved, when two people do not talk there can be no reconciliation. I believe the same applies on a tribal or national scale. Now that the last conflict (Northern Ireland) appears to have ceased permanently I hope that a sincere and strenuous effort will be made by all peoples of these islands to look deeply into our shared past so that we may find resolution and healing for all our people and the land with it too.

Tlachtga, and the Ancient Roots of Halloween/Samhain

First published on Druidry.org, June 2012

Most people have some awareness of the origins of the fire festival of *Samhain*, the time that is known in common parlance as Halloween. *Samhain* is the word for November in *Gaeilge* (Irish) and is thought to be derived from *sam-fuin*, meaning end of summer.

The modern celebrations of Halloween are derived from the traditions of the British Isles and no doubt similar traditions around a festival of the dead existed throughout Europe. More than anything, the modern celebrations are influenced by the importing of North American practices, which are themselves the distortion and adaptation of customs exported to the New World, primarily by the Irish and Scottish emigrants. In terms of modern Paganism, the main themes of this fire festival are as follows:

Death and rebirth – At this point in time (end of October) the natural world appears to be dying, the *Mabon*, or Child of Light, passes beyond maturity into death and the otherworldly Cernunnos archetype retakes his place as consort to the goddess. This is otherwise symbolized by the time of the Crone, Hag or *Cailleach* who will re-emerge in spring transformed into the youthful form of the goddess. This was also a time of collecting the last of the harvest (*Samhain* being the last of 3 harvest festivals) and the time at which animals were culled prior to the onset of winter.

Festival of the dead – The acknowledgement of the ancestors and the dead in general was central to *Samhain* celebrations and offerings of food were commonplace throughout the British Isles. A person's failure to pay appropriate respects to the dead (such as eating offerings of food) was thought to result in themselves being ostracized from such festivities when they too became deceased. Other customs and precautions such as throwing out all dirty water and proper attention to the hearth were observed — the consequences of failing to do so are described in the Irish myth *Eachtra Nera* where a hanged man's spirit spits water over the members of the household he has entered causing their death.

Funeral games and divination – This was also a common time of divination and prophetic vision, *Eachtra Nera* again being a prime example, Nera sees a vision of the possible events of the Samhain a year hence, an attack on the king's *dún* (residence) by the *sídhe* (fairies). This was common time to play divinatory games or perform divination charms, particularly related to marriage or love. Indeed, the *Báirín Breac* (fruit loaf) containing a mock wedding ring is a survival of such customs and is still commonly eaten in Ireland today. Trickery, cross dressing — particularly of young boys to confuse potential thieves among the *sídhe* was common. Suspension of normal order and time, removal of doors, moving of signs was indicative of the removal of barriers between the material realm and the otherworldly realm. Such activities as 'trick or treating' are descendants of the *buachaillí tuí* — a group of disguised revelers who represented the spirits of the dead accompanying the goddess of the land in the form of a mock horse character *an Láir Bhán*, or the white mare. Apple bobbing is again a descendant of earlier apple games, apples being a clear link to the otherworld in Celtic mythology.

Sacrifice – The slaughtering of animals at this time was highly practical but it is also a time when offerings were made to the gods to ensure the return of the vital forces in nature and to protect the people and their means of survival through the dark and harsh winter months. Sacrifice of pigs was common into the medieval era and it is likely that in earlier times humans were also sacrificed — archaeological remains supports this theory. Sacrificial rites remain in Ireland even now in the form of 'Bleeding for St. Martin', albeit a Christianised form of sacrifice of a hen or cockerel at the beginning of November.

Sacred fire – It is a common custom to light *Samhain*/Halloween fires even now for Celtic peoples of all religions, however, in the UK the date has been displaced to 5th November in commemoration of the attempted blowing up of the English Houses of Parliament by Guy Fawkes in 1606. This tradition of *Samhain* fires is recorded as directly descended from the ancient *Samhain* fires of *Tlachtga* (Hill of Ward) in Co, Meath, Ireland, although it is likely similar fire traditions existed throughout the British Isles. The Druids lit a sacred fire, probably at the new moon (end of Oct/start Nov). *Tlachtga* was on the horizon from Tara, some 12 miles away, perhaps the Tara fire was lit once the *Tlachtga* fire was seen or the fire was brought from *Tlachtga* to Tara, possibly by boat and Loughcrew (*Sliabh na Caillíghe*) after that. Many Druids in Ireland believe this to be true, although this is impossible to prove, and re-enact it yearly.

Tlachtga was the sacred place of Druids, Tara (*Teamhair*) was the seat of the *Ard Rí* or High King, who feasted surrounded by the *Rí Tuaithe* (provincial kings) and *flatha* (nobility), symbolically demonstrating the unity and stability of the people at this time of growing darkness, chaos and threatening forces within nature. However, it was *Tlachtga* where the first fire was lit at this time and then after the lighting of the Tara fire the fires would be lit all over the country. The sunrise and moon rise at *Samhain* form an alignment from *Tlachtga*, to the quartz standing stone in Cairn L of Loughcrew (*Slieve na Caileach/Sleive Bearra*) and Lambay Island (off the coast of Dublin). Interestingly, the Mound of the Hostages (at Tara) is also illuminated by the sunrise at *Samhain*. This alignment continues west across the country also intersecting 'Lugh's Seat' at the end of the volcanic 'Pillars of Samhain' and the cairn of *Mór-Ríoghan* above the Keash caves.

Now called the Hill of Ward, after a former owner of the 17th century, *Tlachtga* is a hill fort consisting of a series of four concentric banks with a central platform. It was disturbed in 1641 during Cromwell's invasion but has never been properly excavated, although it has been suggested that there is a barrow burial there, probably dating from the Bronze Age. The person who is buried at *Tlachtga* is most likely an important figure, perhaps even a king or queen, but that will remain a mystery until a proper archaeological dig takes place.

There are three wells within a few hundred metres of the site, one near the main road from Athboy (*Atha Buí*) is relatively modern but is perhaps fed from the older nearby well also to the west. To the south lies a more ancient and much larger well that retains its old name *Tobar Draoithe* or "The Druids' Well", which most likely was the main well associated with and used for practices at *Tlachtga*. Modern Druid ceremonies at the new moon make use of this well, whilst the more general public gathering on October 31st at *Tlachtga* (that has now taken place for over a decade) uses the roadside well on the road from Athboy.

It is well known that *Tlachtga* was one the great assemblies (*aonach*) of the Gaelic people, in 1168 Ruaidrí Ua Conchobair (last *Ard Rí* of Ireland), presided over a national synod of kings and prelates at the site. The rulers of the intermittent kingdom of *Mide* also sat here, although *Tlachtga* is often associated with the province of Munster and the medieval kingdom of *Brega*. Ceremonies centred around the lighting of the winter fires are said to originate from *Lugh Lámfhota*, (the *Tuatha Dé Danann* hero of the second battle of Moytura and later high king) around

1450BC. This being the case, the tradition of *Samhain* fires is some 3,500 years old.

As for *Tlachtga* herself, there are several stories relating to this goddess, the most recent being that of the medieval *Metrical Dindshenchas* (place lore in verse form) and *Banshenchas* (women's lore), both of which refer to *Tlachtga's* father *Mog Roith* as being a student of Simon Magus, and also describe Magus' three sons raping her at *Imbolc*. She gave birth to triplets at *Samhain* at the site that bears her name and died in the process. This version of the story was most likely ecclesiastical fantasy, appearing to be based on a medieval tale of the beheading of John the Baptist, in which *Mog Ruith* takes on the role of executioner. In the *Banshenchas* version *Tlachtga's* story is partly merged with the myth of Etain and Midir, also the unknown martyr that *Tlachtga* is said to have slain may be a confusion with the account of her father described above.

The earliest form of *Tlachtga* was a Druidess type goddess that arrived with the Firbolgs, long before the *Tuatha Dé Danann* and Milesians. The meaning of her name is 'Earth Spear', probably relating to lightning. She was described as daughter of the chief Druid *Mog Ruith* of Munster who lived in the time of high king *Cormac McAirt* (mid-3rd century AD), although he may well have been a god in an earlier form, his name means 'devotee of the wheel', which probably relates to the sun.

Tlachtga is said to have created a pillar stone called *Cnamhcaill* meaning 'bone damage' out of a fragment of *Roth Ramach* her father's wheel. It is said to kill all who touch it, blind those that gaze upon it and deafen those that hear it. This pillar is thought to represent lightning, which would tie in with the meaning of her name, as lightning was likened to a spear thrown at the ground. *Tlachtga* was most likely not only an ancient goddess, discredited and demoted by Christian scribes, but a goddess of death and rebirth, the sun and lightning.

Whatever the circumstances of her death, *Tlachtga* is said to have given birth to three boys — *Doirb*, *Cumma* and *Muach*. In the oldest version of the story, they became rulers of Munster, Leinster and Connaught (three of the provinces of Ireland). It was said that while their names are remembered that Ireland would be safe from domination by strangers. Of course, they were indeed forgotten and Ireland, as we all know, fell under the yoke of the Normans. Her triple birth and subsequent death resembles *Macha*'s double birth and death from grief, giving her power to the land in the process, leading some to see *Tlachtga* as a form of the triple goddess.

So, it become clear that *Tlachtga* is intimately linked with the symbolic death and rebirth of the land at *Samhain*, perhaps this is why her story was rewritten to diminish her impact and ensure that she and her sacred temple were forgotten by mainstream society. They did such an efficient job that most modern Pagans are unaware of either her, the ancient temple or her links with *Samhain*, a festival that is celebrated worldwide by Druids and Wiccans and Shamanic Pagans. Despite great efforts to eliminate *Samhain*, (as well as other Pagan traditions) there is still a direct link between the ancient sacred fire of *Tlachtga* and the modern lighting of bonfires, between the ancient festival of the dead and our modern pageantry of ghosts, ghouls and other such fun and games.

Perhaps now it is time for *Tlachtga*, this almost forgotten goddess, to retake her rightful place within Celtic culture and for a renewed understanding of her significance in Paganism, the history of the land of Ireland and also the Celtic customs and traditions that survive to this day in the British Isles and beyond.

Modern Druidry in Ireland

First *published in* Brigid's Fire *magazine,*
August 2010

Over the last twenty years there has been a slow and steady increase in Paganism in Ireland which has gathered pace in the last decade. Wicca, introduced to Ireland by Janet and Stewart Farrar, is perhaps more established than any other form of Paganism here, although Druidry (also encouraged by the Farrar's) has grown significantly in that time.

The seeds of the Pagan revival in Ireland were sown not here but in the UK in following the repeal of the Witchcraft act in 1951. Following this repeal two strands of esoteric thought emerged into the mainstream via two men who have become very well known in magical circles.

The first person was Gerald Gardner, author of several books, most notably *Witchcraft Today* which blew the lid off what had until then been a religion practiced in total secrecy. It was Gardner who coined the term 'Wicca' and almost single-handedly created a new form of the ancient Pagan religion that existed throughout Europe up until the middle ages. It is from Gardner's foundation that the Wiccan religion has grown, evolved and spread throughout the western world.

Ross Nichols. a contemporary and friend of Gardner, was instrumental in the mainstream Druid revival in the UK and played a part in its revival in Ireland via the Fellowship of Isis. Ross Nichols was chairman of the Ancient Druid Order (a Freemason like Druid order), which claims its origin in the 1700s. However, Ross left the order in the 1960s and established the Order of Bards, Ovates and Druids (OBOD) which was set up as a vehicle for returning to Celtic spirituality. From this other splinter group other groups such as BDO formed and a number of other orders have since sprung up in the UK, America and beyond.

The re-emergence that took hold in Britain transferred to Ireland to some extent, although this process was to some degree hampered by the much later repeal of the Witchcraft Act (1983) in the Republic. Subsequent to the British Pagan revival, which is largely focused on British traditions, the Irish revival has gathered pace but this seems to have taken place in a slightly different way to in Britain.

The Druid revival in Britain could be described as pan-Celtic — it draws on the traditions of Wales, Scotland, Cornwall, Northern England, Brittany and Ireland. Druidry in England itself, lacking its own sources due largely to the influence of the Romans and later on the Saxons and the Normans, has tended to draw mostly on Welsh tradition.

Ireland, in contrast to England, despite conquest and many attempts at cultural domination has retained the bulk of its Celtic cultural heritage and still retains the native language in pockets around the country. Druidry here was not suppressed by the Romans, who maintained only a trading relationship with Ireland, instead it was gradually absorbed and replaced by Christianity over a period of several centuries, seemingly with little violence. The remains of Druidic tradition here were still in evidence in the 17th century at the time of the demise of the Bardic schools following the flight of the Earls. In more recent centuries the total dominance of Catholicism largely eradicated Druidic thought and beliefs, but with some of the more secular aspects such as laws, folklore and some customs remaining but generally in a form that is detached from their original context.

From my observations of Druidry here most Druids seem to fall into one of two camps — those who take a nationalistic or purist approach to Druidry, based on a desire to resurrect Irish practices and the other camp being those who are somewhat more eclectic. Many feel a desire to develop and unearth the indigenous Druidry rather than simply copying the established systems of non-Irish organizations such as ADF, OBOD or BDO etc. For others, the sources — modern or ancient, Irish or British, Celtic or multi-faith, is not so important, the spiritual journey and the attitude being of greater priority than concerns about cultural integrity, learning and technique.

One major ideological difference it seems would centre around the magical systems employed. Most of western esoteric tradition has its roots in kabalistic magic which originates in the middle east, however, this is not the case with Celtic magic. The Druids and Shamans of the pre-Christian period had a system that shares some of the concepts found in Kabbalistic magic, Alchemy and Witchcraft and also in Hellenic and Vedic culture. However, the expression and practice of these concepts is in most western magic is often quite different from what we know of Druidic culture. A basic example of this would the elements, Kabbalistic magic has four, Chinese has five and Celtic magic had three — sky, sea and land, or nine if you consider the concept of *dúile*.

There being a vast treasure trove of written material concerning early Irish culture and still existing folklore and tradition that could be said to be indigenous, some Druids feel that there is no need to 'borrow' ideas from other Pagan traditions, including those of the international Druidic revival. Much as there is a strong case for continued rediscovery of Irish Druidic heritage that is buried just under the surface, there is also a case for a more inclusive approach that also respects and values the contribution of other sources.

I personally believe that there is room to accommodate both extremes and those that fall between two stools. Although a fudged consensus pleases nobody, I think that as mature spiritual practitioners we should be able to 'agree to disagree' and find common ground where it does exist.

The Druidic community here is small and comprised of small orders and groves that usually work entirely independently. Following the demise of the Convocation of Druids of Ireland (CDE) there has been no umbrella organization either to represent the Druids of Ireland or even to provide networking opportunities to the Irish Druid community.

Consequently, Irish Druidry remains isolated and somewhat stagnant. I feel that it is important that Druidry here develop its own unique character and find maturity as a path on its own terms, and this process can be facilitated by dialogue between the disparate groves and orders of this island. The disagreements and confrontations that have occurred in Irish Druidry in the last few years may have been a necessary part of a growing up process but they have done nothing to foster links within Ireland or abroad and this is a problem that is in need of addressing.

For some reason, Druidry in Ireland has been particularly plagued by politics and dogmatism. Perhaps when one looks at the turbulent and troubled history of this island, made worse by infighting and disunity, it should not be such a great surprise. Given that the groves and orders here are all relatively young it may take some time and communal efforts to re-establish a form of Druidry that can be identified as Irish. I hope that as this process happens and Irish Druidry gains maturity that its practitioners and organizations will have the self-confidence to be uniquely Irish yet also be respectful and open to interaction with international Druidry and other religious paths.

A Re-evaluation of the Ogham Tree List

First published in Journal of Ogham Studies *magazine,*
June 2016

It is not well known amongst those interested in Celtic Spirituality that the modern interpretation of the Irish Ogham alphabet is largely based on the ideas of Robert Graves, following the publication of his magnum opus *The White Goddess*. Those in academia generally have different ideas about Ogham in general and most differently on the possibility of there being a lunar Ogham calendar or indeed the attributing of arboreal or plant characteristics to the entire 20 or 25 letters of the alphabet. As a generalisation, it appears that some people with an interest in Ogham, including many writers and Druidic orders, seem happy enough to go with the 'accepted wisdom' that can be found in many books and on the internet. However, I believe that a re-evaluation of the kennings and the general ethos of the *beith-luis-nin* or Ogham alphabet, based purely on the evidence and not whimsical notions, is long overdue. Firstly, we must thank Graves for a re-introduction of Ogham into modern culture and specifically the area of Celtic Spirituality.

However, much of his work was erroneous and speculative, which he admitted himself subsequent to the publication of *The White Goddess*. One of his prime sources for his 13-month lunar calendar was O'Flaherty's *Ogygia* (published in an English translation in 1793). Of course, scholars were and are aware that there are actually 15 consonants, which instantly destroys Grave's theory, based on a mistake in O'Flaherty's work. Any tree calendar, viable or not, is an entirely modern invention. There is no evidence that I have found in academic work or translations of the ancient manuscripts that suggest that such a thing ever existed prior to Graves' suppositions. Having dismissed the idea of the calendar, let us now turn our attention to Ogham as a tree alphabet. Scholars such as McManus tend to dismiss Ogham as a tree alphabet, citing the fact that only eight of the letters actually refer specifically to trees. Although this is in fact correct, as McManus himself acknowledges, the kennings often allude to trees or could possibly do so.

Another scholar, MacCoitir, has re-interpreted the old-Irish kennings, specifically in reference to trees — which gives a complete list of trees and bushes, not including plants. Having studied his work, I find his arguments and re-interpretation to be convincing, however, given the cryptic nature of the three *Bríatharogam* (word-ogham) lists, it remains somewhat open to question. It would be nice to say that there is a definitive and correct interpretation of the letters' meanings and their correspondences, but unfortunately it is not that simple and the best we can achieve is a model of best fit, based on the original source material. Unfortunately, the most common Ogham list is based on evaluations of translations of medieval Irish into modern English. This standard list has not been challenged for quite some time, but that changed in 2003 with the publication of Niall MacCoitir's work.

What MacCoitir has done is return to the early legal tracts such as *Bretha Comaithchesa*, cross-referencing it with the oldest extant versions of the *Bríatharogaim Maic ind Óc, Bríatharogaim Con Culainn* and *Bríatharogaim Morainn mic Moín*. He also points out that much of the terminology surrounding Ogham refers specifically to the parts of trees/bushes, which is further indication that the alphabet is almost definitely a tree alphabet. Let's look at some specific examples. The letters themselves are referred to as *feda* or *fid* in the singular, which means respectively 'wood' and 'tree'. The consonants are also called *táebomnai*, which translates into 'The side of a tree-trunk'.

The *druim* (edge/ridge) on which the letters are written was originally vertical, like a tree trunk, with the horizontal *druim* coming into favour with the use of paper or vellum. The spines or lines that comprise the individual letters (on the *druim*) are referred to as *flesc*, which translates as twig. So, from the above terminology it is quite clear that the alphabet has a connection with trees and bushes. However, the most common Ogham lists to be found in books and on the internet includes plants — vine, ivy, heather, fern, reed and honeysuckle. For starters, reed and fern do not have either a trunk or twigs and so can be immediately dismissed so far as I can see. Heather does not have a trunk and whether you could define its low, fine growth as twigs remains doubtful. The remaining plants are not trees, they are parasitic in as much as they need a host to climb up — either a wall or a tree in most cases. On the basis that the plants mentioned above are not trees and do not possess the qualities associated with the Ogham terminology one is left with the task of looking for viable alternative interpretations, based on the source material — which is exactly what MacCoitir has done.

His first discrepancy with the standard list is not in fact the removal of a plant — it is a substitution of one tree for another, namely *Nin* — the Cherry in place of Ash. This was rather a bold move considering the widely accepted interpretation of *nin, nuin* as 'Ash'. The word actually translates as 'branch-fork' which is indicative only of a tree/bush. Therefore, we must rely on the three *Briatharogam* for some indication of what tree it should actually be. The three word-oghams in Irish are — *Costud Síde, Bág Ban* and *Bág maise* which MacCoitir retranslates as 'staple enjoyment or supply of the otherworld', 'boast of women' and 'boast of beauty' respectively. These are all rather cryptic but indicate a connection with the otherworld (realm of *an sídhe*), femininity and beauty. Cherry traditionally possesses these qualities but Ash does not. Hence, I would have to agree that Cherry is the correct choice and that Ash should be placed elsewhere.

The next discrepancy is *Muin*, which is most often given as Vine as suggested by the medieval *Auraicrept Na N-Éces (The Scholar's Primer)*. However, the word-oghams for this especially vague — *Tressam fedmae, Ardam maisse, Arusc n-airlig, Conar gotha*; which mean respectively 'Strongest in action', 'Most noble goodliness', 'Proverb of slaughter/rottenness' and 'Path of the voice'. To further complicate matters the word *Muin* can mean 'neck', 'love', 'trick' or possibly 'thicket'. MacCoitir suggests thicket as the most likely meaning, given its arboreal nature, and also points out that 'strongest in action' and 'proverb of rottenness' could relate to purgative properties which the Buckthorn tree is well-known for and Vine is not. Vines are not native to Ireland, introduced in the late Roman era, however, Buckthorn has a long history of medicinal use in Ireland up into modern times. *Muin* is, in my opinion, the most difficult tree to place due to the vague and multiple associations, however, I am confident that MacCoitir has correctly identified Vine as a medieval error.

Gort is commonly identified as Ivy, again listed as that in *Auraicrept Na N-Éces (The Scholar's Primer)*. This word actually means 'field' and the word-oghams *are Milsiu férai, Glaisem gelta, Ined erc* and *Sásad ile*; meaning 'Sweetest grass', Greenest pasture', 'Suitable place for cows' and 'Satisfaction of all' respectively. These meanings are again rather vague but would tend to indicate a tree (if any) that can be associated with fields and cows. Firstly, Ivy is not a tree, it does not grow free-standing in fields and it is not eaten by livestock. Gorse or furze, in contrast is commonly found in fields, it is a small tree that has traditionally been used as fodder for livestock, including cows. Gorse was also valued on good land as beneficial due to its multiple uses — such as fodder, bedding, dye, beer, fertilizer and hedging. This is a much better fit than Ivy, which itself might often have been confused with another parasitic climber Honeysuckle — *Edlenn* and *Edeand* being similar in pronunciation.

Onn was identified as Gorse or Heather by the medieval glossators, however, the word in Old Irish clearly means 'Ash tree'. The word-oghams are *Congnaid, congnamaid ech, Fétham soíre* and *Lúth fían,* meaning 'Wounder/helper of horses', 'Smoothest of Craftmanship.' and 'Sustenance of warriors.' At first these correspondences may appear to be not much help, but ash was used extensively in carpentry, hurley making, for spears and as fodder for horses (dried leaves). Ash fits at least two of the word-oghams whereas Gorse is a far harder fit.

Úr is often given as heather, a small low-growing shrub, but the word means 'clay' or 'moist/fresh'. This would appear to fit well with the first of the word-*oghams Úaraib adbaib; Gruidem, guirem dál, Sílad cland* and *Forbbaid ambí,* meaning 'In cold dwellings', 'Most devoted sharing', 'Propagation/dripping of plants' and 'Shroud of a lifeless one.' Elm is native, like heather, but it is a tree and is especially well adapted to damp and cold conditions as well as being full of sap. In modern Irish the elm is referred to as *Crann Úr,* which further strengthens the argument for the placement of Elm here instead of Heather.

Of the five supplementary letters, used for rendering Greek and Latin words, MacCoitir disagrees on two of the commonly accepted lists. The first is *Uilen* (UI), which means 'elbow/angle'. The word-ogham *tuthmar fid* or 'most fragrant tree' is presumably why it is often given as Honeysuckle. Of course, Honeysuckle is not a tree, but Juniper (which is also fragrant, especially when burned) is a small tree, which is actually also referred to by the medieval glossators in the context of this letter. According to Fergus Kelly *Crann Fir* is the Juniper, the word *fir* or *fiar* having the meaning 'bent or twisted', which fits with its characteristic as well as the word *Uilen* of similar meaning.

The second of the supplementary letters he replaces is *Emancholl* (EA), which means 'twin of hazel'. It is frequently listed as Beech, which can easily be dismissed as a poor choice. Beech was introduced into Ireland in the late medieval period by the Normans/English, it is not native to Ireland and only became widely established by the time that the Ogham alphabet was no longer in common use. Hazel on the other hand is native to Ireland and fits no worse with the word-oghams for this letter, which are totally cryptic.

So, having presented my own interpretation of the evidence presented, mostly by MacCoitir, I hope I have argued a strong case for re-evaluation of the commonly accepted Ogham list. I would suggest that although a 'tree calendar' is clearly a modern innovation, there is a very strong case for beith-luis-nin as an entirely 'tree' alphabet. Many writers concur with John-Paul Patton's belief that Ogham is a system of knowledge that extends beyond the trees themselves. I would agree with this claim, however, I think the empirical evidence suggests that the root of this knowledge and usages lies in the tree list itself. I'd suggest that the lore and correspondences that exist derive in some way from the tree list and hence, selection of the correct trees is essential for the correct use of Ogham. Clearly the choice of trees could have an impact on groupings of knowledge and particularly in the use of Ogham in herbalism and as a divination tool. In that sense it is absolutely critical that the right trees are selected otherwise the entire set of correspondences for that letter will be incorrect.

I am not going to claim that these letter interpretations presented here are definitive or entirely correct. I do believe that these amendments are more likely to be the correct one than the common interpretations. I also believe that the commonly accepted list is anachronistic and at the very least, it needs a fresh look by both Celtic scholars and spiritual practitioners who actually make use of the Ogham system itself. To date, the work of McManus, Kelly, MacCoitir and Patton remains largely unknown outside of academic circles, which perhaps explains why most modern spiritual practitioners continue to use a long-established Ogham list that most probably is incorrect. I would like to see thorough re-evaluation by academic and spiritual organisations and a new consensus reached on what the correct attributes of all questionable letters are. Basic definition is an area of Ogham that has been taken for granted and hence almost completely overlooked until recently. However, given the immense impact acceptance of a new list would cause, it is an area of Ogham studies that urgently needs attention.

Naked Ireland, and How We Got Here

First published on Indymedia.ie,
July 2013

A brief history of the deforestation of Ireland and why it happened...

It is well known that Ireland has a very low level of tree cover, among the lowest of any European country — in 2012 it had risen to almost 11% although it is still way below the European average of 30%. Of course, about half of this 11% is Sitkha Spruce, which is non-native and causes acidification of the soil.

So, we currently live in a country that is fairly naked — stripped of the great forests that once covered most of the country. Today most mountain ranges and hills are bare, populated with sheep and cattle instead of trees. It seems that the bulk of our tree populate the 'long acre' i.e. the side of the road or ditches separating fields.

In my travels around the country I've noticed that many of these roadside and ditch residing trees are in a terrible condition — swamped with Ivy, sometimes damaged by wire and fence-posts or miscellaneous injuries caused by pruning or wide/high vehicles.

So how did we get to a landscape that is so bereft of trees and where trees are so poorly valued? The roots of this problem can be traced back to the Norman invasion of Ireland from 1169.

Henry II was accepted as ruler of Leinster by Ruairí Ui Conchobhair (Rory O'Connor) the *Ard Rí* (High King) at the treaty of Windsor in 1175, however, the Norman ambitions did not stop there. Subsequent English rulers attempted to expand their territories in Ireland by a combination of military conquest and exchanging traditional royal titles for Earldom's under English law.

The Gaels of the time lived a semi-nomadic existence, very much in harmony with their environment; their culture was completely rural and made good and sustainable use of the woodlands, bogs and lakes, with the Gaels being intimately acquainted with the lands they lived in.

Of course, the invaders, although militarily more advanced in terms of conventional strategy and war technology, were not accustomed to either the landscape or the Gaelic style of rural existence. After initial success the Normans met with stiff resistance to their advances as the Gaels became used to their techniques and began use the natural environment against their enemy.

...by usage and experience the experience the natives gradually became skilled and versed in handling arrows and other arms. Frequent encounters with our men and their many successes, taught them how to set ambushes, while themselves guarding against them.

...the king of Uladh, came to them, however, on that night, and gave him battle. The Foreigners were defeated, and put to much slaughter.

In the late 12th century Giraldus Cambrensis' *Topographia Hibernia* described Ireland and its people, somewhat fantastically in places, but it does give an early insight on some aspects of life here:

Ireland is a country of uneven surface and rather mountainous. The soil is soft and watery, and there are many woods and marshes. Even at the tops of high and steep mountains you will finds pools and swamps. Still there are, here and there, some fine plains, but in comparison with the woods they are indeed small.

The Irish legal codes (commonly referred to as Brehon Law) gave protection to the natural environment with harsh fines for abuse of trees, based on their perceived value ranging over four categories from Nobles of the wood to Bushes of the wood. Norse and Danish immigrants also observed a respect for the woods and brought relatively small change to the appearance of the country; this was not the case though with the Normans and subsequent waves of English colonisers.

Having realised that the Gaels were able to mount guerrilla warfare from the relative safety of the forests and mountains the Normans were effectively under siege until they began to dismantle the native habitat.

The woods and bogs are a great hindrance to us and help the rebels. Much good could be done by Irish churls felling, dressing and burning the trees in heaps. This couldst be done whilst leaving sufficient timber for the use of the country, if a tree is left standing every twenty yards. (Eoin Neeson citing CSPI).

By the 14th century the Anglo-Normans (or English) were increasingly under pressure from surprise attacks in transit and even rapid full-frontal assaults on their towns from Irish armies that seemed to be able to disappear into the mist and woods just as quickly as they had appeared.

The Irish were able to keep livestock and grow vegetables and grains in the lands as yet unexplored by the English and lay in vast stores for the guerrilla campaigns. It was the woodlands and these stores that the English eventually began to target in their efforts to subdue the native people:

In searching the woods and bogs we found great store of corn, which we burnt... We continued burning and destroying for four days... The enemy in these parts chiefly depended upon this country for provision. I believe that we have destroyed as much as wood have served some thousands of them until next harvest. (Sir Henry Sidney, 1556)

Although highly successful, these tactics were carried out intermittently and not followed up on, so that gradual de-colonisation had reduced 'The Pale' significantly. However, Tudor king Henry VIII began to take a serious interest in the unruly English colony and through new laws, 'Surrender and Re-grant' and vicious military campaigns, he began to turn the tide.

It was under Elizabeth I that the great destruction of the Irish wilderness began, first in her attempts to crush the Fitzgeralds of Munster and later on in Connacht and Leinster. Woodlands were chopped or burned, villages and crops burned also in an all-out war of attrition...

At this period it was commonly said, that the lowing of the cow, or the voice of the ploughman could scarcely be heard from Dun-Caoin to Cashel in Munster. (Annals of the Four Masters, 1616)

This culminated with the defeat of the O'Neills of Ulster in a desperate war that cost Elizabeth an astronomical sum of two million pounds and almost bankrupted England. Unified resistance was broken but small clans and communites held out in the mountains and woodlands — perhaps the most famous example being Fiach O'Byrne of Glenmalure, who was eventually hunted down and killed in 1597.

Under Cromwell the uprooting of the people from their *tuatha* to Connaught enabled their lands to be pillaged, taken and exploited for a quick profit. Although 'Tories' continued to attack the English settlers, as the woodlands began shrinking and converting to plantations, resistance became increasingly difficult.

With resistance effectively crushed, it was possible to fully exploit the natural resources of Ireland and begin the wholesale transformation of the landscape:

adorned with goodly woods even fit for building of houses and ships, so commodiously, as that if some princes in the world had them, they would soon hope to be lords of all the seas, and ere long of all the world (Edmund Spenser)

Of course, it is well known that Elizabeth made use of Ireland's huge forests to help build an impressive navy. Speculators bought vast acreages and had many thousands of trees felled for export, in almost all cases failing to plant any new ones. Although even in these times it was becoming noticed that a huge natural resource was being denuded and wasted...

There are forests in this kingdom of many thousand acres, some principal ones ought to be reserved for the use of the Crown, and not wasted, as they are now by private men, who purchase them for trifles or assume them upon tricks and devices from the simple Irish (Eoin Neeson citing Chichester)

Although much of the woodland was felled for warships (2,000 trees to make one 74-gun ship), it appears that demand for barrels and casks, and also the iron industry, by far outstripped the destruction wrought by shipbuilding.

For example, in the late 1630s the export of pipe-staves for barrels and casks reached almost 5 million — a 'pipe' being big enough to hold 126 gallons. The seemingly endless supply of wood meant that English colonists effectively cornered the market, until the trees eventually ran out.

Leather tanning, which utilised bark from living oak trees led to the debarking of such huge quantities of oak trees that attempts were made to prohibit the practice. Ironworks also had a terrible impact on the Irish woodlands given that six tonnes of wood were required to make two tonnes of charcoal, which was then able to produce one tonne of iron. Mass clearances for iron making carried on until the use of coal finally reached Ireland — by which time most of the forests had gone...

The great woods which the maps do represent to us upon the mountains between Dundalk and Newry are quite vanished., there being nothing left of them these many years since but only one tree standing close by the highway, at the very top of one of these mountains. (Boate's Natural History of Ireland)

The 'Penal Laws' further reduced the land in the possession of the Catholic Irish so that by 1800 only 5% of Ireland's land was in Irish hands and that land which was taken was most often commercially exploited, with only the big landlords maintaining forests, solely for their own enjoyment of hunting in an otherwise ugly and stripped landscape. Despite encouragement from the government for landowners to improve their land, by planting trees, perhaps only 2% of the land area had tree cover at this time.

The establishment of the Irish National Land League in 1878 and the Irish Land Commission in 1881 gave some hope for the native Irish to reclaim the land that was in the possession of landlords, but by this time the majority of the country had been cleared. Many lakes were filled in and bogs dried out for economic exploitation and what was being planted from the early 1800s onwards was mostly conifers.

This process, as we all know, continued into the 20th century so that the bulk of Irish woodland remains coniferous to this day. The situation is improving, with a growing awareness of broadleaf and native species amongst both government agencies, companies and the general public, but with the last-minute reprieve of Ireland's woodlands harvesting rights being sold off to help fund deficit payments it shows that there is still no room for complacency!

References:

Murt MacGarraidhe – Strangers at Home

Niall MacCoitir – Irish Trees, Myths. Legends and Folklore

The History of Religious Intolerance
How Religious Intolerance Has Helped Bring
Us to the Edge of Destruction

First published on globalresearch.ca, February 2018

In the world before Christianity and Islam took hold, far more religions and philosophies existed than do now. Around the middle of the first millennium BCE Daoism, Buddhism and Zoroastrianism began to become established and quickly spread in Asia, no doubt impacting on already long-established religions of the time but without such wide-reaching repercussions.

These new religions appeared in a world where a vast number of religions already existed. The Mesopotamian religion, is the oldest known and recorded organised religion, consisting of worship of some two thousand deities. Although not explicitly tied to the state and rulers (as was the case with Egypt) it was deeply embedded in the culture of the Sumerian, Akkadian, Babylonian and Assyrian empires over some four thousand years, spreading its influence over a vast region and, it is thought, influencing Canaanite, Greek and possibly Egyptian and Jewish religions during that time.

Like many other religions it co-existed with others and was transmitted by cultural shifts brought about by war and trade as various empires expanded and collapsed. Whether it was state sponsored or the 'official' religion throughout its empire, as in Egypt, is unclear but it does appear that their religiosity was at the core of their culture. In Egypt, their polytheistic religion, although transforming over time was clearly tied to the monarchy (Pharaohs) and implemented by a highly organised, state sponsored, priesthood, deeply embedded within the social and political hierarchy. As a great imperial power, its religion had a significant impact on other cultures and religions such as Greek polytheism and possibly some aspects of Christianity. Certainly, the cult of Isis was widespread across the Greco-Roman world, throughout the Mediterranean region and also in parts of Africa.

Although it is generally regarded that religious intolerance was the norm in antiquity, it was not always the case. In India, Buddhism and Jainism, alongside Hinduism, were allowed to flourish in the Mauyra and Gupta dynasties. In China, Buddhism coexisted with Daoism and Confucianism along with folk religion over two millennia, with very little suppression and intolerance in that time period. In the Achaemenid empire of Cyrus the Great (after 550BCE), religious tolerance was enshrined in the laws passed, covering an area thought to contain half the population of the world at the time. Within the much later Sassanid empire (around 400CE) Judaism, Manichaeism and Christianity were tolerated alongside Zoroastrianism which was dominant in western Asia. During such times both the environment and people were able to prosper — free from the constant destructive onslaught of war.

Unfortunately, the situation was not to last. Both Zoroastrianism and Manichaeism, from being hugely popular faded into obscurity due to violent competition with Christianity and Islam. The political and religious union of the Roman empire, following Constantine, left little room for toleration of rival religions, including the Greco-Roman Paganism that had been so dominant for over a millennium. In Armenia and Georgia both Zoroastrianism and Paganism suffered as the state chose to enforce a policy of Christianity as the official religion, while at the same time centralising and consolidating economic and political influence. The 5th century ushered in a new era of religious persecution which also served to consolidate social and political power.

Islam quickly spread beyond Arabia following Muhammad's death in 632, swiftly taking the Byzantine and Sassanid empires by storm, although Byzantium survived in gradual decline for another eight hundred years. Although current troubles surrounding Islamic extremism may lead many to think otherwise, Islam has historically had a more tolerant attitude to other religions than Christianity. Zoroastrianism, which was dominant in western Asia was persecuted by Islam and actively discouraged for a millennium. Despite this, today in Iran (often considered a pariah state) Christianity, Zoroastrianism and Judaism coexist peacefully alongside the majority religion of Islam, albeit with less rights.

At the end of the 11th century Pope Urban II initiated a Christian war against Islam in defence of Byzantium to reclaim the Holy Land. Two hundred years of Crusades ended ultimately in failure and led to the destruction of Byzantium in 1453 and Muslim incursions into Europe thereafter. Apart from a few decades, the Muslim Ottoman (Turkish) empire was at almost constant war with Christian Europe, until its final demise at the end of World War I. During the Crusades, and up until the end of the 17th century, Christians took the opportunity to also persecute Jews, with mass expulsions and massacres throughout Europe during much of that period.

The Muslim world also came under attack from the Mongols during the 13th century, the low point of which was the destruction of the 500-year Caliphate and city of Baghdad — bringing to an end the Abbasid dynasty and what was considered the golden age of Islam. Most of the Mongols were Tengrist but Genghis Khan permitted and encouraged religious freedom across his new empire, so long as he faced no resistance. Tough resistance from Muslim rulers led to a typical Mongol response, a bloodbath across the Islamic world, which almost destroyed Islam in Asia. Freedom of religion generally allowed Tengrism,

Christianity, Buddhism, Judaism, Manichaeanism, Taoism and Islam to coexist peacefully, although gradually three of the four Mongol Khanates became Muslim, with the Chinese Khanate adopting Tibetan Buddhism.

With the discovery of the Americas and subsequently, the rounding of the Cape of Africa (Good Hope) in the 15th century, the Spanish and Portuguese unleashed an unprecedented wave of Christian oppression and religious intolerance far beyond its previous domains. Beginning with Columbus' genocide in Hispaniola, religious persecution, enslavement, murder and environmental destruction took place across the New World and coastal Africa. Soon to be joined by other emerging imperial forces, such as England, a wave of colonisation, extermination and forced conversion took place, over hundreds of years. The repercussions of this are still very much in evidence today with continents environmentally ravaged and many peoples becoming extinct, diminished and relocated, with their indigenous cultures and religions completely or nearly destroyed.

Despite a gradual move towards secular governments throughout the world, individual, organisational and state sponsored religious intolerance has continued to plague the world into the modern era. Some the most horrific religious oppression in history has occurred in the last century or so with the genocide of Armenian Christians by the Ottomans and the Nazi Holocaust against primarily Jews and Jehovah's Witnesses. Religious and social oppression of Australian Aborigines, Native Americans, indigenous tribes in South America, in apartheid South Africa and throughout the former Soviet Union and China has all taken place within the last hundred years.

Even now, the world has witnessed the barbarism of Daesh (Islamic State) in the Middle East and the recent oppression and migration of the Muslim Rohingya people in Myanmar by the Buddhist majority. Although only recently re-ignited this new horror is part of a long conflict that originated during World War II. Having been on opposing sides during the war, the Buddhist regime and the Rohingya have been in sporadic conflict since 1947, culminating with the mass eviction (in 2017) of Rohingya people into neighbouring Bangladesh.

Currently there are estimated to be some ten thousand distinct religions in existence in the world, despite the eradication of many faiths during our tumultuous history. Unfortunately, we have still not figured out a way to co-exist in peace both on an international level, between theocratic states, or within individual religious communities.

Part of the problem, no doubt, is created by the adoption of religion at a state level. Where secularism or at least state guaranteed religious tolerance is the norm the level and frequency of religious intolerance is lower. Throughout our sad collective history there have been brief islands of calm, religious plurality and toleration, instigated at state level, that prove that peaceful co-existence was and still is possible.

Many religions claim to have the right answers, to be the one true religion or to have the sole authority of the divine. Given that there are so many religions in the world, it seems rather bizarre that just one could rightfully lay claim to exclusive divine approval. In truth, what religion a person adheres to is largely dictated by social and geographical factors — the community and location in which one grows up.

If one is able to put aside the correctness of polytheism, henotheism (many aspects of the one) or monotheism, all religions point to the hand of the divine in the creation of the universe and life within it. In a certain sense all religions can be said to be both right and wrong at the same time, in that they describe or allude to the divine truths of our existence, but in a way that can hardly be satisfactory to all.

All religions have ideas about morality and decency but these are not necessarily the same and indeed are quite often contradictory. For instance, murder would generally be considered wrong, almost universally, however, there are circumstances such as 'honour killings' in some religious cultures that are considered acceptable. However, in some religions even to kill a fly would be considered a great sin. So, who is to decide what is correct and what is not, who has a divine mandate and who does not?

As human beings we are somewhat like goldfish in a small tank — with our limited perception we attempt to understand the world around us and ourselves, to discover the nature of life and the universe and to find meaning within the chaos and confusion of life. Like the goldfish we are limited by our intelligence, our senses and our placement within a universe that is bigger than our imaginings. I believe that it is true to say that our ability to comprehend the mysteries of existence are very limited, perhaps more so than we can possibly realise.

The belief in one true religion has been the cause of conflict the world over or been the justification for it. Religion has been misguidedly been used to justify war and colonisation, economic predation and the ecological destruction that accompanies it. While humanity has been foolishly arguing, fighting and jostling for dominance in the world we have been distracted from the raging fires that now surround us, that we have created ourselves.

It is clear that the 'end times' talked of in many faiths could well be upon us, but if that is so, it is surely not due to an act of God but as a result of our own carelessness, stupidity and obsession with competing with our fellow humans. At this time, we have the capacity to destroy the world with nuclear weapons or to poison it for many thousands of years through the careless use of nuclear power. We have taken warfare to new depths with increasingly efficient ways to slaughter one another, even without the direct involvement of human soldiers any more. Worse still, through over-population and over-exploitation of nature we are pushing the world towards ecological collapse; which could bring extinction for many species, including our own.

While our governments waste fortunes on larger and more dangerous armies, economic hardships and poverty continue to plague the world — the poor suffer the ravages of climate change while a powerful minority continue to feed their insatiable greed for more. Instead of being united by faith, albeit of different strands, peoples are often divided and turned against each other, to the benefit of their manipulators and to the detriment of humanity and the world at large.

In truth we have reached a great crisis for humanity and for the world — 'climate change', caused by our short-sightedness, is merely one of the symptoms of our disease. It is well past the time when we should put aside our religious and ideological differences and focus on the great problems of our time i.e. saving humanity from itself.

In the past empires and civilisations collapsed due to economic, religious and ecological factors, in addition to military failures. Such collapses were localised not systemic, but now we no longer have the luxury of repeating the mistakes of human history. If we continue down a path of violence, destruction, vast inequality and intolerance then there is little hope for humanity. History has proven that times of peace, cooperation and toleration are possible. If we can overcome our differences, while there is still time, and truly work together in cooperation to transform our societies then we at least have a chance to save humanity from an avoidable tragedy.

Ogham — Respecting an Ancient Alphabet

First published by Pagan Dawn *magazine,*
November 2020

I felt compelled to write this following reading a recent speculative and inventive piece on *ogham* (Old-Irish *ogam*). I have to admit I was quite dismayed initially, having spent a large portion of my Druidic studies on *ogham,* I was more than a little displeased by what I read.

I am not a reconstructionist but I have to say that some efforts in the field of Irish (and also Welsh) language and culture are little more than cultural appropriation as they come from a place of ignorance, although well-meaning. It often becomes clear that inventive people often have not read the source material, do not understand the language at all, how to pronounce it or how to use it. Therefore, I have to question their right to transform and mutate an ancient tradition and expect it to be taken seriously, or given any legitimacy at all.

Sticking with Irish, the basis of *ogham* — the language has changed greatly over time. Irish now has several more letters than it used to. Up until the creation of the new modern alphabet *An Caighdeán Oifigiúil* ("The Official Standard") you would never see letters W, X, Y, Z, or H, J, K. Irish has 4 modern dialects, so spellings still vary. However, in the 1960s the old semi-Roman script was abandoned for modern standard European letters, but you can still see the occasional road sign or shop sign in the old script which made use of a dot, called a *bualte* (pronounced bwill-cha) to represent H.

The modern alphabet in *Gaeilge* (Irish language) was called *Beith-Luis-Nin* (like ABC — literally B-L-letter) and uses the following letters only — **a á b c d e é f g h i í l m n o ó p r s t u ú**. For loan words one can use **j k q v w x y z** although you rarely see them, as they are used for just a handful of words. This is the starting point from which we should try to understand *ogham*, a word that has no English translation. Please note that the modern Irish word is *ogham* and not *ogam*, which would be a much older form. If you are going to use *Gaeilge* at all it is best to try and be consistent — using entirely old forms or entirely modern forms, wherever possible.

My own *Gaeilge* is poor, perhaps the level of a 4- or 5-year-old, however, I know enough to know when the language is being abused! *Ogham* has 20 letters in total — no H, no K, no Z, no Q no W etc.! For additional Latin sounds the *Forfeda* were created (the last group of 5) **ae io ui ó ea** at an unknown later date. Try writing English words with only 20 letters and you will soon release that *Gaeilge*, and certainly not *ogham*, should be not be interchanged with English and used willy-nilly, like some kind or word toy.

This language and system are far older than English — the *ogham* system is at least as old as 4th century CE and probably much older. *Gaeilge* is many thousands of years old, like its distant cousin Welsh or rather *Cymraeg / y Gymraeg* and should not be bastardized by well-meaning but ignorant misuse! The same applies to *ogham*, which unfortunately has suffered greatly in this area.

Mis-spelling of the letter names is common in books on *ogham*, as is the inclusion of letters that don't even exist in *Gaeilge* — Q, W, Z, for example! The use of word-oghams (*Bríatharogam* plural *Bríatharogaim*) the two word meanings, often referred to as 'kennings' has been extended and messed with into modern times. The original word-oghams were written in Old-Irish and translated into Middle-Irish, presumably by Irish monks. These texts are found in the *Book of Ballymote* and other places, the most famous being *Auraceipt na n-Éces* (*The Scholar's Primer*), first published in 1917 and translated into modern English by George Calder. I have a copy of this myself, although few people have actually read it, that I know of.

The three lists from which we derive some understandings of *ogham* are *Bríatharogaim: Morainn mic Móin, Mac ind Óc, Cú Chulainn*. Whether these 3 lists actually relate in any way to Morainn, Angus MacOg or Cuchulainn is unknown, but these are all poetic and when translated into English have questionable meaning or relevance. This has led to a century or so of argument about correct interpretation. Scholars cannot even agree on whether or not *ogham* is a tree alphabet.

However, Old-Irish words associated with the construction are almost all tree related — *feda* the groupings of five, means wood; *fid* for individual letters means tree, *nin* has a dual meaning of letter or branch fork; *tábomnai* the word for consonants also means the side of a tree trunk; *flesc* the lines of the letters themselves also means twig and the line that the letters are drawn on is *druim* — which means back or edge.

The *druim* runs from bottom to top traditionally — you start the word at the bottom! On paper it is acceptable to work from left to right instead but never, never, ever — top to bottom, on paper, wood or rock! One should never try to write English or other non-Irish words in *ogham*, apart from being a misuse of the system, it doesn't work for many words anyway — try writing LOVE in *ogham* and you just can't but you could write the Irish word for love which is *grá*!

While it may be pleasant or amusing to play with and extend the various *ogham* types such as cow-ogham, bird-ogham etc., this is not a silly game, these had a real purpose in ancient Ireland and one should not trivialize or bastardize a tradition that is unique throughout Europe. If you wish to explore *ogham*, I suggest you learn something about it before you begin to play with it — anyone with an ounce of sense does not jump into a Ferrari after one driving lesson, taken in a Fiat 500! Feel free to explore *ogham*, revive it and add to its usage (if you have the skill to do so) but please do so with respect and from a position of knowledge and understanding, not one of ignorance and folly.

Uncovering the Origins of Halloween

First published in Indie Shaman *magazine,*
June 2021

Anyone involved in Shamanism or indeed the Pagan movement in any way will be aware of the festival of *Samhain,* more commonly known in modern parlance as Halloween. To most Pagans it is the Celtic New Year and many regard it as the most important festival on the modern Wheel of The Year.

In truth, for many Shamans, or those that incorporate Shamanic techniques into their spiritual practice, it makes perfect sense that Samhain would be a significant time, given that psychopomp work and working with the spirits of the departed is a major part of the Shaman's role. However, although it does not have huge practical bearing on how one works in this area, I feel it can do no harm to have a deeper understanding of where this festival of *Samhain* comes from and what are its most important aspects.

Sound knowledge and a deeper understanding of the past can only be a benefit in relation to our own practice and helps inform our actions, and also create a deeper connection with the ancestral legacy of indigenous European spirituality that has barely survived and been revived in recent decades.

It would appear to be that *Samhain* or a localised version of it has been celebrated across the entire world for millennia. In western Europe, where European Pagan traditions survived the longest, Celtic survivals and written accounts are mostly to be found in Ireland and to a lesser extent also in Britain, Brittany and a few other countries. Similar traditions have also survived to some extent in Norse and Slavic countries, the Alps and other more remote parts of Europe, but often fused or combined with Christianity.

Indeed, this is also true in the Celtic fringes of Europe, where much of the survivals have a mildly Christian gloss over what were clearly overtly Pagan traditions that both Catholic and Protestant Christianity failed to suppress. In the case of Ireland, we are especially lucky in that some ancient texts survived, now translated into English (or other languages), in some cases being accounts or stories from a time long before they were first codified.

Samhain is the word for November in *Gaeilge* (Irish) and is thought to be derived from *sam-fuin*, which means end of summer. Theories are that the festival lasted for the entire month, three days or one day — the most likely seems to be a three-day period of celebration and rituals for the dead, in my opinion. The main themes of this fire festival, from the surviving source material and traditional survivals seem to be death and rebirth, sacrifices/final harvest, sacred fires, divination and funeral games:

Death and rebirth

At the end of October the natural world appears to be dying off with the loss of leaves, the beginning of frosts and noticeably shorter days. The Child of Light (*an Macan/Mabon*), passes beyond maturity towards death and the otherworldly Cernunnos archetype retakes his place as consort to the goddess. The goddess of the Earth is generally symbolized at this time by the *Cailleach* in Ireland and elsewhere as a hag/crone archetype, who will re-emerge in spring transformed once more into the youthful form of the goddess. The acknowledgement of the ancestors and the dead generally was central to *Samhain* celebrations and offerings of food were usual throughout the British Isles. Failure to pay appropriate respects to the dead was thought to lead to offenders being barred from these festivities when they joined the afterlife. Superstitious customs abounded that had to be adhered to, in order to avoid bad luck or even death. Throwing out all dirty water and proper attention to the hearth was observed — the consequences of failing to do so are described in the Irish myth *Eachtra Nera* where a hanged man's spirit spits water over the members of the household he has entered causing them all to die!

Sacrifices/Final Harvest

The slaughtering of animals at this time was both practical and spiritual — offerings were made to the gods to ensure the return of the vital forces in nature and to protect the people and their means of survival through the dark and harsh winter months, while old and sickly animals were slaughtered for meat, some of which would be preserved for winter food. Sacrifice of pigs was common into the medieval era and it is likely that in earlier times humans were also sacrificed. Sacrificial rites involving hens or cockerels remain in Ireland even now in the form of 'Bleeding for St. Martin', albeit in Christianized form but transposed to the beginning of November (St. Martin's Day). This was also a time for collecting the last of the agricultural harvest (*Samhain* being the last of three harvest festivals). An interesting tradition is that blackberries had to be collected before Halloween Night (*Oiche Shamna*), otherwise the Devil would have spat or urinated on them!

Sacred Fires

It is still a common custom in Ireland to light *Samhain*/Halloween fires even now, however, in the UK the date was long displaced (to 5th November) in commemoration of the attempted blowing up of the English Houses of Parliament by Guy Fawkes, from 1606. Onwards. The tradition of *Samhain* fires can be directly traced back to the ancient *Samhain* fires of *Tlachtga* (Hill of Ward, in Co, Meath, Ireland), although it is highly likely that similar fire traditions existed throughout the British Isles and perhaps even most of Europe. The Druids lit a sacred fire on

Tlachtga at *Samhain*, which was visible from Tara, some 12 miles away, and probably the Tara fire (in the presence of the High King/*Ard Rí* was lit subsequently. Today the bonfire is still very much part of Halloween, bringing light, purification, warmth and protection on a physical and spiritual level, as we cross into the darkest times of the year, or to the more secular minded it is a bit of fun and celebration, accompanying their fireworks, candy apples and trick or treating.

Divination

This was a common time of divination and prophetic vision as the veil between worlds was considered to be at its thinnest — a liminal time when communing with the spirit world was at its easiest. The tale *Eachtra Nera* is a prime example of this going back into Irish pre-history: Nera sees a vision of the possible events of the *Samhain* a year hence, an attack on the king's *dún* (residence) by the *sídhe* (fairies). Some of the divination practices have evolved into games, some of which were related to marriages — divination regarding love was extremely popular in Ireland and Britain, right up until the first half of the twentieth century, when many Halloween/*Samhain* traditions began to fall into disuse or were forgotten completely. Indeed, the *Báirín Breac* (fruit loaf) containing a mock wedding ring is a survival of such customs and is still commonly eaten in Ireland today, the finder is said to be likely to marry before next *Samhain* comes around.

Funeral Games

This was a common time to play divinatory games or perform divination charms, particularly related to love — with apples, nuts, coals and even some rather strange games revolving around lime kilns. Apple bobbing is again a descendant of earlier apple games, apples being a clear link to the otherworld in Celtic mythology. Trickery, cross dressing — particularly of young boys to confuse potential thieves among the *sídhe* was common. Suspension of normal order and time, removal of doors, moving of signs was indicative of the removal of barriers between the material realm and the otherworldly realm. Even now, in Ireland, young people often turn road signs to point the wrong way at Halloween, a continuation of the old tradition of turning normality on its head. Such activities as 'trick or treating' are descendants of the *buachaillí tui* — a group of disguised revelers who represented the spirits of the dead accompanying the goddess of the land in the form of a mock horse character *an Láir Bhán*, or the white mare. The hobby horse or a more ghostly version can still be found today, in some cases displaced to the Solstice/Christmas, but still performing the same function as leader of the otherworldly spirits.

These traditions are mirrored in remnants across Europe, many exported to the New World and re-imported from USA/ Canada. However, we can find similar indigenous traditions in the Americas, that relate to the dead, mostly notably from Mexico, similar ideas can be traced to indigenous African religions and the practices of their descendants found in North and South America. The Mexican festival of the dead in fact fits so well with the European traditions that it has blended somewhat with modern Halloween, with Day of the Dead parades and cultural emblems such as the painted skulls being exported to the rest of the world as part of modern Halloween celebrations. The same can be said to of Voodoo (derived from African Vodun) and Santería (Catholic/African syncretism), both of which have made their way into modern Halloween celebrations.

Samhain Deities

Perhaps least known of *Samhain*/Halloween traditions relates to the deities, particularly of Ireland. The *Cailleach*, who I mentioned earlier, is perhaps the most well-known association, certainly among Pagans and Shamans — but also related to this time of year are the gods associated with death and the otherworld, *Donn* and *Manannan Mac Lir* and, of course, *Tlachtga*, the goddess associated with the sacred fires.

Tlachtga was both a goddess and the sacred place of Druids and it was *Tlachtga* where the first fire was lit at this time and then after the lighting of the Tara fire the fires would be lit all over the country. The sunrise and moon rise at *Samhain* form an alignment from *Tlachtga*, to the quartz standing stone in Cairn L of Loughcrew (*Slieve na Caileach/Sleive Bearra*) and Lambay Island (off the coast of Dublin). Interestingly, the Mound of the Hostages (at Tara) is also illuminated by the sunrise at *Samhain*. This alignment continues west across the country also intersecting 'Lugh's Seat' at the end of the volcanic 'Pillars of Samhain' and the cairn of *Mór-Ríoghan* above the Keash caves so clearly the hill named after *Tlachtga* was a place of no small significance.

Ceremonies centred around the lighting of the winter fires are said to originate from *Lugh Lámfhota*, (the *Tuatha Dé Danann* hero of the second battle of Moytura and later high king) around 1450BC. This being the case, the tradition of *Samhain* fires is some 3,500 years old. Recent archaeological digs at *Tlachtga*, over 2014–'16, confirm an early use of the sight into the bronze age, with it continuing to be used up until the end of the Pagan era.

It is well known that *Tlachtga* was one the great assemblies (*aonach*) of the Gaelic people, throughout the pre-Norman history and notably in 1168 when *Ruaidrí Ua Conchobair* (last *Ard Rí* of Ireland), presided over a national synod of kings and prelates at the site. This was the last time of significance that the native Irish made use of this site, until the revival of its use in modern times.

As for *Tlachtga* herself, there are many stories relating to this goddess, including from the medieval *Metrical Dindshenchas* (place lore) and *Banshenchas* (women's lore), both of which also refer to *Tlachtga*'s father *Mog Roith* and to a contemporary sorcerer of Jesus of Nazareth: Simon Magus. These stories describe Magus' three sons raping *Tlachtga* at *Imbolc* and he gave birth to triplets at *Samhain* at the site that bears her name, dying in the process.

Fragmentary information about *Tlachtga* and her father is woven into stories that are most likely ecclesiastical fantasy, a Christian gloss intended to diminish and discredit two deities of significance to the Pagan predecessors. It is probable that earliest form of *Tlachtga* was a Druidess type or a tutelary goddess that arrived with the Firbolgs, long before the *Tuatha Dé Danann* and Milesians set foot in Ireland. The meaning of her name is 'Earth Spear', probably relating to lightning. She was described as daughter of the chief Druid *Mog Ruith* of Munster who lived in the time of high king *Cormac McAirt* (mid-3rd century AD), although there are other references to *Mog Ruith* at different time periods — he may well have been a god in an earlier form, his name means 'devotee of the wheel', which probably relates to the sun.

Tlachtga is recorded to have made a pillar stone called *Cnamhcaill* meaning 'bone damage' out of a fragment of her father's wheel — *Roth Ramach*. It was said to kill all who touch it, blind those that gazed upon it and deafen those that heard it. This pillar is thought by some to represent lightning, which would tie in with the meaning of her name, as lightning was likened to a spear thrown at the ground. *Tlachtga* was most likely not only an ancient goddess, discredited and demoted by Christian scribes, but very possibly a goddess of death and rebirth, the sun and/or lightning.

Tlachtga was recorded as giving birth to three boys — *Doirb*, *Cumma* and *Muach*. In the oldest version of the story, they became rulers of Munster, Leinster and Connaught (three of the provinces of Ireland). It was said that while their names are remembered that Ireland would be safe from domination by strangers. Of course, they were indeed forgotten and Ireland, and the country fell under colonial rule as prophesized.

It is now clear that *Tlachtga* is intimately linked with the symbolic death and rebirth of the land at *Samhain*, perhaps this is why her story was rewritten to diminish her impact and ensure that she and her sacred temple were forgotten? They did such an efficient job of suppressing *Tlachtga* that many Pagans do not know her name, her ancient temple or her links with *Samhain*. However, despite great efforts to eliminate *Samhain*, (as well as other Pagan traditions) there is still a direct link between the ancient sacred fire of *Tlachtga* and the modern lighting of bonfires, between the ancient festival of the dead and our modern pageantry of ghosts, ghouls and other such fun and games.

The traditions of *Samhain* — the fires, the food, the games, divination, honouring the dead, the celebrations have somehow survived, in many cases somewhat detached from their original meaning. However, digging a little deeper does reveal where the modern practices derive from and what their original significance was. Despite the best efforts of religious oppressors, intolerant of anything that they could not destroy or appropriate, the ancient festival of the dead is anything but dead — it is alive and kicking and reconnecting with its ancient Pagan origins!

Kerry: A Kingdom Worthy of the Name

First published on thehistorypress.co.uk,
July 2019

Kerry is the most westerly county of Ireland, in the far south west and it has long played an important role in Ireland's history. Although humans arrived in Ireland some six thousand years earlier, the earliest clear evidence of farming in Ireland was found at Ferriter's Cove on the Dingle Peninsula, where a flint knife, cattle bones and a sheep's tooth were discovered, dating from approximately 4350 BCE.

Even today county Kerry is full of megalithic monuments such as burial tombs and stone circles, as well as later monuments and ring forts from the copper and bronze age. The Dingle peninsula, also known as Corca Dhuibhne, is reputed to be where the Celtic Milesians (Sons of Mil) arrived and where they fought and defeated the *Tuatha Dé Danann* to successfully establish the culture from which the Gaelic people of Ireland were descended. In fact, Mil's Egyptian wife Scotia, whose descendants went on to give her name to Scotland, died fighting the *Tuatha Dé Danann* and she is reputedly buried along with her horse just outside Tralee. The stones marking the graves are still there today and an obelisk memorial, not far from the site was erected a few years ago, created by local stonemason Billy Lean and artist Elena Danaan.

This and other great battles occurred in the *Sliabh Mish* mountains which were named after Mish the princess who according to legend lived to great age as a wild woman on top of the mountains. Caherconree a mountain peak in this mountain range is home to the remains of a ringfort called *Bóthar na gCloch* (road of the stones) which is bordered on three sides by steep cliffs and was the fort of Cú Roí Mac Dáire, a great king and warrior with magical powers, who was killed by the famous Ulster hero Cú Chulainn. At the end of the *Sliabh Mish* range lies the Conor Pass, near Dingle town, which is Ireland's highest mountain pass and Mount Brandon, which has been a sacred mountain since Pagan times and is still visited by pilgrims today.

As well as these mountains, Kerry possesses the MacGillycuddy Reeks range, which features Carrauntoohil, Ireland's highest mountain, at 1040m tall. The MacGillycuddy Reeks, close to Killarney, stretch across 12 miles of the Kerry countryside and also includes Ireland's second and third highest mountains. This range is also home to Ireland's highest lake, Cummeenoughter, which is also known as 'The Devil's Looking Glass'. The famous mountains the 'Paps of Anu' in east Kerry, overlook *Cathair Crobh Dearg*, or 'The City' which is possibly one of the oldest sacred settlements in Ireland, which has given rise to a wealth of legends featuring giants, St. Brendan and the Red Branch Knights, during its long history.

County Kerry has been referred to as 'The Kingdom' since the 1st century AD when the O'Connor chieftain Ciar took control of the territory between the Shannon estuary and the Maine river in the south. Before this, the territory was known as *Clar na Cliabh* or The Plain of Swords, but thanks to the O'Connor's it became known as Ciar Raigh which translates as 'Ciar's kingdom' or possibly 'Ciar's people'. Ciarraigh later became anglicised as Kerry, but was still referred to as 'The Kingdom' ever since. It is also said in Kerry that, "There are only two kingdoms, the Kingdom of God and the Kingdom of Kerry."

Kerry has a rich history dating from before the Norman invasion and continuing into modern times — from the exploits of the Fitzgerald dynasty, the famous Earls of Desmond, right up to the War of Independence and the Civil War. Kerry is also a treasure trove of folk customs, superstitions and stories, such as belief in the Pooka (*púca*), curses, the fairies (*sídhe*) and various traditions relating to good and bad luck associated with the fireplace or days of the week. Kerry is home to Ireland's oldest known fair, the Puck Fair (which is some 400 years old) that takes place every August in the small town of Killorglin. Kerry is also home to Ireland's oldest surviving thatched cottage (about 300 years old), at Finuge Cross, near Listowel town.

Anascaul, on the Dingle peninsula was the home of Tom Crean, one of the greatest explorers of the Antarctic, who was a colleague of both Scott and Shackleton on several freezing and highly dangerous voyages of exploration in the early twentieth century. Kerry was also home to several heroes of the Irish revolution, including Roger Casement and Michael Rahilly both of whom lost their lives as a result of their brave actions.

In the modern era, Kerry was known as a favourite place of comedic film star Charlie Chaplin, who holidayed in Waterville for many years in his later years, as well as ancestral home of Pierce Brosnan, the famous actor who starred in *James Bond* movies as well as many other successful films. It is also famous as home of the Rose of Tralee festival, that attracts people from all over the world, not to mention the location for famous films such as *Ryan's Daughter* and several of the *Star Wars* films.

Both now and in the ancient past Kerry has been a vibrant and interesting place, with a history that few regions of the world can equal. With its stunning scenery and rich cultural heritage no wonder it is one of the most visited parts of Ireland.

A European Samhain
Ancient Halloween Traditions from Ireland and Beyond

First published in irishcentral.com, October 2021

Although a vast number of Halloween/*Samhain* traditions come from Ireland, many of them also come from Britain — Scotland, Wales, Cornwall and parts of England. Similar traditions have also survived to some extent in continental Europe, particularly Brittany.

Halloween bonfires were a big tradition in Ireland on 31 October. In Britain, particularly England and Northern Ireland, the tradition is displaced to 5 November with children begging 'a penny for the Guy', which is a stuffed effigy of Guido (Guy) Fawkes to be burned on the bonfire, although in Northern Ireland this was/is sometimes an effigy of the Catholic Pope.

On the Isle of Man, New Year's Day was regarded as 1 November until relatively recently. The mummers play, a form of re-enactment of old Pagan beliefs, would take place with mummers going from door to door on Halloween, singing a song, 'Tonight is New Year's Night, Hop-tu-Naa!' Children also participated by going around begging and saying rhymes or giving some other kind of performance.

Also popular throughout Ireland and the British Isles was for young people to get up to harmless mischief — for instance removing doors from sheds, moving items to unusual places and letting cows out of a field, etc. It was common for young people to impersonate the spirits of the land, but now the American custom of dressing up in scary costumes has become popular.

Joe McGowan recounts in *Echoes of a Savage Land* how it used to be growing up in Sligo (north-west Ireland):

Years ago there were no trick-or-treaters in Sligo. But the spirits were out! Evidence of the previous night's activities greeted churchgoers as they walked to mass on All Saint's Day; carts left with one wheel or no wheels, gates missing, cabbage-strewn roads... A favourite trick was to fasten the front and back door of a neighbour's house from the outside and then climb up on the roof and block the chimney, sending clouds of smoke into the kitchen below.

Another choice prank was to take the cart up to a gate, bringing the shafts through the bars and then harness the ass to the other side. This was quite an unusual sight in the morning and very funny, to everyone except the owner of the team.

...a farmer well known for his bad humour kept the whole parish amused for days with his efforts to chase away a 'strange' horse, which was later revealed, after a shower of rain, to be his own horse, disguised by a coat of whitewash.

In modern Ireland such pranks are still fairly popular — such as turning road signs to point the wrong way or leaving traffic cones in silly places. More common generally across Ireland and in most countries is the 'trick-or- treat', which more often than not involves a treat. However, some tricks do happen — like blue mouth or pepper sweets and being sprayed with water pistols and being targeted by firecrackers or buckets of water, etc.

In Ireland the *Tuatha Dé Danann* were considered to have power over the fertility of the land, and similar beliefs existed in parts of Britain. It was thought necessary to placate them as they could bring either prosperity or plague and famine — sick cattle and poor harvests. People acknowledged this power and made offerings on the ground, usually of milk, sometimes meat (pork most often) and also cakes. This would occur at the four Celtic feasts, including *Samhain*.

It was also common at *Samhain* for people in masks (mummers) and suits, traditionally of straw, to go around villages and towns to beg for food, drink or money. If people were stingy, they were thought to receive bad luck and misfortune in the year ahead

A very similar tradition survives today in Dingle, Ireland, on St Stephen's Day/Wren Day (26 December), perhaps again transferred from *Samhain*. Teams of people (including musicians) representing different streets or areas of the town (mostly men) go around the whole town in straw costumes and get progressively more drunk. When teams encounter one another, they have a mock battle. After it is over, those not fit only for bed retire to the pub and more drink is taken.

In some cases, the *Samhain* or Christmas/New Year processions involve a horse character, often with snapping jaws, called the white mare, hobby horse, *Lár Bhán* (Irish) or *Mari Lwyd* (Welsh), representing the *sídhe* (*Tuatha Dé Danann*) spirits of the land riding forth across the land. In Limerick it was called the 'Blanket Horse' (*Capall an tSusa*) and across the country the horse's entourage were called names such as strawboys (*buachaillí tuí*), guisers, hugadais or visards. To show disrespect to the *Lár/Láir Bhán* and its entourage was to invite famine, disaster and general bad luck on yourself and your household.

Some believed that at *Samhain* the fairies could turn the yellow-flowered weed, ragwort (gone to seed usually), called *buachalán buí*, into spirit horses and use them to ride about all night long. Sometimes a human might be able to join them, so long as they did as they were told. In one story, a young fellow is invited by the king of the fairies to ride with them on a white calf but told not to speak. In their adventures they ride over to Scotland but after the young man lets out an exclamation about the calf making an excellent jump the fairies all disappear, leaving him a journey of more than a day to get back home to Ireland.

It was considered advisable to stay well clear of graveyards on Halloween night as the dead might well rise. Some considered that to see a ghost or risen dead person at *Samhain* would cause instant death!

Staying clear of ringforts, barrows and burial mounds was also considered to be a wise move, as it was often believed that lights and sounds of dancing and laughter could be heard at *Samhain* as the *sídhe* came out into the world. It was also thought that the spirits of the dead could emerge into the world of the living through these places. Equally, the *sídhe* or the dead might kidnap the living, bring them gallivanting or even back to the otherworld:

It is considered on All Hallows' Eve, hob-goblins, evil spirits and fairies hold high revel and that they are traveling abroad in great numbers. The dark and sullen Phooka (púca) is then particularly mischievous and many mortals are abducted to fairyland. Those persons taken away to the raths are often seen at this time by their living friends, and usually accompanying a fairly cavalcade. If you meet the fairies, it is said, on All Hallows' Eve, and throw the dust taken from under your feet at them, they will be obliged to surrender any captive human being belonging to their company.
(Lageniensis, *Irish Folklore*, 1870)

In Britain and Ireland new fire was brought into the house from the bonfire to light the hearth fires that had been put out before nightfall. This on a smaller scale echoes the lighting of the royal fire at Tara (probably from the *Tlachtga* fire) and the subsequent lighting of fires across the country. This tradition has been transferred to Christmas in many cases with the lighting of the Yule log. In Ireland, fires are far less common than a few decades ago, but in Dublin in particular, the Halloween bonfire tradition still survives, although it is discouraged by police, for health and safety reasons.

The Christianisation of Ireland

Previously unpublished

It is widely held that St. Patrick converted the Irish to Christianity, en masse, by himself almost overnight, but this is part of the legendary saintly history or hagiography of Patrick, rather than anything based in truth.

For a start, we can be confident that Ireland had interactions with Christianity before the arrival of the adult St. Patrick (supposedly a former child slave in Ireland). This is widely attributed to Palladius, but Britain the closest neighbour of Ireland had been home to Christians for hundreds of years, long before the official uptake of Christianity in 325CE throughout the Roman Empire. Of course, Britain did not become entirely Christian, particularly the northern kingdoms where Rome struggled to have influence, and indeed it slipped back into Paganism to a large extent, with the exist of the Romans and the arrival of the Saxons.

In Ireland, the old order, that of Druidry, had persisted for centuries, perhaps millennia before Christianity arrived and, of course, it did not vanish almost over-night as Roman Catholic tradition would have us believe. Archeological evidence would suggest that a complex religious structure, with religious centres and temples already existed across Ireland, however, Christianity lays claim to many sites that predate it. Examples of sites that were almost certainly or extremely likely to be pre-Christian are Clonmacnoise, Glendalough and Skellig Michael.

The stonework to be found in these places includes clearly non-Christian symbols and iconography and often massive differences in the age of the stone structures. A perfect example of this is Skellig Michael that has a small graveyard for the monks, however, some of the buildings within the monastic enclosure and the stairs itself may well be of much earlier date, but, as with all stone, it is difficult to prove the age without distinguishing features. Also, outside the main monastic enclosure is a stone that bears clearly Pagan symbolism, including the circled cross — a Pagan symbol that long pre-dates the crucifix that came into fashion after the earlier Christian symbols such as alpha and omega or the fish symbol. Finally, Skellig Michael is mentioned in the Pagan lore of Ireland as a place of the god Don and also in accounts of the arrival of the Milesians, an event that happened many hundreds of years before Christianity arrived in Ireland.

Common understanding is that the ancient Irish were illiterate but it is clear from *The Annals of The Four Masters* that King Cormac Mac Art was literate and ordered the writing down of all the knowledge of Ireland in around 200CE, his own wisdom is preserved in a codex that bears his name. Another ancient tome claims that St. Patrick burned over 400 Pagan books — which immediately undermines the notion that the pre-Christian Irish were uneducated and illiterate savages. If there were no books why would Patrick need a fire upon which to burn the knowledge and histories of the Pagan order he sought to suppress?

St. Patrick may well have been responsible for the sea change that saw Ireland transformed from Christian to Pagan, as taught to all Irish school-children, but this transformation was far from immediate. Ireland's own history proves this, with accounts of Pagan conversion reaching 200 years or more after Patrick had arrived in 432CE. One good example is the supposed trip of a somewhat elderly St. Brendan (died approx. 577CE) to Valentia Island, where he is said to have converted two elderly Pagans on their death bed. St. Brendan's Well (*Tobar Olla Bhreanain*) features several crosses from probably the 7th or 8th century, but the main structure appears to be much older, with a modern well superimposed on it. Also surrounding the site are many large stones, some of which may have once been upright, although that is difficult to prove. Given the story, I imagine that this place was a holy well before it became a Christian holy well, and it was most likely appropriated by St. Brendan on behalf of the Church, as was the case with so many places across Ireland.

Another example would be St. Columba or Colmcille, who was thought to have lived 521–597CE, a missionary but often stated as a former Druid who converted. Clearly, if this story has any truth, then the Druids were still a force to be reckoned with perhaps 100 years after St. Patrick arrived, even longer maybe.

The strongest evidence of the survival of Paganism is to be found in the land of Ireland itself — in the soil of Éire, through the archaeological record of burials. There is very strong evidence of Pagan style burials continuing alongside Christian style burials for hundreds of years after St. Patrick arrived in Ireland. The grave goods accompanying Pagan burials often make it easier to place the time frame and there is strong evidence of some Pagan burial persisting as late as 800CE in Ireland.

What is clear to me is that the Christian hagiography surrounding St. Patrick and the conversion of Ireland is mostly, if not entirely fictitious. Not only did the country fail to convert within St. Patrick's own lifetime, but it clearly took centuries after for that conversion to be completed or at least officially completed, outside of persistent underground Pagans. It is clear that an extensive religious structure existed long before Christianity arrived and that much of it was taken over and appropriated by the Christian Church, with its former history and legacy erased completely.

One must also question the notion of a peaceful conversion — indeed St Patrick's battles with the Druids were violent and are perhaps indicative of a less than peaceful conversion of the population. Can we name any other country with a claim to an entirely peaceful conversion to Christianity? I cannot think of one and in most cases, the baptism into Christianity is one of fire and blood and cruel murder of those who would not yield — throughout Europe, North Africa, Asia and the New World of the Americas. Christianity is a religion soaked in the blood of conversion by the sword, and I very much doubt that violence was not used in Ireland, as it has been throughout the Christian world.

I have nothing against St. Patrick, or the existence of Christianity, in Ireland or anywhere else. However, I think it's about time we had an honest re-evaluation of the life and deeds of this man and the pseudo-history that surrounds him. The Pagan past of Ireland is far from being shameful, just as the Christian history of Ireland is not without shame, particularly in the last 100 years. No religion is perfect, but the story of the erasure of one religion to be replaced by another is one that has not been told in this country with any degree of honesty — that is something that badly needs to change.

Where Does Halloween Come From?

First published in thehistorypress.co.uk, 2021

Halloween is one of those annual celebrations that we just accept as part of the year, like Christmas and Easter, often without question — it is just something that happens at the end of October. However, much like Christmas and Easter, Halloween is specifically placed at a time of year that was intended to supplant an earlier celebration from the pre-Christian era.

While Christmas is linked with the winter solstice and the birth of the Child of Light, often called *Mabon, an Macan* or *Mapanos*. Easter is linked to the spring equinox, falling on the Sunday following the full moon after the equinox — which is why it is different every year. Halloween is short for All Hallows Eve, which is on the 31st of October, the day before All Souls Day.

Halloween was introduced by Christian authorities to replace the ancient festival of *Samhain* (as it was called in the Irish language, *Gaeilge*). *Samhain* today is the name for the month of November, as well as the ancient festival of the dead. In Scotland it was called *Samhuinn* in Scots Gaelic and in Welsh it *is Calan Gaeaf* and in Gaul it was referred to a *Samonios*, referred to on the Coligny Calendar in the phrase TRINVX SAMO SUNDIV, which translates roughly as "the three nights of the end of summer".

Generally, it is regarded that *Samhain* derives from the words *sam-fuin*, meaning the end of the summer, which would tie in with the Gaulish terminology. Although in modern terms, summer ends in August, the Celtic year was split into two halves rather than four quarters. The end of October was pretty much the cut-off point for any good weather, a dramatic shortening of the day, the falling of the last leaves and the end of any harvesting of food. So, purely from a practical point of view, it makes sense to have regarded it as the end of summer (*samhradh*) and the beginning of winter (*geimhreadh*).

In neo-Paganism, the Celtic New Year is at Halloween/ *Samhain*, the 31st of October, although this is not the universally accepted date for *Samhain*. There is strong evidence to suggest that pre-Christian Celtic peoples of western Europe not only celebrated the festival of *Samhain*, but that they also regarded it as the New Year. In Celtic culture the day began at sunset and ended the following sunset — night preceding daytime. It was the same with the cycles of the moon — the dark moon being the beginning of the month and also with the year — the beginning of winter being the beginning of the year.

Although Paganism almost completely died out in most of Europe, the festivals and traditions of Paganism survived, not just into the Christian period, but into the modern era. To a large extent the strongest cultural survivals of *Samhain* / Halloween can be found in Ireland, Britain and Brittany, where both the languages and cultural traditions hung on despite very deliberate and harsh attempts to eliminate them.

All of the traditions that we find surrounding Halloween are Pagan in origin, somewhat mutated in some cases, but clearly derived from Pagan belief and folk practice in every case. In essence, *Samhain* is a festival of the dead and traditions regarding the rites of passage for deaths and regard for ancestors are something that is not easily eliminated in any culture. The various Christian churches, outlawed and prohibited customs such as lighting bonfires, leaving offerings for the ancestors, parades, games, divination etc. but to a huge extent the populace ignored these dictates, especially in more rural areas.

In the end, the Church was forced to give up and appropriate much of the traditions of *Samhain* under the banner of All

Hallows Eve and All Souls Day, but this was not particularly successful in modifying the behaviour of ostensibly Christian parishioners — who still believed in fairies, the returning of spirits of the ancestors, the Celtic otherworld and the art of divination at such an auspicious time. Although one can detect some of these traditions begin to die out from after World War I and World War II particularly, the knowledge of them is well recorded, leading to somewhat of a revival, particularly in the 21st century.

To a large extent the traditions of *Samhain* were exported to North America, Australia and New Zealand by Irish, Scottish, Welsh, English and Breton emigrants. These traditions carried on fairly undisturbed into modern American culture, and in many cases becoming fused with Central/South American ancestral/Day of the Dead traditions that are very similar in nature, as well as those exported from Africa via the slave trade.

What is clear is that the native spirituality of western Europe, at least with regard to the Festival of the Dead, has a lot in common with the native traditions of Central/South America (such as Peru, Brazil and Mexico) and the native traditions of western Africa. In modern Halloween traditions one can find symbolism and practices from syncretic beliefs of Santería, Candomblé, Voodoo, Hoodoo, Vodun and Aztec religion sitting alongside Celtic symbolism and practices — much of which has been re-imported to not only Europe, but many countries around the world.

One could say that the pre-Christian Festival of the Dead is a tradition that just refuses to die, despite extremely vigorous attempts to stamp it out of existence. Not only in Ireland, Britain and Brittany were these belief and practices suppressed but throughout Africa and the New World, where they either already existed or were brought over along with the slaves who survived the horrendous journey.

Today the celebration of Halloween (and *Samhain*) is accepted as a part of the yearly calendar, a bit of harmless fun — but its roots lie in deeply spiritual, serious practices and beliefs that come from traditions that are much older than Christianity. So, Halloween is actually a lot older than we might at first think and its traditions have survived a long history of persecution and oppression. In Ireland the ancient bonfires can be traced back to *Tlachtga*, both a Goddess and a place (in County Meath) where the Druids lit sacred fires, at least as long as 3500 years before today.

Halloween/ *Samhain* is a tradition that has defied the best attempts to destroy it, and may well remain with us for thousands of years yet to come.

FOI and the Goddess Revival Movement

First published in Pagan Dawn *magazine,*
May 2022

The Fellowship of Isis (FOI) is now an international esoteric organisation that spans the globe, with over 25,000 members, but it's origins can be traced back to an obscure castle in a tiny village in county Carlow in Ireland.

It all began with the Durdin Robertson family, an Anglo-Irish family that can trace it roots back to the Norman Esmondes who arrived in Ireland in 1192 and who built the first castle on which Huntington Castle now stands. The current castle, which was built in 1625, houses the original Temple of Isis in its basement, which may have one time served as a dungeon. In in the corner of this temple lies an ancient holy well, dedicated to the goddess Brigid, a part of the temple life that has always held great significance for both the founders and members that attend or visit the temple. In 1963 Lawrence Durdin-Robertson, together with his wife Pamela and sister Olivia, formed the Huntington Castle Centre for Meditation and Study. This small group would be the nucleus from which the FOI would eventually emerge.

Although all three played their part, initially Lawrence (a former Anglican priest) was the driving force behind the fledgling goddess spirituality emerging from Huntington Castle in the tiny village of Clonegal. He began to write on the divine feminine from 1970 onwards, publishing a series of books and became a declared priest of Isis on 1972, although it was not until the vernal equinox of 1976 that he formed the Fellowship, in conjunction with Pamela and Olivia.

This may sound somewhat mundane from our current standpoint, in the early decades of the next century, but at the time it must have seemed quite a revolutionary and extremely eccentric act to most people. One must bear in mind that Ireland, a deeply conservative and slow changing country, was still very much in the grip of the Roman Catholic Church at this point and this would have gone very much against the grain.

I never met Lawrence or his wife Pamela, but I did meet and get to know Olivia and other members of his family, after my first visit to a ceremony at Huntington Castle in 2003. Even at this time, when I mentioned 'The Castle' to a man from a nearby town, he declared that they 'were all nuts, witches and devil worshippers'. Clearly, almost 30 years after the foundation of FOI some people in the area continued to have a very low opinion of the Robertsons and what they had created!

Nonetheless, despite the disapproval of many locals, those in surrounding towns and undoubtedly the Catholics hierarchy, FOI gradually grew from small gatherings of sometimes less than dozen people to a swelling congregation, continuing to grow after the death of Pamela in 1987. Pamela came from a Scottish quaker family and her influence highlighted the reverence and importance of the natural world within FOI. Subsequently, in 1992 The Druid Clan of Dana (*An Clann Draoidheachta Danann*) was established by Olivia and Lawrence and it was stated "The purpose of the Druid Clan of Dana is to develop nature's psychic gifts."

The following year, 1993, Olivia was invited to attend the Parliament of the World's Religions Centennial Session, as representative of the Fellowship of Isis, along with other appointed FOI delegates. This was the first time that the religion of the Goddess was publicly acknowledged as a world faith at this parliament. Olivia was one of two women and sixteen men who addressed the opening plenary from the platform and she gave the blessings of Isis to the world in her speech.

Almost exactly a year later, in August 1994, Lawrence passed away, leaving the Fellowship solely in the hands of his sister and co-founder Olivia, by which time both had written several books and a multitude of essays, rites and a complete liturgy. The FOI began to grow at an exponential rate, attracting people from the UK in great numbers and as far away as west coast USA and Australia.

By the time that I first visited the Temple of Isis in 2003, FOI had become a major player on the world stage of esoteric organisations, having exceeded anyone's expectations and defied the ill will of many. My initial impressions of Olivia were that she was highly eccentric and perhaps a little nutty, but clearly a woman of great intelligence, gravitas and love of life. She radiated an immense positivity that was almost tangible but underpinning her irreverent and humorous exterior one could detect a very deep and profound inner spiritual strength.

Olivia was often surrounded by followers, worshipers almost, the curious and opportunists too, but beneath the good cheer and seemingly randomness of much of her directions and endeavours, flashes of her unadvertised qualities would sometimes emerge. I remember her once dealing with an attendee/member (who had got out of line) with just a few words. It was instantaneous, direct, succinct but amazingly powerful, like an extremely polite bolt of lightning, that vanished as quickly as it arrived.

Like the divine goddess, that so inspired Olivia, she was many things to many people and hence she was in constant demand from members, the congregation and a steady flow of journalists and film-makers. I was fortunate to be able to spend some time with her by myself or with her and a small number of others, which revealed a more pensive and quiet side to her nature. Eventually, in 2009, she initiated me into the Druid Clan of Dana, where-after I was lucky enough to be invited to drink tea on rare occasions in her sprawling kitchen.

By this time Oliva had become quite the celebrity — travelling to America to visit various FOI centres and also becoming a regular and revered guest of the annual Goddess Festival in

Glastonbury, England. Despite being in her 90s, Olivia was remarkably spritely and incredibly sharp mentally and she loved to travel, meet people and continue to lead the ever-growing ceremonies at FOI Foundation Centre at Huntington Castle.

Towards the end of her life, there were clear rumblings regarding the future of FOI and certain events led to a reduction in open invitations to The Castle for a while and also the updating and strengthening of the FOI Manifesto and Code of Ethics. Unfortunately, in 2013 Olivia fell and broke her leg, leading to a prolonged hospital stay. Shortly before she was due to be allowed to return home, she suffered a severe stroke which led to her passing over a short time after. By the time of her passing, the notion of a goddess movement, of the acceptability of the divine feminine had transformed from a hopeful dream to a genuine reality.

Olivia might be regarded by some as a proto-feminist — she was scholar, worked successfully in education and was a successful author of both fiction and non-fiction long before FOI was even imagined. Her aim, spiritually speaking, as far as I recall, was to restore balance to spirituality that had become dominated by a male-centric, patriarchal viewpoint, which was dragging the world downwards into a spiral of self-destruction. Although the focus of all three founders was clearly on Isis, the fellowship has always acknowledged a wide variety of divinities, including the masculine gods. One could say the aims of the FOI are restoration and achieving a holistic balance, as opposed to replacement of one form of worship with another, that is equally one-sided.

I cannot speak of the other two founders, who I did not know personally, but of Olivia I can say that she was incredibly humble and self-effacing, given her undeniable influence and torch-bearing for the re-emergent goddess spirituality. The legacy of FOI and Olivia Robertson is undeniable, with the small dreams of three people in a miniscule village, creating a ripple that would eventually become a tidal wave in time. Olivia was well aware of what they had achieved, by the time of her passing, and she was keen that the work should continue long after her death. From her perspective, her personal celebrity and influence were of no real importance — what mattered to her was the Work, the unfolding of the Divine Plan and she felt she was merely fulfilling her role in helping that to manifest itself.

We are all here to do what we can, in the time that we have, Olivia and her co-founders were an inspirational force that is greatly missed, but their influence is still here and will remain so, the work continues and we must all play our part in day by day, as Olivia said:

To touch one heart is to touch the world. (*Bealtaine* 2013)

Reconstructionism versus Romanticism

First published in Pagan Ireland *magazine,*
September 2021

As with many spiritual paths, Druidry or Druidism is divided into at least two camps. Broadly speaking these can be defined as 'Revival Druidry' and 'Reconstructionist Druidry', with perhaps a third camp (which I find myself in) being a mid-point between the two.

The idea of Reconstructionism is perhaps a reaction to the whimsy, inaccuracy and scant attention that is sometimes paid to historical fact by many practitioners, writers and leaders within the revival movement of the past 300 years or so.

The Druid Revival can be said to date back to English antiquarian and eccentric John Aubrey (1626–1697), who seemingly had no awareness of the dying Gaelic, Celtic culture across the water in Ireland, that actually had some genuine antecedents in its past. He and his follower William Stukeley were fairly obsessed with Stonehenge and the romance of the Druid, from Romano-British and Romano-Gaulish times.

However, it was an Irishman, with somewhat more credibility — John Toland, a genuine philosopher and historian who is credited with organising the first Druid meeting in 1717. Toland was author of *History of The Druids,* published in 1726, four years after his death, which includes a detailed biography but gives no mention of this supposed Druidic meeting at Primrose Hill, London.

Toland at least knew the genuine history of Ireland and its ancient peoples and is perhaps one of the few credible people named in the early Revival Druidry, which is filled mostly with eccentrics and fraudsters, such as Edward Williams (Iolo Morganwg).

The romanticism of the 18th century has been built upon by more romanticism from the Celtic Twilight (W.B. Yeats and Augusta Gregory in particular), despite the huge mass of academic work and translations undertaken during that period, by the likes of Mayer, MacAllister, O'Curry, Rolleston, Stokes etc., which shed genuine light on the *as Gaeilge* survivals of the mid to late medieval period. This was further compounded by more recent erroneous interpretations and writings of others, such as the infamous Robert Graves, in his highly subjective *The White Goddess*.

So, what is my beef with Reconstructionism you may ask? While a return to the original source material, twinned with a greater understanding of the archaeology makes perfect sense, what has happened is that some in the 'Reconstructionist Camp' have become incredibly puritanical, closed to new ideas and alternative interpretations of the Druidic faith.

Neo-Druidism is not a replica of the original Druidism and it never can be, as we have an incomplete picture of the original, which is separated by a gap of approximately 900 years (800CE–1700CE) by my estimation.

Obscure Pagan paths that have survived in Europe and Asia have evolved with time, as is to be expected, but Reconstructionist Druids allow for no such evolution, development and growth, unless it comes from some newly found text. Surely some middle-path, where the past and the present understanding can coexist, has merit? I'll let you be the judge of that though.

The Forgotten Irish Influence on British Neo-Druidry

First published in Moonscape *magazine,*
June 2023

Much of what is referred to as the Druid Revival, which started in late 17th century England and began to take shape in the early 18th century is attributed to three main figures — the antiquarian John Aubrey (1626–1697), William Stukeley (1687–1765), who was much influenced by the former, and lastly by Edward Williams (Iolo Morganwg 1747–1826).

These three eccentrics were English, apart from Williams, who was Welsh, a 'scholar', collector of literature, master forger and laudanum addict who spent several years in debtors' prison and became best known for founding the modern Gorsedd society and establishing the *Eisteddford* (Bardic competitions) revival, as well as his fraudulent book *Barddas*. John Aubrey, somewhat less disreputable, was a pioneer of archaeology (Avebury and Stonehenge), antiquarian and folklorirst (known for his book *Monumenta Britannica*), who none-the-less lost his fortune and large estates he inherited through a series of law suits.

Meanwhile, William Stukeley, again more reputable that either Williams or Aubrey, was both a medic and an Anglican clergyman, and graduate of Cambridge University, who continued Aubrey's investigations of Avebury and Stonehenge. He is largely credited with the main influence on romantic, revival Druidism/Druidry, possessing fanciful ideas about Druid origins in Pheonicia and links to Biblical pseudo-history, while also styling himself 'The Druid Chyndonax'. Having become a Freemason in 1721 and soon after, a Master of a Masonic Lodge, he was greatly influential on the Masonic interest in Druidism that persisted throughout the 18th, 19th and early 20th centuries.

Much of his ideas, often conjecture, have made their way into modern Neo-Druidic thought and practice.

However, another figure, less mentioned, looms large in the history of the Druid Revival, but is mostly briefly mentioned merely as founder of the first known revival group 'The Druid Circle of the Universal Bond', in London, in 1717 — one John Toland. He is also credited as first Chosen Chief of The Most Ancient Order Of Druids (1717–1722) by the modern order (TDO). Despite these landmark moments, Toland (1670–1722) is largely forgotten or ignored, despite having by far the best pedigree — as an academic, philosopher and historian of his time.

Toland was born, in Ardagh, Co. Donegal, Ireland, just 60 years after the collapse of the Gaelic Order, following the flight of the Earls in 1607. The old Gaelic Order was a system of culture, government, nobility and royalty stretching continuously back into the Pagan era, that survived fairly intact until the end of the Elizabethan conquest. Toland, a Catholic, would undoubtedly have spoken *Gaeilge* (Irish) as did over 80% of Irish people at the time, but he also knew English.

At the age of 16 he converted to Protestantism in order to attend university in Glasgow (it was illegal for Catholics to attend higher education) and thus he began an illustrious career (mostly in England, Germany and Netherlands) as a rationalist philosopher and freethinker, author of some 100 books, as well as myriad pamphlets and papers. Toland's major historical work *History of the Celtic Religion and Learning Containing an Account of the Druids* was published four years after his death in 1726, largely forgotten until a revised version was published in 1815 as *Toland's History Of The Druids*, which is also largely forgotten today.

Toland's work was based on a deep understanding of history and philosophy, not least of the country of his birth, where the Bardic culture and Druidic remains had been snuffed out only one generation or so before his birth. Unlike the usual suspects of eccentric British Druidism — his knowledge was based in a genuine and recently extinguished Gaelic past, still remembered, rather far more questionable ideas.

Toland was considered quite scandalous in his time, too progressive, too modern, heretical at times — infuriating senior clergy in both Ireland and Britain. He also wrote and spoke extensively on politics, proposing then radical ideas supported by Robert Harley, head of the English Country Party. His idea that neither ecclesiastical or monarchic governments were inherently good, or divinely sanctioned, was considered outrageous by many, but (to me at least) many of his ideas are influenced by early Irish Gaelic literature such as 'The Wisdom of Cormac'.

Why then is such a luminary ignored or forgotten by the Druids and Druidic establishment of our own day? Now recognized in philosophy and academia as a man ahead of his time, he has yet to be acknowledged for his role in Neo-Druidism or insights into Irish Druidism — both have largely been ignored, even to this day. Isn't it time that John Toland was given his due, in the light of his unique position in the history of Neo-Druidism?

References:

Toland's History Of The Druids — *John Toland (1726, Reprinted James Watt, 1815)*

John Toland, the Druids, and the Politics of Celtic Scholarship — *Justin Champion (Irish historical studies: joint journal of the Irish Historical Society and the Ulster Society for Irish Historical Studies, 2001)*

John Toland — *Michael Brown, (Dictionary of Irish Biography, 2009)*
The British Circle of the Universal Bond (An Druidh Uileach Braithrearchas) — *The Ancient Druid Order 1.3 (Brochure, The Druid Order, 1976)*

Metaphysics

Science and Religion

First published in Immrama *magazine, 2004*

In the modern world the scientific and religious view of the world would appear to be at opposite ends of the spectrum, however, it was not always thus and the divide between these views points is decreasing.

In ancient times the idea of subdividing knowledge as we do now was not common. Pre-Christian peoples of Europe (at least among the higher strata of their societies) were acquainted with knowledge — the Greeks, Romans, and Celts plus further afield, the Persians, Egyptians and Sumerians had an understanding of astronomy, mathematics, architecture, medicine and engineering and even electricity (e.g. the 'Baghdad battery') yet they were also highly religious societies.

As late as the renaissance people of learning were often versed in all the 'arts' by which I mean knowledge in a wider sense; two very famous examples of this are Leonardo da Vinci who was an accomplished artist and scientist, and Michel de Nostradame (Nostradamus) who was an excellent physician and also a seer. In medieval times and earlier all aspects of knowledge were studied in a more holistic approach to life, as such the work of the magus or alchemist was as much a scientific undertaking as it was a spiritual one. It was mainly the prohibition of scientific thought by the Roman Catholic church that forced a gradual change of view, those who wished to acquire a better understanding of the physical nature of the universe had to pursue their studies in secret or openly reject the Church. In addition to this, the wide acceptance of the ideas of 16th century philosopher René Descartes served to widen the gap between religion and science. Descartes believed that the mind was divisible from the physical world and that physical matter is more or less clay to be manipulated as we see fit. In essence Descartes divorced the natural physical world from divinity, connecting only the mind or soul with higher powers, i.e. God, this idea has evolved to create a purely rational way of life that denies the relevance of spirituality in the apparent world.

The logical conclusion of this process of rationalism is where we have arrived at today — human society with scant regard for the physical universe and a very weakened sense of interconnectedness or equilibrium between the physical and spiritual planes of existence.

One might think that the schism between science and religion is complete but recent events (by that I mean the last few decades) have caused a remarkable turnaround. Quantum leaps in physics have led to a complete reconstruction of physicists' view of the universe and a more complete picture shows an indefinable factor at work in much of the laws of nature, what is often referred to as 'the hand of God'. Such facts as light being both a wave and a particle (which is supposedly impossible), water being able to retain information, the change in nature of sub atomic particles that occurs as a result of observation etc. defy human logic but have been scientifically proven.

This shift in understanding has prompted many hardened atheist scientists to declare that God actually does exist being that there can be no other explanation for some of phenomena that exists in the universe. Their ideas of what God is may differ greatly from that of the common concepts, however, there is a growing acknowledgement in the scientific community of a greater force at work that is as yet beyond human understanding.

It is my hope that the two strands of human understanding of the world around us — science and spirituality will unite again once more to give a more complete picture of the nature of existence; perhaps in order for science to develop as it has, it was necessary for this schism to occur. Unfortunately, because of this schism many scientists have rejected religion in the past, as a parallel to this religious people often have a tremendous scepticism and fear of science as if it were innately dangerous or somehow wrong.

In my experience many of the Pagan community have a blind faith in their religion and a distrust of science, a perfect mirror of the scientist's rejection of God and blind faith in science. As spiritual beliefs become stronger, this is often coupled with an absolute rejection of science and all that it has brought us — a perfect example is the person who will consult an untrained sales assistant in a health food shop but refuse the advice of a doctor who probably underwent 5–7 years training before being able to practice. I'm not saying that natural therapies are inferior; they are, after all, the foundation on which modern medicine was built, what worries me is the superstitious fear of knowledge derived from science — which I see as akin to fear of voodoo. (Note: Voodoo or Voodun is an African/Afro-American Earth-based religion not to be confused with Hoodoo which is an American magical system based on African, European and Native American magic).

Some philosophers have argued about the moral aspects of science and technology (e.g. *Futureshock* by Alvin Toffler discusses this in detail), and many people believe it to be morally suspect. I believe that science is neutral, to me it is the gift of the Gods and may be used both to benefit or bring harm as we see fit. The Greek god Prometheus was credited with giving man the gift of fire, perhaps the very first technology we possessed, for which he suffered eternal torment. However, we possess an ability to learn and manipulate the physical world far beyond any other creature, surely that is a gift of knowledge that the divine meant us to possess. It is the application of our knowledge that is the crucial factor — for example, a sharp knife in the hands of a chef is a useful tool, in the hands of deranged criminal that same knife becomes a deadly weapon.

As a person trained in scientific methods, whilst also practicing my religious beliefs as a Pagan I attempt to marry the two ways of thinking to obtain a balanced and hopefully better understanding of the world around me.

One of the greatest problems facing the human race is to learn how to live in balance, both science and religion indicate that the universe attempts to maintain an equilibrium — a state of perfect balance. Unfortunately living within that state of harmony has proved to be very difficult for us as a species, we live at odds with the natural world, dominating and destroying it but at the same time hopelessly weak before it when it unleashes its raw power. Within our own sphere of human interaction, we are still horribly off kilter, unable to live in peace, unable to accept different modes of thought, religion, lifestyle or even minor differences of physical appearance.

It will take every ounce of all that we possess spiritually and intellectually if we are to survive our own inadequacies and evolve beyond the dangerous semi-savage state that we are currently in.

Learning to throw aside our preconceptions but at the same time drawing on all the vast resource of physical and metaphysical knowledge that humanity has accumulated might be a way forward for us. Most essential of all is that we regain some humility and realize that to the gods we are like foolish children in need of help, only when we accept how little we really know will we begin to learn the true meaning of our existence.

Rites of Passage

First published in Brigid's Fire *magazine,*
February 2011

These are times of great change, ecologically, economically, politically and not least spiritually. If one had predicted the amazing loss of faith in the institutions of religion and government say 20 years ago there would have been nothing but howls of derision and laughter. However, here we are now in 2010 and the great edifice of public respectability is crumbling under the weight of its own corruption and failure to engage with the people of this country in any meaningful way.

I am not for a moment suggesting that neo-Paganism is going to fill the obvious void left by the mass exodus from Roman Catholicism, but it is one of a number of spiritual paths that is on the increase and will play its part in providing an alternative for those that still feel the need for spiritual/religious input in their lives.

This is an interesting time for Paganism here, thanks to the efforts of PF Ireland, legal marriage ceremonies can take place for the first time. Another recent development is Ireland's first ecological burial ground, which caters for all denominations as well as humanists or atheists. This presents the opportunity for genuine Pagan burials to take place for the first time in well over a millennium rather than the embarrassing after-thought tacked onto the obligatory Christian burial that people of many faiths have received in the past — regardless of their wishes. For example, a good friend of mine told me, the story of how her dear friend was given a Catholic burial despite the fact that he was a lifelong Sikh!

Such important rites should and must not be allowed to be enacted by default or the rights and religious freedom of any faith be trampled on. After all, our constitution enshrines the right to religious freedom for all the people of Ireland; although this was written with the Catholic/Protestant divide in mind, it is equally applicable to all religions and should be applied equally.

So, perhaps now that opportunity beckons, it is time to get our house in order with respect to rites of passage? Given the multitude of beliefs and strands within Paganism it is not possible, nor should there be, standardized rites and procedures. As a former Catholic I am well acquainted with the Church's rites from birth to death, as is generally the case with anyone who has grown up in that environment. Neo-Paganism being still in its infancy the rites of passage are not so clearly defined and also vary enormously from one tradition/path to another.

In modern Christian tradition baptism is performed either at birth (in the case of illness) or after a few months. In much earlier times this was generally performed on consenting adults; the baptism of infants, which is in reality a form of initiation, was introduced to prevent their souls entering Limbo in the event of their untimely death. Interestingly there is no such rite in Islam or Buddhism that I am aware of, although the Jewish act of circumcision is performed on infant males (this barbarous act actually has some basis in penile health) and *mikvah* or ritual immersion is practiced as a means of purification although this is repeatable at appropriate times unlike baptism.

In pre-Christian Ireland and Wales, it is recorded that Druids baptized children, in Ireland they sang the *baithis geintlídhe* over the child at a river or stream. I could find no reference to the age at which this was performed but if it was also a name giving this was probably performed on new-born. Speaking personally, I feel that any form of initiation performed on the newborn or those who are unable to make decisions for themselves is an act of violation and should not happen. If I were asked to dedicate/ initiate an infant to a particular path or to a particular deity

I would refuse to do so. I do, however, feel that a blessing and name giving is fair enough and provides an opportunity for a communal rite without infringing the individual's right to self-determination. In some initiatory rites (such as described some 1800 years ago by Apuleius on his acceptance into the cult of Isis) baptism is part of the ritual, apparently common enough in religious cults of the pre-Christian era, however, this was entered into by sentient individuals of their own volition.

Introducing children to religious beliefs is a difficult subject, there is a thin line between passing on traditions and indoctrination, which brings me to the next rite — Greening. As an alternative to receiving 'Holy Communion' some Pagans offer Greening to children of the usual ages 7–8. Having not witnessed this myself I cannot say too much about it, however, I can appreciate that both family and the child themselves may feel it appropriate for some act of commitment to their path, although I again would be hesitant about initiation.

I would consider late teenage a time from which it might be appropriate to offer initiation, unlike the Catholic rite of Confirmation which usually takes place at 12–13 in this country. I am aware that in some other less predominantly Catholic countries this takes place at 14–15, a step in the right direction but in my opinion still too young for most teenagers to make a definitive commitment to any spiritual path. In Wicca 'Coming of Age' ceremonies including 'Dedication' might be offered at the onset of puberty, however, this does not require the same level of involvement as initiation. In many cases this is perhaps sufficient for people who do not wish to make a serious spiritual commitment and also is a sensible intermediate stage on the way to initiation for those who choose it.

From discussion with Wiccan friends and from my own experience of Druids and Shamans I am aware that there is no clear point of entry for initiates as regards age, it seems to be at the discretion of the individual priest/priestess, coven, grove or order and, of course, depends on the readiness/willingness on the part of the neophyte.

If rites in Paganism are to be taken seriously, I feel that it is important to avoid the nonchalant attitude often exhibited by Christians and sometimes in other long-established faiths. 'Going through the motions' defeats the object of participating in religious rites and so I would consider that initiates (young or old) should be required to exhibit their sincerity before being allowed to participate in what should be a sacred moment in their life.

As regards marriage, this is now a well-established rite within Paganism; what is new here is the legal status that has been granted via the Pagan Federation. In legal terms there are only two sentences that are required, the remainder of the ceremony is at the discretion of the participants so I believe, which hopefully means that all shades of Pagan can be catered for. It will be interesting to see how this unfolds and I have high hopes that this will give Paganism a level of credibility and toleration that it has not been afforded in the past.

As I mentioned at the beginning, the opportunity for unimpeded death rites presents itself. Restrictions of the law with regard to manner of burial or cremation obviously have to be observed and so potential celebrants need to be aware of this in performing a rite of death. As far as I know it should be possible for family to perform their own rites (if any) at the new burial ground in Killann (Wexford), perhaps dispensing with the need for a facilitator altogether!

This is an exciting time to be a Pagan both as an individual and also as a facilitator/priest/ celebrant etc. especially as we move ever closer to equal status with other religions. I can only hope that this will lead to greater freedom and greater religious tolerance both in Ireland and the wider world, which in both cases is sadly still beset by religious intolerance and violence.

Celtic Cosmology — An Introduction

First published in Aontacht *magazine, April 2013*

As a general rule, it would be fair to say that most non-Pagans have little or no understanding of Pagan theology/cosmology. In the absence of any information to the contrary, they often tend to be rather fearful and perhaps unwilling to investigate. This being the case, they would more than likely be surprised to find out that there is no unified theology or cosmology within Paganism, moreover they'd be surprised to learn that several quite different streams of belief and practice exist.

Within Paganism itself, the most well-known cosmological system is the Hermetic tradition, i.e. that of the ancient Greeks, in part derived from the Egyptians. Combined or intertwined with this is the Jewish mystical school of Kabbalah, elements of which are to be found in Witchcraft, Alchemy, Freemasonry, Golden Dawn etc.

Much of this esoterica made its way across Europe to the British Isles via the Greeks, Romans and later on the Normans and the influx of Hermetic refugees caused by the crusades and the eventual fall of Byzantium. However, within Europe there are two indigenous streams of Paganism that have survived (partially) with relatively little outside influence, these being Norse and Celtic cosmology. In both cases this is most likely due to the physical isolation of being on the fringes of Europe and in the case of Scandinavia, the extreme weather probably deterred most invaders or would-be colonists.

What remains of Celtic cosmology is somewhat fragmented, for several reasons. Due to the colonisation of Europe by the Romans much of Celtic culture was almost completely eliminated — e.g., in Cisalpine Gaul, Gaul and Iberia where the Celtic languages and religious practices quickly fell into disuse.

In the British Isles, Ireland in particular, the influence of Roman culture was much weaker which enabled Celtic language, custom and religion to outlive the Western Roman Empire. What is now England was heavily Romanised, however, some elements of Celtic culture did survive although this was again diluted by the influx of Germanic and Norse invaders from the 5th century onwards.

The arrival of Christianity had an obvious impact on Celtic religion more so than it did on any other aspect of Celtic life, however, dating of Pagan burial sites in Ireland shows that Pagan practice continued alongside Christianity at least into the 8th century CE. A brief comparison between Roman Catholicism and Celtic or Norse Paganism clearly indicates that much of the celebrations and customs of Paganism were simply assimilated or re-assigned by the Church, probably out of necessity. So, in a distorted form, much of Paganism has in fact survived into current times.

Further to the above, Norman and subsequent English colonisation of the entire British Isles forced the remaining Celtic countries into retreat and eventual collapse of their systems of government, agriculture, language and culture in general. This culminated in a ban on *Cymraeg, Gaeilge* and *Gáidhlig* which lead to the destruction or loss of much of the written and oral culture of the Celtic people.

So, unlike Buddhism, Hinduism, Judaism or Christianity, for example, there is no one text or set of texts that embodies the theological or cosmological system of the Pagan Celts. What remains is a partial picture of Celtic belief, which has been used to reconstruct Celtic Paganism in the modern era — a process that is still continuing today.

In common with the pre-Socratic model of the four (or five) elements, Irish culture relates to the physical word in terms of four and five but also three and nine. There are four cities mentioned in the *Yellow Book of Lecan*, from which the *Tuatha*

Dé Danann came — each in one of the cardinal points of the compass. Four Druids were associated with each city, as were four hallowed objects, the treasures of the *Tuatha Dé Danann*. Although the text is not explicit, the most common directional association is that shown below.

City	Treasure	Direction	Element	Province	Quality
Falias	Lia Fáil (stone)	North	Earth	Ulster	Battle
Gorias	Spear of Lugh	South	Fire	Munster	Music
Murias	Cauldron of Dagda	West	Water	Connaught	Knowledge
Findias	Sword of Nuada	East	Air	Leinster	Prosperity

In addition to the four main compass directions, the Irish cosmology includes five others — roughly translating as: above, below, outside, inside and through. These nine directions correspond with what is known as *Dúile* (nine elements), which includes the familiar air (sky), fire (sun), water (sea) and earth (land).

These nine elements of *Dúile* relate to the cosmos (*Bith*), the three realms within the cosmos and the three cauldrons within the human body, with three of these elements relating to each cauldron. This is most easily illustrated by the table given below, that I have borrowed and modified (from Searles O'Dubhain).

Dúile

Body Part	Cosmic Part	Direction	Tool/Property	Cauldron
Cnaimh (Bones)	Cloch (Stone)	Thuaidh (North)	Lia Fail	Coire Ernmae
Colaind (Flesh)	Talamh (Earth)	Faoi (Under)	Nemed(grove)	Coire Ernmae

Gruaigh (Hair)	Uaine (Plant Life)	Amach (Outwards)	Ogham and Herbs	Coire Ernmae
Fuil (Blood)	Muir (Sea)	Siar (West)	Cauldron of Dagda	Coire Goriath
Anal "Breath"	Gaeth (Wind)	Oithear (East)	Sword of Nuada	Coire Goriath
Imradud (Mind)	Gealach (Moon)	Isteach (Inwards)	Well of Segais	Coire Goriath
Drech (Face)	Grian (Sun)	Dheas (South)	Spear of Lugh	Coire Sois
Menma (Brain)	Nel (Cloud)	Thrid (Through)	Inspiration	Coire Sois
Ceann (Head)	Neamh (Heaven)	Os Cionn (Above)	Torc/Halo	Coire Sois

The *Dúile* and the three cauldrons of wisdom (*Sois*), vocation (*Ernmae*) and Warming (*Goriath*) relate to the head, body and blood of a person, which in turn is related to the three realms of sky, land and sea. Hence it is clear that three was a very important number in Celtic cosmology — three cauldrons, three realms and nine (3 x 3) elements. Indeed, this continued to be theologically significant into the Christian era and even today the trefoil (three-leaved shamrock) is a symbol associated with Ireland.

The three realms of sky, land and sea are representative of the upper world (*Magh Mór*), middle world (*Míde*) where we usually find ourselves and the otherworld (*Tir Andomain*). Personally, I would say that these three realms co-exist here and now in the same space, it is a matter of perception that shields us from seeing the greater reality. In the Welsh tradition these three realms are near enough the same but are shown as three concentric circles — *Annwn* (otherworld), *Abred* (middle) and *Gwynfyd* (upper), with the space beyond (*Ceugant*) being the infinite or godhead.

The three realms are alluded to in Celtic myth, the otherworld in particular and it is also represented by the *Bile Buadha*, or

Tree of Power/World Tree, which is similar in concept to the Norse *Yggdrasil*. The sacred tree or *Bile Buadha* relates to the five ancient provinces as described in *Settling of The Manor of Tara*, each of which had its own *Bile*. These are roughly the same as the four modern provinces (shown earlier) with the addition of Míde or Meath — the sacred tree *Craebh Uisnigh* being located at Uisneach the 'navel of Ireland', sacred and royal centre. So, to the four provinces shown earlier we can now add:

City	Treasure	Direction	Element	Province	Quality
Uisneach	-	Centre	Spirit	Míde	Kingship

This Celtic concept of the universe unifies the three realms of existence with the human existence via *dúile* (element) and the *coire* (cauldron) but it also connects via the *Bile Buadha* to the five provinces and cardinal points. Connecting all of existence is *neart* or *nwyfre* (Welsh), which roughly means life-force or the spirit that flows through all things. This whole concept can be described as *Dán*, which is somewhat similar to the Chinese concept of Tao — everything is interconnected, everything is animated by spirit.

This belief is clearly illustrated by Brehon Law, which gave usage of the land among the community (*tuath*) rather than our modern concept of ownership. It also treated animals as persons to the extent that a hen could be punished for trespass, snatching and wasting or bees must provide honey as compensation for stinging a neighbour or passer-by. This view of the world and all that is in it as deeply connected is beautifully described by the ancient poem the *Song of Amergin*. Amergin, the Milesian (Gaelic) *Ollamh* or chief Druid is also credited with the ancient tract *The Cauldron of Poesy* which is a metaphysical discourse on the three cauldrons and the nine elements.

This view of our existence endured through the Christianisation of the British Isles and indeed through colonisation by the English.

Clear evidence of this is the survival of belief in the *sídhe* and the otherworld in folklore and literature. As late as the end of the 1800s the Gaels of Scotland preserved their language (*Gáidhlig*) and beliefs, although superficially Christianised. Alexander Carmichael saved the sayings and practices of the last generation of islanders and highlanders who retained these traditions in his collection *Ortha nan Gaidheal (Carmina Gadelica)*. One of the best examples of this being a direct reference to the three realms:

Neart mara dhuit	Power of sea be with you
Neart talamh duit	Power of land be with you
Neart néimhe	Power of sky
Mathas mara dhuit	Goodness of sea be with you
Mathas talamh duit	Goodness of land be with you
Mathas néimhe.	Goodness of sky.

This deep connection with the realms of existence is borne out in the seasonal cycles of the Celt and their respect for the sun, moon, stars and the earth and all that lives upon it. Their most important celebrations were tied to the natural cycles and to the deities of the land itself, a model which has fortunately been retained and is commonly understood (in various forms) by Pagans as the 'eightfold wheel of the year'.

So clearly, we can see that Celtic cosmology has a unique view of the world that has somehow survived the contraction of the Celtic world. Unique as it is, it is perfectly possible to integrate this worldview with the more common classical tradition. The Irish Order of Thelema does exactly this and thereby combines indigenous belief and practice with the generally more familiar hermetic structures.

In my own practice I work within a framework of the five elements and the three realms and three cauldrons and I find that the two models are entirely compatible in an Irish context when considered in terms that I've outlined above.

At the end of the day, finding a meaningful and practically workable spiritual experience is more important than the restrictions of theological dogma. Although I do not advocate a 'pick and mix' approach to spirituality — without disrespecting or defiling discrete magical and spiritual systems one should be free to work with what one fully understands in a way that is beneficial to the connection with spirit, deity or whatever you might define as cosmic. Although the ancient Celts were hardly syncretic, they clearly recognised the interconnectedness of all existence, like the branches and the roots of the cosmic tree that stretch into the furthest reaches of the universe. I am sure that were they around today they would embrace tolerance, shared wisdom and be open to the positive influences of the world that surrounds them.

Dealing with Death

First published in johnhuntpublishing.com,
November 2013

In Ireland the month of November is called *Samhain* in the native tongue but it is also the name for Halloween. Today most people celebrate Halloween with 'Trick or Treating' and bonfires on 31st of October (5th of November in UK), not realising that these are modern forms of ancient religious celebrations associated with the coming of winter and the festival of the dead.

At this time people were aware of the literal death of the year — the end of the harvest and the trees and plants dying or becoming dormant. In Celtic belief the year (which was split into two halves) began as the darkness began, just as the day began as soon as the sun set. Elsewhere in Europe and indeed as far away as South America, this time was a celebration of the ancestors and an acknowledgement of the role of death in our lives.

Of course, until very recently, death was an every-day part of human life — before proper sanitation, vaccines and antibiotics the Western death rate was incredibly high and people were used to accepting the likelihood that many of their friends and family would die during their own lifetime.

These days people are often completely shocked and unprepared for death. This is perhaps understandable in the case of those who die young, who we no longer expect to receive an early death, but in the case of the elderly many still have tremendous trouble in dealing with the inevitable passing over of loved ones.

Personally, I feel that this inability to handle an important part of our lives is directly due to the removal of the ritual and close proximity formerly associated with dying. Although far less common now, the wake, where the deceased is still kept in the house (in an open coffin) for up to three days still happens in Ireland. In less traditional Irish families and in other countries the deceased are often spirited away to a funeral parlour and not seen again until the burial/cremation.

This ancient funereal custom forces a finality on those left behind and also offers a very direct and immediate opportunity for grieving. During the period of the wake there is a great deal of eating, drinking (both tea and alcohol) and also lots of chat about the deceased that may include both crying and laughing in large amounts. In both Celtic Pagan and Christian belief, it was considered that the dead person was hopefully moving on to a better place and hence the wake and post-burial gathering often centres around happy memories and celebration as much as it does mourning.

Rather than sweeping it under the carpet or denying the gravity of the situation, the Irish tradition confronts the death head on; so, by the time of the 'removal' and the actual funeral many of the family and friends are already well advanced in the process of saying goodbye to the deceased.

This appears to me to be a very healthy way of dealing with death, even if it does often involve excessive drinking. In fact, the drinking itself can be cathartic in that is loosens people up and enables expression of emotion that might otherwise be difficult for some. This form of funereal tradition is respectful and very much deep rooted in community, not least because of the long-held beliefs in regard to ancestors.

In many places around the world this time of the year is a time to remember our ancestors — where we came from. This has been a strong tradition in Celtic countries until the very recent past, however, respect for the ancestors is still equally important to other cultures today e.g. China, Japan and many other Asian countries.

We may now live in a global village, with family ties across different countries and different cultures, but it's still important to remember where we come from and that without our ancestors we would not be here. Like all things that live we will also die, and it will eventually be our time to join them and become ancestors ourselves.

Re-uniting the God and the Goddess

First published in Aontacht *magazine,*
December 2011

Over the last two centuries there has been a gradual re-emergence of the feminine in modern human society. This began very slowly and gently and has gathered great pace in the last hundred years, the last fifty especially. With this revitalizing of women has also come the revitalizing of the many faces of the goddess — the divine feminine.

This is a wonderful development and long overdue after millennia of patriarchal society that has brought humanity and the planet to the edge of collapse. This necessary development has empowered women but unfortunately it does not seem to have done the same for men. Instead of welcoming this change from a position of inner strength and self-knowledge many men have reacted by becoming more aggressive or by becoming overly passive. What the feminine renaissance has clearly demonstrated is something that is not often highlighted — the fact that men too need a renaissance, but one of a very different kind.

Maleness has been hugely damaged by such a long period of negative role models, abuse of each other, the planet and a failure to deal honestly with the inner life. That the masculine in humanity is degraded is undeniable, but simply embracing the re-emergent feminine energy alone is simply not enough to heal men. Men comprise roughly half of humanity, and by extension if men cannot also re-find a place in the world, humanity will remain damaged as a whole.

The re-emergence of the goddess is vital to re-dress the terrible imbalance of the past, however, I believe that ultimately, we have to find a path to re-uniting the god and goddess and man and woman as equals in a way that will bring harmony. From looking at ancient forms of religion it is clear that there was a dynamic beyond patriarchy or matriarchy — a form of spirituality that embraced both.

In the earliest form of Judaism there were two gods — male and female, although at some point the goddess became forgotten. From Egypt, Ra and Isis are known today as the god of the sun/creation and goddess of the earth respectively. Less familiar to most are their opposite gender counterparts — Nut, goddess of the sky who enrages Ra but later assists him, and also Geb — Nut's brother, father of Isis and also god of the Earth. In Irish mythology we also see overlapping deities — Grainne, the solar goddess and Lugh, the solar god; Morrigan, goddess of war and death, Donn — god of death. In Hindu culture each god has a female consort, from whom his power emanates, for instance the god Shiva's creative force is embodied as the goddess Shiva. Looking now at Taoism, the Yin/Yang symbol succinctly depicts the intertwining of the divine male and female energies to create a whole. It is interesting also to note that the very centre of the black half is white and the very centre of the white half is black — simply demonstrating that aspects of the one are contained in the other.

There are probably many more examples of this type of duality, a double polarized but non-linear relationship between dark and light, female and male, goddess and god. Unfortunately, despite the fact that this model of deity still exists it seems to be largely ignored or forgotten by most men and women.

It is interesting to note that this spiritual energy is embedded in the fabric in the universe in what physicists call the torus energy — two half spheres meeting but apparently externally not connected, however, they are connected internally through a central vortex. This energy form is found in the atom, an orange, a human aura, the earth's magnetic field, the sun's energy flows and even in the structure of galaxies. Even more startling is the fact that this energy matrix was depicted in the temples of the ancients, indicating that they knew of its existence, perhaps not in terms of physics but certainly as a spiritual principle.

Although women are undoubtedly regaining their power, many men appear to be lost in hostility or have capitulated to such an extent that they have lost their own power. Just as polarization towards male energy was and is dangerous, I think that a polarization towards female energy could be differently but equally disastrous.

However, it is not for women to rediscover what the divine masculine should be or what maleness really is. It has often been said that girls grow up to be women but that boys do not necessarily grow up to be men. I agree with this statement wholeheartedly — men need a second birth. This second birth in older cultures took the form of an initiation into adulthood if you will, otherwise the boy often remains the perpetual child.

Just as women have had to strive to re-establish themselves over time, most often with the objection of men, men themselves need to wake up to the fact that they were already lost long before women had the confidence to point that out. Embracing the feminine in women and also the feminine side within men is an essential part of the healing process. Beyond that, it is also necessary for men to rediscover their maleness and the true virtues of the god energy. Without positive male role models that process is very difficult and often leads to the maturing of men in mid-life or sometimes not at all.

Although women should be critical of men's inadequacies, it is not always constructive. It is the initiated man, the elder, the man who knows himself who should be the one to take younger men aside and show them what it really means to be a man, in cooperation rather than in conflict with women.

In order for many men to acquire that knowledge in a world of corrupted male leaders and negative role models it is often necessary for men to undergo a soul-destroying ordeal, a divine dismemberment if you will; an event shown in myth by the death and rebirth of Osiris. Life can be a hard teacher and without an appropriate teacher, men are forced to learn maturity the hard way — usually much later than their female counterparts. Hence it is a real necessity for men who understand what real male strength is to 'break-in' boys and young men, which will save them and the people they touch from the damage done by a perpetual child who is masquerading as an adult.

Ultimately both men and women have to undergo spiritual Alchemy — the resolution of the many parts known and unknown within ourselves — male and female, our shadow self, our Ego etc. The first step in discovering the philosopher's stone or metaphysically turning base metal into gold is the acknowledgement that we must undertake that journey of integration and self-discovery.

It seems to me that far more than men, women have 'stepped up to the plate' and are willing to explore a new and healthier dynamic in human interaction. Now is the time for men also to 'step up to the plate', not submissively or disgruntled, but fully engaged in the process of understanding what it means to be human and what we are all here to do. If life can be described as a dance, then it really does take two to tango, whether that means finding a life partner, learning to relate to others or integrating aspects of the opposite sex into our own psyche.

It is my feeling that only through healing the rifts between men and women, re-uniting the god and goddess, can we save ourselves from an endless cycle of imbalance and perhaps even extinction. One can only hope that each of us will find the divine spirit in ourselves to make sure that equilibrium with one another and creation as a whole becomes our new reality.

Virtual Reality
Do Druids, Shamans & Witches Fit in
This New world?

First published in Indie Shaman *magazine, July 2022*

Much has been made of virtual reality (VR) and augmented reality (AR) in the last decade, but it is only really now, in 2022, that this is becoming a genuinely viable way of interacting on a wider scale, especially since Facebook launched its Metaverse.

While many people are ready to embrace this, there are others such as myself, who are very skeptical about how useful or beneficial it is for society in general and for the esoteric/magical community in particular. One must remember that the world of computing only became part of mainstream society in the early 1980s, in terms of human history that is but a flickering of the eyelid. For the vast majority of human history, we have had little or on technology and managed to survive somehow.

I am not opposed to technology, as I believe it is neutral — a knife is a useful tool in the hands of a skilled chef, in the hands of a murderer it is not a benefit at all, quite the opposite! So, it's not just a question of what the technology does, but how it is used and what effects it has on the physical, intellectual and spiritual aspects of human existence.

In the case of computers, they are incredibly useful tools that can save time and effort and be of particular benefit to people with some kind of difficulties or a disability. Computers have aided people to speak, to gain mobility, to make non-functional limbs work again or operate prosthetic limbs. With the advent of the brain-computer interface (such as Neuralink) we are now seeing all kinds of possibilities for disabled people that were previously in the realm of science-fiction.

On a more mundane level computers have revolutionised communication, with the mobile phone being a far more powerful computing device, on a scale of hundreds of times better, than home computers from the early 1980s. We can now talk to people on the other side of the world via video links, almost as if they were just sat in another room. This has great advantages for those who cannot travel due to disability or even lack of time or financial viability.

As regards spiritual practice, communications technology has enabled us to share ceremony, courses, events etc. across vast distances and also in cases where a pandemic has prevented 'real world' meet-ups. This is, of course, a great benefit as it is both cheap and convenient and provides a means of interaction to anyone who can afford a 'smart phone' and internet services. Of course, this is only realistic for those living a Western lifestyle — the vast majority of people on this planet do not own a 'smart phone' or have regular and consistent access to the internet.

I have seen a lot of discussion of this topic online in recent times — with people advocating for more on-line interaction, especially from a lack of opportunity/disability angle. The other side of this is, clearly, the lack of tech availability due to poverty and low development in more than half of the world — which no-one mentioned or seemed to factor into their arguments. Poor people have a right to a spiritual life too, and in the case of over half the world, they do not even have the option to attend a Shamanic conference online or take part in an online Druidic ritual, as they are confined to physical reality only.

There are pros and cons to this argument about access and availability, but clearly it is a great benefit to those who are restricted physically in some way, assuming they can afford and access mobile phone technology. However, this is not where the contention ends, there are other factors which are perhaps more subtle but more indicative of how humanity is faced with difficult choices about its future.

One aspect that was discussed on forums etc is the interface between our own selves and the world that exists outside of our minds and physical bodies. Up until now there has only really been one choice — to exist in the physical world and to exist to some extent (or even totally) outside in nature, for most people. We now have the option of moving our lives temporarily, occasionally, often, or even semi-permanently into an artificially created reality.

We do not yet know what effect living in a virtual reality or augmented reality world will have on us physically, mentally or spiritually, as it is far too early to know — we can only try to predict what the long-term effects will be. Already, studies on the use of social media over the last 30 years, particularly on young people, seem to indicate a negative effect in terms of mental health, ability to concentrate, ability to retain information and to communicate effectively in 'real world' face-to-face situations.

Some might suggest that we are already losing some of that which makes us human, and that this will only get worse and accelerated if we choose to dive into the Metaverse and other forms of virtual reality. Can we say with confidence that religious and spiritual interactions will not be affected by functioning in an artificially created universe? Will we still be able to connect with the natural world from within it? Also, when we leave this virtual world and return to the natural physical world, will our ability to interact with nature, people and the world of spirit be unaffected? Or will it be damaged and diminished?

We do not know the answers to these questions as yet. I, for one, would urge caution as we enter an unknown area of existence, with many possible problematic factors to be studied and assessed. It takes long enough to learn the skills of the Druid,

Shaman or Witch, for most people and already many modern people already struggle to find or refind a strong connection to spirit/deity and the land. There is a strong argument that modern humans are alienated from the land and nature by our technological lifestyles, so if this is true, then is virtual reality going to make this situation even worse?

This is a new area of human experience that really overlaps with science-fiction, transhumanism, the idea of cyborgs, artificial intelligence and human-machine synergy. This may seem exciting and wonderful to some, but to others it is a frightening dystopian future that may lead to the end of humanity as we now know it. I cannot say, which vision is right, but I can predict that it will cause a split between those who wish to remain solely in the 'real world' and those who wish to engage with new virtual worlds and supplement their human existence through technological advances.

Already I have seen red flags raised, particularly from the gaming community, about personal safety and the greater ability of people to disguise themselves in virtual worlds — where they can behave inappropriately with little hinderance or consequences. There are already cases of tragic consequences for some young people who have been preyed upon, often when they entered adult arenas in the VR worlds already in existence. Who is going to look after us in the virtual world, or is it just going to be an uncontrolled, free-for-all? When you consider the magical world already has its inherent dangers with journeying, dealing with entities, use of spells, how do we factor all this happening in a VR world where people can appear to be anything that they wish to be?

There is also the question of money, sharing and selling of data (information) and the role of big tech companies and government in this new and emerging technology. Will notions of privacy have to change within the VR and ER worlds? Do we wish to interact in a spiritual world where commercial entities

218

are involved, such as Meta or Microsoft for instance? In this world are we free agents, are we able to do or buy anything we want? Do we (as human avatars or something else entirely) in fact become digital commodities ourselves?

A very interesting film *The Congress*, starring Robin Wright, looks at many of the issues I have discussed. It begins with focus on Aaron, a young disabled boy (played by Kodi Smit-McPhee) who becomes part of the new virtual world, where he can live without the difficulties of his physical life. His mother undergoes a journey into this new world, which is part playground and part nightmare. I will not ruin this film for you, but suffice to say, it throws up many questions and in my opinion is perhaps the best and most thought-provoking film on this subject matter.

Clearly humanity will continue to evolve, but the question is how? Do we remove ourselves from technological influence completely? Do we limit our interactions with technology such that it cannot influence our thinking and behaviour, or do we dive right in and embrace this new age of artificial intelligence and artificial reality?

Personally, I have serious concerns about how it will affect wider society and also the much smaller esoteric communities that I am a part of. Already, in recent years, I have seen friendships end, whole communities damaged through social media interactions. I have lost some friendships through social media communications, mostly due to misunderstandings and the inability to fully communicate in the way that would be fully interactive if it was face-to-face. This makes me rather sad, and I wonder if these problems might only get worse if we start to interact with each other mainly through VR and ER environments.

As part of my beliefs and my way of life, I choose to interact with nature, I choose to be part of nature and spend much of my life immersed in it. I do not think I will be spiritually, intellectually and emotionally able to continue in that fashion if I find myself engaged with, or hooked up to, a virtual world and virtual communications on a regular basis. I fear that I would start to lose myself and a sense of who I am and my place in this world. For me, Druidism/Druidry and Shamanic techniques I avail of, are powerfully grounding and give me a sense of connection to the world, and also a means of understanding myself and my place in the Creation.

I wonder, if we go down this virtual road, what will happen to our sense of self, our spirituality, or connections and to our very humanity? Will it change the essence of who we are? I know who I am and what I want and what I need. I for one will not go down this road any further. If I have to say goodbye to people as they head off into the VR universe then that will make me sad and I will feel a sense of loss undoubtedly. However, I do not think that this is the right direction for me, or humanity at large. This is a choice we will all be faced with fairly soon. What will you choose to do?

Druid Ethics

Kingdom of the Blind

First published in Immrama *magazine,*
December 2005

It would appear that the age of Aquarius is ushering in a new era of spiritual awareness and a redefinition of our relationship with spirit, something that is long overdue. This may well be the case but one must wonder have we really progressed in our attitudes? Or have most of us really just swapped one set of outdated dogma for a facile, self-serving sense of spirituality that fits perfectly into the 'me' culture that is so widespread in western society?

To see examples of this all one has to do is visit any book shop or health store to see the plethora of self-help and self-development books which are mainly geared towards the unfulfilled yet self-obsessed individual. These usually offer a quick road to happiness, a kind of cure-all, in much the same way that carpet-baggers in the wild west of America flogged snake-oil to the gullible a century or more ago. What seems to be lacking is any real substance and in particular, what people most need — the cold hard truth. The answers to the problems that trouble the human soul are not to be found in a sound bite or a quick fix guide. The solutions are not to be found in a book, some pointers, signs and assistance perhaps, but the core hard work of spiritual growth takes place on an internal level on your own personal quest.

Modern spiritual movements mainly veer towards quick methods of obtaining our goals without the proper respect paid to why, how or the journey of achieving those goals. Unfortunately, modern Paganism also seems to have been infected with this "quick fix" attitude, largely due to the rash of frothy and populist books published in recent years.

Many writers seem to be cherry picking information to present without giving the underpinning of basic knowledge and groundwork for the acolyte to work their way through. The Angel and Fairy genres seem to me to be particularly guilty of irresponsible attitudes and some writers who have reached guru status seem to be jumping on every new spiritual bandwagon. Unfortunately, many inexperienced Pagans do not have the wit to know when they are being fleeced and will tend to stick with authors that they know and buy every book and accessory available.

I have no problem with writers or practitioners achieving success, what I do find upsetting though is the blatant exploitation of their exalted position to increase sales and workshop attendances. Of course, as Paganism is not structured in the same way as a conventional religion there is no authority to endorse or police unethical or exploitative behaviour. With the inevitable thirst for new fads the publishing and conference industries are hardly going to take the high moral ground when unscrupulous writing occurs; in fact, they are generally so lacking in understanding of the subject matter that they are not in a position to pass judgment on the quality of their writers' works. Their main concern is usually profit, hence the book-shelves are crammed with accessible but insubstantial works which often have a short lifespan.

The fundamental problem lies with us though, the consumer; if we are not so gullible as to believe or demand a pile of rubbish it would not be so widely available. It really is up to individuals to develop a sense of proportion and discern for ourselves what is genuine and what is insincere. This brings to mind the Monty Python sketch from *Life of Brian* — Brian standing naked at his window addresses the crowd "You're all individuals, don't let anybody tell you what to do. You've all got to work it out for yourselves!" To which the crowd cheer followed by cries of "Tell us more oh master!". It is a strange paradox that in learning to see our own spiritual path we more than likely need the help or instruction of others before we can become able to stand on our own two feet, but this does not mean that we should accept all that is put before us without question.

I do believe that no matter how inexperienced or unconfident an individual is, all one needs to do is consult the inner voice or intuition to know if this 'help' is appropriate and of spiritual benefit. Here again lies another problem — this inbuilt 'bullsh*t detector' is a of variable strength from one person to another, hence the startling array of fools stumbling around in a spiritual wilderness, willing to sign up for almost anything. I would suggest that the most crucial thing to remember is the old adage "A little knowledge is a dangerous thing". It really does seem that in the current social and spiritual landscape the one eyed are the one's wearing the crowns.

Truth against the World?

First published in Goddess Times, *October 2006*

Recent events in the Druidic community have compelled me to take a firm position in support of what I think is right and attempt to uphold one of the basic principles of Druidry (and life in general) — the truth. As people, honesty and trust are the basis of any good relationship, how much more so is that required of those who profess to follow a spiritual path? Much of the human world is tinged with cynicism — this is due to the gap between word and deed, how many of us can truly say that we trust our politicians, civil servants and religious leaders?

As Druids, our first concern should be truth in word and deed, the two are inseparable. Sun Tzu (in *The Art of War*) wrote that deception is of key importance in war; if that is so, then perhaps during war is the only acceptable arena where untruth can be permitted. As a general principle, honesty should be adhered to, except perhaps in the direst of life-threatening circumstance such as during war. As Druids, if we are to deserve the respect of the public, other Druids and other spiritual paths we must be seen to uphold that principle.

In a recent trip to Uisneach with other Druids I went wandering by myself after the ritual was over. As I made it over the brow of the hill near the royal ruins, I came across the broken stump of a large oak tree, which was split, charred and smoldering. The rest of the tree was lying in the next field, together with a small ash tree that it had brought down, wisps of smoke were still rising from the fallen oak trunk. It was quite clear that the oak had been struck by lightning very recently (the fire did not reach the ground), I thought this auspicious and later mentioned it to some of the other Druids who interpreted it in a positive light.

Looking back on events that have taken place since that day, the significance of the oak tree as the tree of the Dagda and the ash as that of the Goddess is not lost on me, or indeed the lightning (Dagda's axe). At the time I was unsure of the meaning but in retrospect I see this as a warning of worrying events that were to follow in the weeks after. In recent days, leading up to writing this I have felt obliged to re-evaluate my own path, after all who am I to criticize others and make demands if my own house is not in order?

Having spent a confused night on the top of Mount Leinster in freezing fog and terrible gales, a troubled sleep which was plagued by disturbing visions and the severe cold I re-emerged in the morning exhausted, starving hungry but spiritually renewed. That night I placed three solemn *geis* upon myself, and in all seriousness if I fail to keep them then I will cease to call myself a Druid. I am sure I will continue to make mistakes and like all those who follow a spiritual path I will be tested by others and by my own shortcomings, but I have committed myself to at least try to live a life of integrity.

At the end of all this, where does it leave me? I realize that, like all spiritual searchers, I must always remain vigilant, be prepared to face my own demons and discover my own truth. If we are not able to do that, how can we uphold truth in a world of dishonesty and trickery? There is a lot more to Druidry, of course, than being guardians of truth, but if we fail in that respect, we may as well forget the rest.

Becoming the Person You Meant to Be

First published on lukeeastwood.com, January 2010

When you were young did you have an image in your mind of the person you might grow up to be? You had hopes and dreams and some of those became a reality while others became just a distant memory. When you look at yourself now and remember the person you had hoped to be how much of a difference do you see? Is it better, is it different, or is it just worse?

As a person with some spiritual awareness, one would hope that it is not the last one, but sadly for many, at some stage, it is just that. In this age of huge expectations, the reality for many people is huge disappointments, but this is largely because our choices and desires are not truly chosen by us. Often our decisions are not our true heart's desire but choices formed by society, other people and what we perceive other people to expect or want of us.

If as you are reading this you perhaps feel that you have strayed some way from the path you imagined taking then relax, take a deep breath, you are not alone. All over the world there are thousands, perhaps millions of people who feel that way, I have been one of them. It is not a space I wish to visit again, and I am mindful to try and keep on the right path as it is so easy to fall. For better or worse, each and every one of us has the power to change ourselves, the life we lead and the world immediately around us.

My own life has taken me through a rollercoaster ride from highs to lows and back again, as part of my journey of discovering myself: Some ten or more years ago I might have written a very different article, I was in a very dark place. I was commuting 5–6 hours a day to Dublin in a stressful job, attempting to get a house built for my young family, trying to maintain a dysfunctional relationship with my wife and my in-laws whilst also separated by long distance from my own family. I had lost touch with my spirituality as it was not 'acceptable' in the circles I mixed in and I got little sustenance from the Catholicism of my early years and that those around me participated in.

Suddenly it all fell apart: I lost my job, my wife asked me to leave, and very soon I found myself alone in a microscopic bed-sit with no money, no wife, no house, no job, no friends, the only thing that gave me a faint glimmer of hope was my toddler daughter who still loved me and did not judge me, regardless of all the madness going on around me.

Things got worse, my attempts to rebuild my life were not very effective, although I managed to set up in business and get enough work to get by, but I became depressed and instead of acknowledging this I began to drink, smoke, I took drugs, used pornography, I sat in on my own and instead of cooking (which I formerly enjoyed) I ate fast food, packet soups and microwave meals. This continued for a while until one day driving quickly on the way to Dublin, I looked at a big truck coming the other way and thought to myself how all that was required was a quick turn of the steering wheel to the right and it would all be over.

Something stopped me, thank goodness, I think it was the image of my daughter alone and helpless without a stable influence in her life and her unhappiness that brought me to my senses. I realized that I had a reached a point where I was a million miles away from the person I had hoped to be or even had been in the past. I had been a fun loving, creative, energetic and positive person — in my work (a professional musician, graphic designer, semi-professional artist) and also sociable and gregarious in everyday life. Now I had become just a sad shell, with no interests, no spiritual life, a failure with no vitality, who literally dragged himself through each day. At that moment I hated myself, I was full of disgust and self-loathing and I couldn't bear what I had become; it was then that I decided that my choices were either death or a fight — a fight to re-find myself, to become a healthy and happy person who wanted to live and enjoy life. I think that I had already decided that suicide, however, appealing at the time, was not an option, which left me with an enormous mountain to climb.

At first, I didn't know where to start, I knew what I wanted to do but I felt so ineffectual and powerless that I seemed to get nowhere. Having considered seeking medical assistance I discussed my depression with my mother, who thankfully was understanding and advised me to leave visiting my GP as a last resort. This turned out to be excellent advice as no doubt I would have been loaded up with prescription drugs rather than given what I needed — a humane helping hand along the path to recovery.

One of the biggest steps was to visit an acupuncturist to try and relieve the monumental stress that I was carrying around with me. It was quite traumatic at first — it prompted my pent-up emotions releasing as well as some physical relief. The therapist's advice to spend just a few minutes each day doing something to make me feel happy was fantastic because even such a small thing seemed very difficult at the time. After a few sessions and gradually following her advice, I began I feel I had a small foothold on the cliff face back to a 'normal' life. I began to visit the beach on a regular basis and often screamed at the sea or threw huge rocks into it. More than anything, my healing experience of the woods and the sea set me on the road to recovery.

I began to remember bits of who I used to be, I remembered how my mother had introduced me to yoga when I was ten or so (although I had not taken it at all seriously). Also, in my early teens my uncle had introduced me to Buddhism, both of these things together with sports had become a major part of my development as a teenager but had become forgotten as my life became increasingly complicated in my late twenties. I now decided that I would go to yoga classes, try to meditate and start running in the mornings. I had also been interested in Celtic culture since childhood and particularly Druidry since my early twenties. At first, I found kick starting myself very difficult: the yoga made me feel better for up to a day but faded quickly, I was unable to clear my mind enough to meditate and the running racked my body with pain. Spending time in the woods and many hours watching the sea was easier and so very therapeutic that it helped me to address rebalancing my body and living a more natural and healthy existence. By now I realized the natural world's ability to heal me, and how important it would become in my recovery.

Gradually over time as the yoga, walks and running began to de-stress and strengthen my body my mind also began to clear and become more positive: I became more outgoing and started to make a few friends. I was still drinking a lot and eating rubbish but I eventually began to see that this was undermining the good work the yoga and exercise was doing, I was also relapsing from time to time into negative thought patterns and a depressed state for days at a time.

I realized that I had no choice other than to keep going, the way back led only to darkness, pain and perhaps death; I had always known that it would be slow and painful but this was a real test of my patience and resilience. Someone had suggested I look at natural alternatives to prescription drugs, which would avoid the, often unpleasant, side-effects, stigma and the permanent 'blot' on my health record. The reality is that most people suffer from depression at some point in their lives, however, that has not stopped people being made to feel ashamed or somehow lacking.

So, I used the internet to research the subject — which revealed some shocking testimony about medical treatment and also about the success, seemingly without problems, of herbs such as St. John's Wort. I had noticed a general tendency in the course of my life to become down in the winter, and this herb seemed to be effective in the treatment of SAD (seasonal affective disorder) as well as clinical depression, and so I decided I would give it a try. I took it for a prolonged period and after its sale was restricted in Ireland, I bought it abroad. After I was better, I took a low dose just in the winter time (Nov–Feb) to prevent the onset of SAD. Now that I work outside all year round, I receive a lot more sunlight and hence I have had no need for it. At the time I had not been aware of the deep significance of St. John's Wort in Paganism both symbolically and as a healing plant, only later as I proceeded with my Druidic studies, did I come to fully understand both its ancient and modern spiritual usage.

Since those early days I changed my diet and began the first of six attempts that it took me to give up smoking. I began daily yoga and began to meditate, write music and poetry, go out to the beach and woods with my daughter, take a renewed interest in spirituality and many other things that gradually made me feel more and more positive.

The spiral was now moving upwards instead of downwards — with each positive step my life became more positive and my capacity to make positive change increased. Now ten years later I have a life that I am happy with, I can look in the mirror and say that I like who I have become. I have changed career to become a horticulturalist, I practice Reiki, I have trained as a Druid with OBOD, I have my own home, a great relationship with my daughter and usually civil relations with my now ex-wife. I am not perfect, I still have flaws and problems like anyone else but I feel that I am much more the person I had always hoped to be. I feel that embracing my spiritual yearnings and finding the strength to follow the path my heart's true desire has been instrumental in my healing. I am no longer living my life to please everyone else whilst making myself miserable: the great mistake of doing that is that it makes no-one happy and serves only to decrease your ability to help either yourself or those around you.

I could not have made this transition without the help and love of key people such as my daughter, my mother and the therapists and friends who have helped me along the road to a happier and healthier life, but ultimately, I had to make every step myself. At the bottom of this journey lies the simple truth that just looking for meaning does not give you health and happiness. It was the striving to be happier, to learn to love myself, to find spirit in myself and the world around me, and the actual living of a better life that brought me back to happiness and thus enabled me to find a deeper meaning to my existence.

We all possess tremendous power to change in both negative and positive directions, and this power feeds itself and grows stronger in whichever direction you choose to take it. This is at the core of any magical practice, but it is easy to forget that our directed will manifests in the astral and physical planes, sometimes in unexpected or chronic forms. The simple choices and reactions each day shape us — which direction will I throw my energy into? Do I want to be happy or wallow in suffering? I had to choose, we all do every day, as the process is never ending if we are to remain in balance. Life will always throw up problems, we cannot control what the fates throw at us, but with proactively choosing our actions, honesty and awareness of the spiritual aspects of all existence, our problems can be turned into opportunities and negativity transformed into happiness.

Druidry — A Force for Positive Change

Originally published in Touchstone *magazine,*
November 2007

In the pre-Christian era, western Europe, before Roman conquest, was ruled by Celtic monarchs/tribal chiefs, relying on the guidance of Druids, who also were responsible for the administration of much of society on a day-to-day level. The Druids were both feared and respected and their strict code of behaviour was adhered to otherwise a heavy price was paid by the transgressor. In modern times the use of draconian practices seems extreme and unnecessary and it is indeed a good thing that the modern practice of Druidry has evolved. It is not much more than 50 years since any form of Paganism has once again been permissible in western society, perhaps it is now time for Druids to once again take a major role in society but in a way that befits the times we now live in?

After thousands of years with very slow technological and social change, mankind has made several 'quantum leaps' in the last few centuries, sadly though our collective emotional, intellectual and spiritual evolution does not appear to have kept pace with the changes in our abilities and lifestyles.

The invention of machines — first steam engines and later the internal combustion engine literally revolutionized the way that we live — enabling us to change our environment and use its hidden treasures on a far greater scale than was previously imaginable. This technology is what has fueled our rape of the land for more and more oil, gas, coal, food and living space and it has also enabled the rapid spread of empires and commerce to areas of the world that were previously difficult to access.

The invention of plastics has further changed society, enabling manufacture of almost anything that can be imagined and giving rise to a disposable culture that is now prevalent in much of the world. Plastic is truly an amazing tool, but unfortunately as it takes thousands of years for it to biodegrade, nearly all of the plastic ever made is still hanging around the landscape, in landfills and in our rivers, seas and oceans.

All of these changes seem to have happened not because they should, but because it was possible. Little thought has been given to the consequences of this wonderful technology and the wisest use of it, it was just used because it had become available, which has led humanity to where it is now — on the brink of ecological disaster.

As Druids we are people with a connection to the land, a love of and understanding of nature — something that seems to be disappearing from mainstream society. I believe that it is no accident that Druidry and Paganism has made a dramatic resurgence since the second half of the last century, this has happened because change is required in our spiritual, emotional and intellectual way of life — and this will precipitate a change in our lifestyles from within.

One could say that western culture has become corrupted and cynical from root to tip — our churches and political organizations etc. no longer command our respect and a great many ordinary people have become complacent and sedated by consumerism or are too disillusioned to try and affect change. From my personal experience this is not so of modern Druids. Most Druids I have met are passionate about life, not just the earth we live on but the whole process of living life as a celebration of existence. Modern Druidry draws on a tradition that belongs in our 'pre-civilized' past but has left behind some of the more violent and no longer relevant values of earlier times.

I believe that the love and passion that is evident amongst Druids is infectious, and that we have the ability to be shining beacons of hope in a jaded world.

I am not suggesting that we should become evangelists and try and convert everyone to Paganism, far from it. One of the core values of modern Druidry is tolerance, which to my view immediately invalidates any expansionist/evangelical attitudes. I do though think that others can be inspired by witnessing us living our lives according to the principles of Druidry and trying each day to bring that into the world on all levels. Ideas are very powerful — if people 'buy into' an idea there is no need to coerce them, as they have made the choice themselves and sown the seeds that lead to changing.

Having come to an awareness of our connection to the earth I feel duty bound to do whatever I can in this lifetime to foster that connection and to attempt to reverse the catastrophic damage that this and previous generations have done. Each practical thing that I change in my life and each time I make a stand against injustice and ignorance it gives me greater hope for the future. I make these decisions for myself and for the good of all existence and that is enough in itself, but if other people around me can see this as positive maybe they will begin to make changes themselves?

Like author Thom Hartmann, I believe that we are all connected in a cosmic-consciousness, and that great shifts in the way human society acts have been achieved from small beginnings. In *The Last Hours of Ancient Sunlight* he cites the example of Mahatma Gandhi who in a totally non-violent revolution changed the course of Indian History, but without maybe intending to do so he instigated the demise of the British and other European empires and also changed attitudes of millions of people worldwide.

If one man was able to achieve all this, by inspiring those around him, surely, we can do the same? Maybe we cannot, to the level of this exceptional person, but enough to make a difference in our family, circle of friends, village, town or city. The world is ripe for change and we have the opportunity right here and now to be a positive force in altering the course of humanity for the good of all future generations and the world itself; I think it's an opportunity that we must grasp.

Shining Your Light in the Darkness

First published in Touchstone *magazine,*
March 2011

These are dark times that we are living in both in a literal sense due to the winter time (in the northern hemisphere) and also in a metaphorical sense due to the unprecedented changes that are occurring in human society at the moment.

The cycles of the year are predictable, winters may be harder than expected, summers may be a wash-out or a harsh drought but they are usually variable within parameters than we can prepare for and adapt to. The cycles of nature can inspire awe, respect and sometimes fear in people, however, we can generally be confident that with common sense, preparation and pulling together that almost all of us will get through the hard times like countless generations before us got through bad years.

In some sense the hardships that nature imposes on us are a lesson to be learned — a reminder of our reliance on the world and our own fragility. As humans we are prone to suffer from hubris and often forget that we can very easily be humbled by nature, a gentle reminder of that fact from time to time does us no harm. This reminder hopefully redirects our attention towards gratitude and the spiritual aspect of life that underpins our physical existence.

Unfortunately, the same cannot always be said of the problems of human society, the dark times of our own making. Recent years have proven challenging — wars continue at the behest of post-imperial powers, environmental degradation has not decreased sufficiently, replacement of fossil fuels has not been instigated in earnest and political and financial crisis appears to be deepening around the world.

It's all rather gloomy, however, this is not the time to become shrouded in darkness and gloom. In fact, I feel that now it is vitally important to see the problems that face us for what they are but to remain positive, hopeful and not allow them to overwhelm us; it is one of the great strengths of humanity that we can solve problems and work together to overcome adversity. To do this does require a certain frame of mind, a sense of hope, positivity and the will to do what one can to effect change for the better.

Personally, I would say I am a hopeful realist — I am aware of the negative and the obstacles ahead but I am always hopeful that they can be overcome or navigated around through positive thoughts and actions. This is where my spiritual life plays a vital role — the maintenance of the light body, the connection with *awen* (*imbas* in Irish) is central to not just magic but to the magic of life — the ability to stay positive and the ability to focus that positivity into concrete actions that tip the scales in your favour.

I would hope that, as Druids, we all have an understanding of this basic premise — that happiness, success, strength and action manifests from the inside outwards into the worlds around us. So, knowing this, I believe that we have an added advantage over those with little or no apparent spiritual life — we learn and use techniques of storing up and working with *nwyfre* (*neart* in Irish) for our own benefit and also for the benefit of the world around us. Of course, people of other spiritual paths also know and work with this energy, but I am not going to discuss that here.

What is most important is not the method by which *awen/imbas* is reached or *nwyfre/neart* channeled. What is most important is the fact that we have the ability to do this — which begs the question how do we use it?

At this time, I see people all around me (especially here in Ireland) who are depressed, defeated and lacking in hope. For some of them they no longer see that the sun still shines every day, even if it is sometimes hidden by clouds. The light of their inner suns has grown dim due to misfortunes, too much negativity etc. and once this has happened the world around them grows dimmer to them, sometimes becoming a vicious circle.

In my daily life and my travels, I am increasingly aware of negativity and fear taking hold of so many people — leading to depression, self-defeating actions and in the worst of cases suicide. Although this can have a temporary negative affect on myself, my inner centeredness that I have gained from Druidry enables me to regain my perspective and hopefully also help others.

In these bleak times it is essential that we not only sustain our own vitality, if we have the power to, we should reach out to others who are suffering. THOSE THAT CAN MUST DO: becoming a beacon of light and positivity for those around us can give the depressed and put-upon an important gift — hope.

Without hope we are all lost, belief that things can and will improve is what sustains so much of human existence, when we give up our fears become a self-fulfilling prophecy. So, if you know people who are suffering, please reach out to them in whatever way you can — sometimes a smile, a phone call, sitting down for a chat or even helping with the laundry might make a huge difference. Often quite simple and small actions can have a great impact on someone's levels of *nwyfre/neart* and their subsequent level of positivity.

Obviously, we cannot just go out and fix everything in a second, but what we can do is by subtle and thoughtful intervention in the web around us raise peoples' energy, quite often without them realizing what we are doing. Everything is connected and small interactions can in time create a great sea change. I believe that our work can be of vital importance in getting our friends, families and communities through the darkness... there is always light at the end of the tunnel but sometimes people need to be shown it.

By using that inner strength and inner light, in a non-patronising and appropriate way we not only empower others to feel more positive about their lives, we become more empowered ourselves — the flow of *nwyfre/neart/chi/prana* is unstoppable and inexhaustible if we are able to keep tapping into it. So be grateful for that great blessing and use it whenever you can to make the world a better place — I believe that that is what we are all here to do!

Éigse Spiorad Cheilteach and the Dangers of Cyberspace!

First published in Touchstone, 2011

On August 6th 2011 the second annual Éigse Spiorad Cheilteach (Gathering of Celtic Spirituality) took place at *Slí na Bandé* (meaning way of the goddess) in Co. Wicklow, Ireland; which I am pleased to say was a great success.

Some two years ago I had the crazy idea of organizing an outdoor event to try and gather together the disparate groups of Pagans in Ireland that largely exist totally independent and often ignorant of each other's existence. I have to say I have been greatly inspired by OBOD's programme of events through the year, which are both excellent and cheap to attend. Sadly, due to many factors such as time, money and distance I have only so far attended one, at *Lughnasadh* a few years ago, it planted the seed of an idea to try and replicate the process here in Ireland.

Although there are over two hundred OBOD members in Ireland most of us do not meet up or even know more than a handful of other members. Thanks to a friend (Pól) there is now a Facebook group of Irish OBODies to try and remedy that lack of awareness, at least among those that are computer literate and who use Facebook.

Much as computers and the internet are highly useful tools, we must not take it for granted that everyone is techno-savvy, as pointed out by Ruis' letter in the September edition of 'Touchstone'. This is where personal gatherings really come into their own and demonstrate that on-line experience is no substitute for the real thing — connecting person to person or to deity, to spirits or to the land.

From personal experience I can state that prolonged and frequent computer/ phone/ tablet usage can have a diminishing effect on spiritual sensitivity and psychic abilities, not to mention physical effects, hence I keep it within strict limits. The electromagnetic energy of cyberspace is different from that of our bodies and other earthly existences — it is a realm of human making, interfacing with the three realms of existence yet it is a completely artificial realm of its own. We do well to remember that fact and not become overly sucked in or seduced by the virtual world, lest we damage our light bodies and our connection to the physical middle realm and indeed the upper and lower realms too.

Some of the themes explored at E.S.C. included making the manifestation of magic a reality in our lives, healing people and places, living off/with the land, the *sídhe*, meaningful connection to the land, journeying through mythology etc. All of these areas had a common thread of practicality and fostering a real connection with the earth and each other as people, something that is vital and cannot be replaced by virtual experiences. This real-life and rooted experience of this day touched a lot of people, myself included and was really cemented by the fireside song, poetry and storytelling in a circle which continued a long tradition in Celtic culture that goes back into the mists of unrecorded history.

This gathering happens on one day only, every August but it would be great to see similar events here for Druids, Shamans and all flavours of Pagan throughout the year. As far I as am aware there has never been an OBOD event in Ireland, something I hope that will happen in the future as a badly needed way of networking; making new friends; sharing and exchanging ideas and celebrating our faith and traditions in a natural and human environment — in the time-honoured oral tradition of our ancestors.

Note: Éigse Spiorad Cheilteach is still running now (at time of publication) although I am no longer involved in organizing it. The first ever OBOD gathering in Ireland took place in 2021.

Meaningful Connection to the Land

Originally published in Brigid's Fire *magazine,*
February 2012

As Pagans we aspire to be connected to the Earth to live harmoniously via a spiritual relationship with deity as we see it — be it goddess and god or various polytheistic forms. This would seem to be an aspiration of virtually all Pagans — Wiccans, Druids, Shamans, Witches etc. and Pagans who wear no particular badge.

Much is talked of or written about fostering this relationship with the land but there is a big difference between thinking, talking and actually making concrete steps to manifest that relationship in a real and permanent sense. For some, religion or spirituality is simply a lifestyle choice, something that triggers certain emotions and fulfills certain needs but which can be picked up and put down again at will. I've heard such people being described derisively as 'weekend warriors' and perhaps such a put-down is not entirely unwarranted.

If we take Paganism seriously as a path in life and not the equivalent to a cynical weekly visit to church, the mosque, synagogue etc.; then that requires a level of commitment way above lip service if there is going to be any real connection, relationship and spiritual growth.

If we look at Earth-based 'indigenous' religions they are all grounded in the mythology of the people and the land on which they live and how they live. Connection and relationship with the land is central and essential in their religious spiritual lives and taking away their history (real and mythological) has been a major weapon in destroying such cultures and communities.

A perfect example of cultural destruction is the colonization of the island of Hispaniola (now Haiti & Dominican Republic) which was once entirely populated by the Taino people. This one-time paradise, occupied by peaceful and welcoming people became a hell under Columbus — leading to mass suicide by those not murdered or enslaved, also the forests were felled and the land denuded. Within sixty years the original population was extinct and the land became totally impoverished. The current population, still victims of Columbus' legacy, are descended mainly from African slaves and most live in desperate poverty to this day.

Lands that have been destroyed like Hispaniola generally have indigenous peoples (if they still exist) that have also been ravaged. Those that have recovered to any extent from colonization have done so through their connection with their past, their ancient culture and the land itself. Looking at Ireland, it is perhaps uniquely placed in Europe as a country that has retained much of its indigenous culture.

The story of the land and its peoples still exists and was written down for posterity in *Lebor Gabála Érenn*, the *Book of Invasions*. A dark and terrible history of this land, it tells the story of the first arrivals from Banba and Parthenon through to the Milesians (sons of Míl) that are the ancestors of the modern Irish race. Despite subsequent invasion by Vikings, Normans (and their descendants) the Gaelic culture has survived, albeit somewhat weakened and in some respects largely forgotten.

We are lucky indeed that this history, both written and oral, together with a vast body of lore and mythology still exists and it is this that bears witness to a relationship with the land that is far deeper and stronger than that of the disconnected and self-absorbed modern age. It is clear that our ancestors lived outdoors to a far greater extent than most of us do now, with many of them living semi-nomadic lives and their relationship with the land was direct. Even recent generations clearly have or had a deep connection to the land, even if they were entirely non-Pagan in their religious beliefs. This is even today evident in the testimony of writers such as Michael Gallagher or Joe McGowan who grew up among people with a genuine connection, love, respect and understanding of the land they lived on.

Sadly, most of us have not grown up with that deep relationship with the land or with a deep knowledge of the lore and myth relating to it. For most of us it is a case of building and fostering that relationship over time. One cannot simply put down the remote control and soda can, drive to a forest and start communing with the land — it just does not work like that! Just like relations with people — who tend to remember neglect, disrespect, ignorance, aggression etc. the land does not readily respond to overtures from those that have a history of not treating it well.

As someone who has worked with the land, like others who have experienced the same thing — I have felt the pain and sadness of the land, which has suffered under much bloodshed and also been abused greatly by humanity. If we wish to commune with the land and the spirits that live on and in it in any real sense then we need to make the changes in ourselves for that to happen and also work to facilitate the healing of the land on a spiritual and physical level. After all, it is us that needs the land and us who relies on it for all things, the land does not need us — it will survive with or without our presence.

First and foremost, in establishing that relationship is humility and respect — understanding that humanity is not the centre of all things and also understanding that how we have increasingly been living for the last few centuries is not respectful to the Earth. We all talk about change, saving the environment, living in harmony etc. but then, talk is cheap. How many of us actually live those sentiments, every day, throughout the day whenever we possibly can? Most of us quickly forget, seduced by the television's siren song or the every-day hassles of modern existence.

We are now at a critical point in human history, a time in which we need to make an existential choice between exploitation and equilibrium. This is more a spiritual choice than it is intellectual — because it is our core beliefs and emotional responses that dictate everything we do. When we wish to change deep within our hearts then the change takes on a character beyond dry intellectualism — a genuine desire to change will manifest itself. The luxury of putting off our good intentions until tomorrow and yet another tomorrow, is rapidly slipping away, like sand through our fingers. If ever there was a time to sincerely decide whether we are of the Earth or simply just on it, then that time is now. So, I implore you, make that choice and live it with conviction in every waking moment, in all that you say and all that you do — only then are we truly worthy of calling ourselves Pagans.

There May Be Trouble Ahead...

First published on philipcarr-gomm.com,
September 2012

Here is a guest post by Druid Luke Eastwood. Luke is the author of the excellent The Druid's Primer.

This is the first blog I have ever written and how nice to be invited to write one as a guest! As we approach the end of the year, I have become aware of an increased tension on many levels — the world economy, Middle-Eastern politics, the worst grain harvest in decades and not least of all — a metaphysical angst surrounding the much-anticipated final days of 2012. Is it me, or is there a growing tension in the air that you can almost taste?

As spiritual tensions rise this seems to be mirrored materially on a macro level around the globe and also a micro level of personal interactions, certainly amongst many of the people I am aware of. It's so easy to take the lower road energetically when under stress, threat or provocation on whatever level, however, it is when we are most sorely tested that we need to take the higher path and reach inside ourselves to find the wellspring of spiritual strength that enables us to do the right thing and retain our integrity.

As pressures increase it tends to bring out either the best or the worst in people and in this case one can only hope that we can all tap into what is best in our own selves and hopefully inspire the same in others. This is, of course, easier said than done, but for the sake of all that live on this planet I believe we should try to meet the challenges ahead with hope, compassion, insight and above all, without fear.

Druidic Living Today — The Fork in the Road

First published in The Cauldron *magazine, August 2014*

The modern Druid movement is an attempt to recapture or recreate something that has been lost — an ancient European, indigenous belief system and culture that has been supplanted by Christianity, technology and rationalism. Of course, this was not the only ancient indigenous culture of Europe and in fact one such culture does still exist today in Europe — the Suomi (or Lapp) people of the extreme north-west of Europe, mostly in northern Finland.

By some miracle this ancient culture has survived into modern times, although almost all, if not all, have become acclimatized to modernity to a considerable extent. Like other indigenous cultures around the world, the Suomi traditional way of life is under threat, which no doubt increases their desire to preserve it. However, unlike other truly indigenous cultures, Celtic culture has lost much of its continuity and hence Druidry/Druidism has in effect been reborn or reinvented since the late Renaissance. Much of the elements of Druid belief and practice still exist in the form of folk culture, the ancient Irish, Welsh and Scottish manuscripts and, of course, the sacred remains that we find in the landscape of the British Isles, although the sum of the parts does not form a coherent, unified whole.

Unfortunately, the passage of time makes it difficult to know what is actually purely Celtic or Druidic and what is a synthesis of Celtic, Viking and English/Saxon/Norman cultures. Given that there are no Celtic peoples that have survived into the modern era untouched by other cultures or the influence of Christianity we can never really be sure of how accurate our reconstructions or re-imaginings actually are.

Some might argue that recreating the past doesn't really matter and that it is the future that we should be concerned about. Although I have a certain penchant for historical accuracy and a desire not to make a fool of myself, I do believe that in a certain sense this view is correct. After all, as a Druid at some point early on, and perhaps even still, one must ask the question: why be a Druid? At the most basic level I would say that Druids choose to be so because of a deep desire to reconnect with an indigenous world view that is increasingly being wiped out by modernity.

Druidry/Druidism is a form of magic but it is much more than this — it is a comprehensive belief system, a religion, a whole way of life. Ultimately, if lived in a way that closely approximates to the values and culture of the ancient Celts then it is a wholesale rejection of modernity and the increasingly nihilistic values of westernised society.

This finally brings me to the subtitle — the fork in the road. I believe that we are at a crucial point in the development of humanity, a place where the road forward splits in two and we must individually and collectively choose which road we are going to take. For the first time in human history, more than half of the population of the globe are urban dwellers and increasingly living in accordance with modern expectations. Meanwhile simple, self-sufficient and ancient cultures that still exist are going the way of the elephant — vastly under pressure and shrinking in number. Such cultures are fundamentally at odds with modernity and the inexorable spread of progress and destruction that accompanies it.

Druidry/Druidism would seek kinship with these cultures and expresses shared values in terms of simple living, preservation of the environment, nature based religious practices and traditional folk culture. However, in most cases, Druids are in fact deeply steeped in the modern world — I myself as I type this onto an old

Apple Mac computer draw on my lifetime experience of modern western culture.

I have made certain choices — such as to live in an old house where I can grow my own food and keep animals, to work in an outside job with the natural world, to minimize my consumption and engagement with the commercial world, etc. Despite these serious and heart-felt attempts to create a life that one could call Druidic, I cannot escape the fact that I have grown up and been educated in a modern western society — even though I am lucky enough to have experienced a rural culture since childhood, that many have not.

The great problem for me, and all Druids, is that this whole movement has developed (in earnest over the last century) parallel to the development of an increasingly secular and commercially driven technological culture. So, while myself and other Druids may have a great desire to live simply and immerse ourselves in Celtic culture, the odds are stacked against us, as we have all been contaminated by the dominant culture that we were either born into or are surrounded by.

As the speed of progress continues to accelerate, I strongly feel that the Druidic community will be forced into a cataclysmic choice, much as the Amish of North America were in the 1860s. In that particular instance the Amish Mennonites attempted to adapt to rapid social change, whilst the Old Order Amish chose to reject modern life and isolate themselves from its influence.

At this point in time the world-wide Druidic community continues to grow, but so too does its engagement with the modern world through the internet: forums, social media, podcasts etc. As people who claim to love and be connected with the natural world it is unnerving how easy it is to spend much of one's time hypocritically engaged in on-line Druidry/ Druidism — an oxymoron if ever I saw one! While it is important that Druids be able to engage with each other and use various mediums to communicate important messages to each other and the world in general, it is far more important that we do not lose the run of ourselves and become engulfed by the very processes that we seek to resist.

Technology and its social effects are now moving at such an incredible pace that it is possible to live almost completely detached from the natural world. People can now move from the house to the car, the office, the shops and back again with little or no contact with the natural world, while at the same time being totally engaged in virtual communication — all thanks to mobile devices. Already we are beginning to see huge changes in how humans socialise as a result of virtual life and the removal of the necessity to engage with an environment outside of total human control.

As a Pagan and a Druid, I find these developments extremely worrying. Whilst I continue to live much as I have done, if anything engaging less with the virtual world as time passes, I am aware of the fact that the world is changing ever more rapidly around me. As a Druid I must ask myself — do I want to be a part of this brave new world? Is there a point where, like the Amish, I have to say 'enough, no further'? I would posit that we are rapidly approaching a point of no return where the connection with the natural world and our ancient selves will be forever severed unless we consciously choose to do otherwise.

Of course, genuinely indigenous peoples are already confronted (sometimes violently) with this momentous proposition and to some extent all people of ecological or spiritual aspirations also face this problem. Speaking as a Druid, this is not simply a matter of ethics but a holistic crisis that affects humanity on a physical, mental and spiritual level.

Do we solve this conundrum by simply running away and living a separate existence like the Amish or do we fight for change and risk being crushed by the juggernaut? There is, of course, a risk in choosing either option — to cut oneself off does not guarantee survival and engagement is equally risky: 'Battle not with monsters, lest ye become a monster, and if you gaze into the abyss, the abyss gazes also into you.' the famous Nietzsche quote succinctly expressing that challenge.

Druidry/Druidism has no universal dogma, no Pope or spiritual leader to dictate on such serious and far-reaching existential questions. Ultimately it is up to each of us to plumb the depths our own hopes and fears and follow our own consciences. Whatever we choose, the time for sitting on the fence is rapidly receding, the future beckons and we must decide what part we will play in it.

The Importance of Truth

First published by johnhuntpublishing.com,
October 2013

Recently I have had to deal with the problem of lying. In ten years of being involved in a Druid grove I've witnessed no troubles with dishonesty, ego trippers etc., until very recently.

The particular person involved is a very affable, likeable person who would have remained popular and widely accepted were it not for the unfortunate need to frequently invent, embellish and exaggerate. In all areas of life honesty is usually the best policy, and in the area of spirituality, especially where it is public, honesty should be paramount.

Modern society is already afflicted with professional liars within the pillars of government, industry, commerce and even within some religious organisations. The Druid movement, still being seen as on the margins of acceptability by many ordinary people, can ill afford to host liars, cheats and dishonourable people amongst its numbers.

For any religion or spiritual path to be taken seriously its practitioners need to be beyond reproach so far as honesty is concerned. People will inevitably make mistakes as is bound to happen in all walks of life, however, that is an entirely different matter from deception.

Druidry being made up of a wide variety of orders and individuals does not have a universal mechanism for dealing with such matters, moreover it seems it is a matter for individuals, groups and organisations to decide for themselves what is morally acceptable. Some might advocate doing nothing in response to wrongdoing, while others (like myself) feel that is usually appropriate to take some form of action — which could be to unveil what is hidden or perhaps even to censure the person who has transgressed.

Whatever action or inaction Druids might consider appropriate, it is generally accepted by Druids that truth is one of the foundations of Druidry/Druidism. If our thoughts and actions are based upon lies then all that is seeded by it can be none other than corrupted — like the proverbial bad apple spoiling the barrel.

These are difficult times to live in on many levels and at such times I believe that adherence to truth and our moral principals is even more important — surely that is when they are most needed.

Three pillars of Druidry, no less three pillars of life: wisdom, truth and love.
The greatest of these is truth, without truth all else has no value.

Tolerance

First published on johnhuntpublishing.com,
January 2014

Well, it's a new year, a new start, with all the hopes that it brings fresh in our minds. Of course, in various places around the world the new year starts at an entirely different time — a reminder that not everyone sees things in the same way or does things in the same way either.

Unfortunately, as the Europeanised countries enter another year, that transition has been marred by violence and war in many places around the globe. In many cases this has been religious in nature — between members of one religion against another, but also internal conflict between two or more factions within a single religion.

Most of us are already aware of what those conflicts are, although some are less heavily publicised than others, so I won't waste time discussing them. What I would like to point out is that all of the major religions of the world advocate peaceful living. It has been suggested by some that both modern and ancient Paganism is inherently violent, just as the same accusation has been leveled against Islam. In both cases this is not the case, although it is entirely true that Pagans and Muslims have often been involved in violence and war over the course of history.

A history of violence can also be found in Christianity, Judaism, Hinduism, Buddhism etc. despite the fact that all of these religions do not advocate violence or killing as a way of life.

As a Pagan Druid I have chosen to follow a particular set of beliefs — I would describe myself as a Celtic Pantheist (although strictly I am a Henotheist) and a Gnostic. Much as this is my path of choice, I am well aware that my choice is no more valid or correct than anybody else's and hence the idea of inflicting violence upon someone else due to their differing views seems ridiculous.

Some Druids are far more eclectic than I am and I might not personally favour their beliefs or practices, however, that does not mean I do not respect their right to interpret 'being a Druid' in their own unique way. The same thinking I extend to all other religions and spiritual paths — something I think that spiritually minded people the world over should benefit from.

Druidry and Buddhism do not prohibit people from including aspects of other spiritualities unlike some others that are strictly anti-syncretic. If it is not contradictory, then syncretic elements may prove complementary. In truth all religions I know of are to some extent syncretic, in that they have been influenced at some point by other religions. Unfortunately dogmatic, blind followers often fail to realise this truth and sometimes also adhere to dogmatic corruptions that enable them to justify terrible acts that go against the core teachings of their own faith.

As a modern Druid, I feel that tolerance and love is a key part of my own path, just as it should also be in all spiritual paths. If we are ever going to see peace in the world, we all need to return to the real fundamentals of our faiths, not fundamentalism as misguided dogmatism. One can only hope that collectively we will all find the grace to do just that.

A Time to Fight

First published on johnhuntpublishing.com,
March 2014

A theme that seems to be coming up a lot right now is the destruction and imbalance that humanity is making in the world. Two particular areas that Druids seem to be getting down and dirty is the campaign to clean up Fukushima and the campaign against fracking.

At the equinox it is a time of balance in the seasons — between day and night but it is also a time to reflect on the balance of nature and how we are sending it out of whack, not to mention the internal balance of our own lives — both externally in how we live and internally in our thoughts and feelings.

We've known for hundreds of years that we've been throwing this planet out of balance, but it is now that things are getting really serious that we are trying to wake up and do something concrete about it. It is a time to fight, to fight for justice and what is right so that everything living on this planet might have a future. That does not mean that we have to be violent and aggressive — violence has a tendency to beget even worse violence.

Fighting can be done in many ways and on many levels and I personally believe that fighting for this planet and all of the life upon it is an important part of the Druid path. Great things can be done without any aggression — Gandhi was a perfect example of the power of non-violent opposition to despotism and injustice, a struggle that led to the downfall of one the largest empires in history — the British Empire. This in turn led to the French and other European empires collapsing.

Those that wish to carry on exploiting this earth relentlessly love it when people react in violent or rash ways, that gives them the perfect opportunity to dismiss any nascent movement as lunatics or even terrorists. So, we must be a little bit cleverer if we want to succeed — we can change the world, we can restore balance. However, perhaps before we each begin our fight, we need to find that point of calm and balance in our own selves and use it to draw strength and wisdom for the battle ahead.

More info on nuclear power: http://www.nuclearfreeplanet.org
More info on fracking: http://www.warriorscall.org

Druid Politics, with a Small 'p'

First published on 'johnhuntpublishing.com',
May 2014

Some people say that religion and politics don't mix and in the modern world religious organisations and their leaders tend not to get involved in politics. Sometimes they like to make some form of social commentary but they rarely go out on a limb and directly confront the political and social actions of governments.

Like many people, religious and otherwise (and Russell Brand), I have come to the conclusion that the political system is so intrinsically corrupt that it is near enough pointless to vote for any political party. We are told that in 'civilized' society we have democracy because we have the opportunity to vote in a new bunch of idiotic cronies every four or five years, but what we really have is a form of fascism.

I don't mean jackboot dictatorship — the common interpretation of that word, I mean fascism in its original definition i.e. a synergistic relationship between corporate interest and government, which is most often enforced by authoritarian leadership. Corporatism has been rising steadily since WWII, with lobbying and influence from the corporate sector affecting virtually everything we do — from the water we drink to the biased opinions foisted upon us by the mass media.

I'm under no illusion that ancient Druidic/Celtic society was entirely democratic, it wasn't — there were kings, chiefs and a hierarchy within society, however, there were means by which even monarchs could be replaced if they failed to live up to expectations. In Ireland Brehon Law guaranteed the rights of ordinary people and even animals, something that was lost under conquest and which people around the world have fought hard to achieve the equivalent of with varied success. Of course, these kinds of laws existing in Ireland, Britain, Gaul and even much later surviving cultures elsewhere (e.g. first nations in USA), were not affected by corporatism as corporations did not exist within them.

Most of us now live in a world where corporate interests are in direct conflict with the interests of ordinary citizens, but unfortunately most governments are more interested in placating the lobbyists than the public that voted them in. That is why I am interested in politics with a small 'p', grass-roots movements and direct action — because the big parties just aren't listening and don't want to know. For that reason, I will be joining thousands like me around the world on Saturday 24th May in protesting against the actions of Monsanto. They are not the only company that has insidious plans to remove our freedoms, but unfortunately, they are one of the most successful at unduly influencing governments. They manage to change laws or bring in new years to enable them to fast-track their commercial manipulation of human behaviour.

There is much wrong with the control mechanisms of modern civilization — it is undemocratic, but it's up to us to make it change. Get out, get active, be the change — if we succeed your children will thank you for it.

Hope in Desperate Times

First published in Touchstome *magazine,*
March 2019

As we approach the third decade of this century, I am very much aware that we are living in times of great change. This is both an exciting and scary time to be alive as we live in a state of flux, with the future of humanity and the planet itself very much at stake. Our future and that of the planet depends on how we collectively deal with the challenges facing us now and in the decades ahead. Most of us are very much aware of the issues of climate change, population growth, ecological crises, globalisation and the expansion of consumerism across the globe. Unless you purposely avoid the news it's pretty much impossible to avoid the increasingly fraught warnings about what will happen if humanity fails to take the right actions.

I feel a sense of anxiety about our collective plight and of my personal as well as our species' failure to do enough to turn things around, up to this point in time. I've noticed this unease in the wider world around me, with a variety of reactions, ranging from ignoring it, increased nihilism (let's party on and let the world burn!), despair, frustration and anger, to determination to do better. It seems to me as if humanity is finally going through the growing pains of an en-masse teenage existential crisis. It would be better for us all if this had happened decades ago, but humanity rarely deals effectively with problems until the wolf is literally at the door.

Back in the 1980s, as a teenager, I became aware of environmentalism, the increasing activity of Greenpeace and the beginnings of a more global economy, which was underpinned by the rapid growth of electronic technology. At the time there were already dire predictions about the problems facing the planet, which I took seriously but many did not. Even to people like myself, the manifestation of these environmental problems looked to be unfolding slowly and there was tremendous hope that society all over the globe would rise to these challenges before they became serious. Like many of my friends I made great efforts to be 'green', to consume less, recycle, plant trees and I became involved in activism for Greenpeace, Friends of The Earth and the anti-consumer McLibel campaign. I felt that I was doing my bit for a better world and this interest fed directly into my spiritual life and my eventual discovery of Druidry, as the path that best embodied my feelings about how to live. Over time I've continued to make a personal effort, as well as supporting organisations fighting bigger battles, and I've tried to remain hopeful about our future.

However, decades later, approaching the age of 50, I often find myself challenged and struggling to retain the sense of hope that filled my younger days. Having spoken about this with other Druids, friends and spiritual people of various faiths I realize that I am far from alone in this sense of apprehension. Clearly my generation and the ones before it have failed to 'step up to the plate' and we have a long way to go to put things right. Sometimes hope appears to be failing me, when I am assaulted by the latest barrage of bad news, but it is then that I have to remind myself that all is not lost. While there are possibilities there is always hope and I am reminded about words from the Order of Bards Ovates and Druids winter solstice ceremony:

The oak is bare, the earth is cold, the sky is black — from where could hope arise? ... My eyes are wet with tears of dreams lost to the dark.

These words are a comfort to me as I remember that every year since life first began, all life on this planet has to confront difficulty. Every living thing (sentient or not) faces the possibility of dying; there is death around us and all the challenges that come with the harshest months of the seasons. In truth, challenges can present themselves at any time, but it is in the darkness of winter that we feel that vulnerability most and are more aware of the fragility in ourselves and the world around us. Despite this, life continues onwards in a never-ending cycle, regardless of losses and failures, hope is renewed, life continues to grow, change and adapt, and obstacles are overcome.

In our mythology we can draw inspiration from tales such as the birth of Taliesin or that of Lugh. In a certain sense Taliesin's story can be viewed as one of horror: Gwion Bach suffers a terrible ordeal in his pursuit by Cerridwen. Cerridwen herself is bereft over the loss of the gift of inspiration for her blighted son Avagddu, who himself could not have been overly pleased. Having endured this and being born again, Taliesin still has to endure a gruesome journey on the sea, inside the darkness of a leather bag. Against all odds, he survives to become the greatest of Welsh poets — proof indeed that a seemingly hopeless situation can be turned around.

Likewise, the infant Lugh, grandson of the terrible Fomorian leader Balor, is born despite the attempts of his evil grandfather to prevent his own prophesized death. Like Taliesin, the infant Lugh escapes death and grows up to join the *Tuatha Dé Danann*. After terrible losses, including Nuada their king, the *Tuatha Dé Danann* are ultimately victorious at the 2nd battle of *Mag Tuireadh* after Lugh slays Balor with a sling-stone. Again, from a perilous start, the prophecy of Lugh is fulfilled against a backdrop of desperate circumstances. Like our ancestors of the past, we can take comfort in these stories of triumph over adversity — themes that continue to play out in both history and modern mythology, such as the defeat of the Nazis or in fiction such as *The Lord of The Rings* or the *Star Wars* saga.

Yes, we live in a very challenging time, it is getting late in the day to address the multitude of difficulties ahead. Yes, humanity is divided and has not yet found a unified approach to protecting life on our planet. No, it is not hopeless. Despite setbacks, disappointments and failures we are still here, we now know that we have all the means necessary to transform our future for the better and there is still time to make these changes. Both as individuals and collectively, humans will continue to have bad days, but that does not mean that we should give up. Even in the darkest of hours and the most desperate of times, there is always hope and we must always keep that flame alive inside us.

On Religious Intolerance

First published in Network *magazine, January 2013*

In the 1st century BCE, the Romans banned Druidic practices throughout Gaul as part of Julius Caesar's efforts to win the seven year Gallic War. The Romans were perhaps the first civilisation to make religious intollerance an official foreign policy (after centuries of multiplicity) and they imposed their Roman pantheon wherever it was practical to do so (places such as the Jewish state of Judea being a notable exception).

Nearly 400 years later in 325CE the Roman emperor Constantine I effectively took over the growing Christian religion (at the Council of Nicea) forcing conformity on the developing churches and beginning the gradual process of making Christianity the official religion of the empire, to the exclusion of all other religions.

During the middle ages, the Celtic Churches of Ireland and Britain were forced to conform to Roman doctrine, 'heretical' forms such as those of the Manichians, Cathars, Coptic Gnosticism etc were either made to convert or violently destroyed.

With the emergence of the reformation, instead of accepting the need for reform the Roman Catholic Church proceeded with a counter-reformation leading to centuries of bloodshed and conflict, the repercussions of which are still with us today. We are all familiar with the 'troubles' in the north of Ireland and even as late as the 1980s Catholic-Protestant intolerance flared up in Fethard in Co. Wexford.

Of course, Christianity is not the only religion to have been subverted for political purposes or used to suppress other religions. In China there was a period of conflict between Taoism and the incoming Buddhism, although this was eventually resolved harmoniously with assimilation of much of Taoist thought into the more dominant Buddhism.

266

In India and what is now Pakistan and Bangladesh there has long been conflict between Hindu and Muslim religions and tension remains high even now. Currently, in Nepal, Buddhists and Muslims are locked in bitter rivalry which threatens to plunge the country into a civil war.

We are all aware of the strife in the Middle East between the Israelis and the Palestinians, which has been almost continuous for over sixty years now. Indeed, the conflict in that region stretches back to the nine Catholic crusades against Islam begun under the auspices of Pope Urban II. Further back still, to the Babylonian capture of Jerusalem in 587BCE there was cultural and religious conflict; with this most famous of cities being attacked or captured 52 times in its almost four thousand year history.

The great sadness of this ongoing religious conflict that still afflicts the world is that things were not always thus. Evidence of the peaceful coexistence of a multitude religions and religious cults exists stretching back into the Pagan (i.e. pre Roman rule). Of course, religion was tied up with politics stretching back into the early city states of Sumeria and Egypt, however, religious zealotry was pretty uncommon, perhaps the notable exception being the reign of Egyptian Pharoh Akhnaten who instituted a monotheistic policy revolving around Aten (Ra sun disc); which led subsequent generations to try to erase him and his revolutionary dogma from history.

Despite the fact that there appears to be more religious strife than ever, due to the almost instantanious reporting or modern media; we are now living in a world where peoples of all races and creeds seek to have the right to practice their religious and spiritual practices without impediment.

This appears to be part of a general trend towards a demand for greater freedom from oppression in all areas of human experience. Just as racial and sexual descrimination has become more and more unacceptable, religious intollerance must also become unacceptable.

I believe that at the core of all religions and spiritual paths the message to mankind is basically the same — a message about how to live in this world and what is important in life. Of course, it is possible to have morality without religious beliefs, but seeing as the vast majority of people on this planet believe in some form of divinety this sense of morality is connected with their religious beliefs in most cases.

Peaceful existence, respect for each other and the world around us are fundamentals of religious or spiritual life, but unfortunately for many this goes out of the window when dealing when others of a different belief system. For many people their views of other beliefs are dominated by fear of the unknown and quite often this is whipped up into hysteria by sensationalism in the media.

Division, hatred and intollerance do not help anyone, it does not make human existence or life on this planet any easier. Surely we have enough problems in the world already without continuing to add religious insensitivity to the mix?

Perhaps it's time that we all reconsidered our perceptions of faiths other than our own and tried to look at them objectively from a position of curiousity or empathy rather one of disdain or fear, usually based on total ignorance. We might find that we have more in common in our beliefs and attitudes than the gutter press would have us believe.

Vested interests, from ancient empires to the present day have always been interested in creating division and conflict where it suited their purpose. However, ordinary people the world over are just people trying to live their lives as best they can, if we give each other a fair hearing maybe we can learn to appreciate what we do share and respect each others' differences.

Leading the Way

First published in Green Egg *magazine, July 2021*

As someone involved in Extinction Rebellion, as a regional coordinator, I could blather on for hours about how we must protect the environment and how bad we all are and point out everything that we are doing wrong. You'll be relieved to read that I am not going to do that. In conversations with younger people, it is clear that they already understand that there is a huge problem, they do not need convincing.

Most people, apart from those living under a rock or who are just bloody-minded, are already on side as far as the need for change. The question is no longer 'do we need to change?' but 'how do we change?'. What people are now looking for is practical and creative solutions to the challenges of being a human in the twenty first century. Given that we are not going to return to the most basic subsistence life (at least not voluntarily) then we need answers and solutions that will enable civilized life to continue without further wrecking our unique and precious planet.

It should be clear to most of you by now that politicians are full of hot air — this issue was a major thing back in the political conferences of the 1990s. Thirty years later they have just talked and talked, procrastinated and placated their rich pals in corporations, with minor tinkering around the edges of the problem. If you intend to wait for the politicians to come up with practical solutions and implement them, you'd be better off trying to hitch a ride to the moon on the back of a flying pig — as it is not going to happen any time soon.

As Pagans we are already supposed to care deeply about this stuff, so in my opinion, we should be one of the groups leading the way and setting a good example on this issue. I remember many years ago, I took out my oil-based heating system and replaced it with a wood burning stove with a back boiler for the radiators, I also planted hundreds of trees a year or two beforehand. At the time my neighbours and some of my friends thought I was nuts, however, a few years later stoves became fashionable and everyone was installing them, often to supplement their oil or gas heating, if not to replace it completely.

My point is that people who lead the charge on change are often regarded not as pioneers but as insane or stupid. Despite this, leading by example is one of the most powerful ways of convincing others to change the way that they are doing things. This applies to many areas of life — what we do with our homes, the things that we buy (or choose not to buy), how we use the land we live on and our relationship with nature.

Lockdown has been an opportunity for people to look at their own lives and re-evaluate, do some soul searching and think about the things that are really important in life. As a Druid, an interest in nature and the environment is a given, so for me it is second nature to spend time in the garden, to sow seeds and put new plants in and to nurture those that are already there. On a deeper level — the relationship between nature and humanity, the magical connection with the natural world and the archetypes of deity we know and worship is something that can be honed and strengthened in a time when we have more time at home. Gardening is one sure fire way, regardless of your beliefs, of making a very visible change, which other people can see too.

If for instance you had an empty lawn in front of your house and transformed it in a few weeks into a mass of flower beds, planted some trees, put up trellis with climbers etc, do you think no-one would notice? You can be sure people passing by will see the changes, hopefully be impressed, and perhaps some of them might be inspired by you to go home and do the same thing to their wasted patch of land.

I wrote *The Druid Garden* with showing people what to do in mind — even if you have never stepped into a garden before with the desire to do any work. It is intended to teach people about the history of gardening and agriculture, about how soil works, how to create a garden from scratch and the properties and care of the plant world.

Some people might respond by pointing out that they have no garden or a tiny 'postage stamp' garden, very little time or no money to spend. These are all impediments, of course, but with a small amount of creativity they can be overcome. For instance — containers, wall hangings, hanging baskets, trellis, window boxes and shelves can all be used to maximise space. Even if you only have a small balcony, you can get window boxes that can be fixed to a balcony railing or bookcase type arrangement can be set up to accommodate several window boxes, hanging baskets can be fixed to a wall.

Even if you have very little money, you can transform a space. Cheap plants are available from many supermarkets (buy them when they arrive in not later) and if you can buy a small pot of rooting powder then you have the ability to get plants for free in the form of cuttings. You can take cuttings from wild areas and if you are fortunate, you will know some people who can donate you some plant material to do this — you don't need much as usually 1–3 inches per cutting is enough.

Gardening may seem hard at first, if you have not done it before, but it is actually quite fun and relaxing once you get into it. I find it very rewarding, but then I do seem to have 'green fingers' anyway, although the most inexperienced and unconfident gardener can learn in a surprisingly short time. The benefits are huge — a beautiful garden full of flowers which feed the bees, a home for a wealth of small creatures, free and healthy food (if you plant fruit and vegetables), herbs that can be used for cooking, medicine and magic, and fresh air, exercise and time in nature.

With a bit of ingenuity and creative thinking gardening can be done very cheaply — it does not need to be an expensive hobby. Apart from providing us with all the benefits I have already mentioned, it sends out a message to the world, to the neighbours and to people passing by — that there is a better way, change can happen and not next decade or whenever the politicians and the corporations decide it can. It can happen now and we can all choose to be part of that if we wish.

Justice

Previously unpublished

In the current climate identity politics has become increasingly influential in notions of justice, morality and equality. While it is clearly well-intentioned in that regard, many would argue that it is divisive and reduces the individual to a single quality rather than a nuanced individual. I personally have not met a person who is solely defined by their skin colour, their sexual orientation, gender etc — people are far more complex than that. Racism and other forms of oppression must be fought — but we have seen the terrible effects of enforced doctrines and over-reaching ideologies in the former totalitarian states of Europe and Asia.

Having been on the receiving end of insults because of my nationality and my chosen religion, I feel for those who have been discriminated against much more harshly than I, some of whom I have witnessed experience this are or have been my friends. It is important to make a stand in these situations and defend people from unfair and often cruel treatment.

But one might ask, is it for government or for any organisation to tell people what to think or how to live? Within the bounds of common decency and obeying the laws, created to protect people, I would say that yes, government and organisations can expect a minimum standard of ethical behaviour. However, this expectation must be kept in check, otherwise it quickly expands into dictatorial pronouncements, social manipulation, censorship and oppression of all those with dissenting views. I am a Libertarian at heart, I believe that people should be afforded the maximum personal freedom possible, within the confines of the law.

Justice and morality are part of the remit of the Druid, but philosophers have argued for millennia over notions of freedom and where to draw the line regarding imposing moral standards on society, while allowing for freedom of thought and expression. No sensible person wants to see discriminatory behaviour, but (in my opinion) in a truly just world no-one is favoured over another based on circumstantial characteristics. If we are to be judged at all, let it be on the contents of our minds, our hearts and our ability to do good in this world.

A Time for Change

Previously unpublished

Having recently passed the spring equinox (also known as *Alban Eilir* or *Cónocht an Earraigh* in Wales and Ireland respectively), now is a time for planting, for growth and for change. In the ancient world the link between human survival and the agricultural cycle was so obvious that there was no need to explain it — it was a given and what was important was the marking and observation of these points on this cycle, in an appropriate and sacred manner.

It is now, in the modern world, that we need to be reminded of our total dependency on nature for our continued existence. In Ireland it has long been a tradition to sow seeds and begin gardening or agriculture on St. Patrick's Day. This, on 17th of March, is only three or four days before the spring equinox, although St. Patrick's major fire lighting stunt at the Hill of Slane took place around Easter, so it is said. Perhaps in times past, the equinox was the start point for agriculture in Ireland and elsewhere too? It makes sense that people would not begin before the back half of March, due to the risk of heavy frost and severe Atlantic storms, both of which can destroy seedlings.

This time of year, is one of hope and in the Druidic tradition it is the time of the defeat of 'an Cailleach', the hag of winter, or her transformation into a young goddess of the land such as Brigid or perhaps even Danu. It is also the time of *'an Macan'*, also known as the *Mabon* or Child of Light, who is represented in Ireland as Óengus mac ind-Óg (Aengus/Angus) stepping out of infancy.

Some Druidic ceremonies, as a symbol of the transition of winter into spring and stepping into the light half of the year, include the sowing of a seed or seeds in the ground or in a pot.

This is a great metaphor for the agricultural year ahead, our hopes for a good harvest and also for our spiritual and personal hopes for the future. In a very real sense, the prosperity of the land and our own personal prosperity are very much entwined, in a spiritual sense, but even more so on a physical level.

In this modern world, if our local crops failed, they could be replaced by food from elsewhere, but if entire regions, countries or continents suffer agricultural failure it leads to famine and death. Our ancestors lived with the shadow of famine lurking not far away — it is only now, in a world of artificial abundance that we can be so blasé about our sustenance. However, I suspect that this abundance may well be a temporary sense of security, afforded us only by the industrial rape and abuse of the planet we live on — it cannot last forever.

Perhaps, for the first time in decades, humans are becoming aware again of their own mortality and fragility, to a large extent because of a pandemic. The Earth has plenty to teach us about the lessons that we have chosen to forget, and which our ancestors were well aware of. So here we are, at a point of balance and a point of change on the wheel of the year, on the wheel of life. There are lessons that can be absorbed and internalized if we so wish, or we can press on regardless and ignore that which the world most wants to teach us. Hubris generally leads to disaster and if we choose to ignore the omens, the clear and present danger of denial, and ignoring the need for change, then we will surely pay a heavy price.

This is a time for change, on many levels. Each of us is called to act, in different ways, and each of us can only really be responsible for our own selves and what we individually choose to do. Will we just stagger on like drunken fools into an unknown future, or will we rise to the challenges? Only we as people responsible for our own choices and as communities can choose the right path, there is no-one else who can do it for us.

The Politicisation of Paganism

First published by Discover Druidry *blog, July 2020*

I'd like to preface this article by stating clearly that I am totally opposed to any form of prejudice and oppression of any group or individual.

In the second half of the twentieth century, Paganism struggled to re-establish itself, with a small minority fighting for its right to exist against centuries of prejudice from a largely Christianised establishment. One could sense a certain unity in recent decades between the disparate groups, sharing a common goal of emancipation for a resurgent spirituality.

Now that those goals have largely been achieved, at least in North America and Europe, attention has diverted elsewhere. I choose to compartmentalise my life to some extent — my work life, my political life and my religious and social life are kept fairly separate, although there are obvious overlaps. I have in recent years noticed an increasing trend of politicisation within the Pagan movement of Ireland, UK and USA. This may have occurred elsewhere, but I am not familiar enough with occurrences in other countries to express any opinion, beyond my immediate experiences.

For a very long time, in Europe, the Christian Church had been directly involved in national and international politics and it took centuries for stable secular government to establish itself. Theocracies still exist, in Islamic countries, arguably in India (Hindu) and some Buddhist countries, which from outside are often looked upon with some disapproval. The norm in these times has become secular government in much of the world, with religious institutions paying little or no role in political matters.

In Ireland, where I live, it has been a hard-fought battle to remove the Catholic Church from its position of influence in Irish politics and as a result secularism, like in Turkey (at least until recently), is now regarded as a valuable commodity that should not be given up lightly.

However, there has been a creeping politicisation within religion, and most certainly Paganism within the last decade. This has probably been the case in other areas of social and personal life, but with religion/spirituality this, for me, has particularly worrying implications. During the run up to the abortion referendum of May 2018, the politicisation within Paganism became increasingly clear. I was involved in the Yes! campaign myself to a small extent, but I chose to do this on a personal basis and not in my role as a Pagan celebrant and organisation member.

Over the last decade the infiltration of politics into Paganism has become increasingly apparent, from both the far-right and the far-left, with both factions becoming more vocal and more vehemently opposed to one another as time has progressed. Particularly worrying has been the resurgence of the far-right, especially in the United States of America, and the gradual emergence of its ideas within some elements of Nordic and Celtic Paganism. This has also occurred in Europe too, but seemingly to a much lesser extent. To counter this, far-left ideology has also emerged, far beyond the usual distain for the far-right extremists, it has been pushing its own agenda within Pagan organisations.

As someone who would describe themselves as a gnostic I find this trend extremely worrying. I have no time for entertaining violence, oppression or hateful behaviour, regardless of which extreme it comes from. We have laws and a legal system to deal with this, which should be availed of to deal with such matters. I like to think I know myself fairly well, I do not particularly like being told what to do, at the best of times, and I like being told what to say or think even less. To be honest, I find both of these factions extremely distasteful and it concerns me greatly that they are both attempting to make inroads into the mainstream and influence the rump of moderate Pagans, who may or may not have any interest in politics. Apart from the obvious vitriol that is exchanged between left and right factions, which itself creates a toxic atmosphere, people are increasingly being coerced (from my experience) to get off the fence and align themselves one way or the other.

I believe in equality, fairness and justice, but I also believe in both the right to privacy and the right to freedom of speech. Increasingly intrusive and bullying practices are being employed and groupthink has become very much the order of the day. Instead of lively debate and impassioned, but civilised discussion, aggressive and abusive arguments are becoming common, especially on social media. It has become acceptable to denigrate those who do not share your opinion, or even those who fail to express an opinion. In the new era of political correctness, both sides regard silence as complicity and, like obsessive Evangelists, scurry to collect every last soul for their cause.

The Conquistadors, failed to see the irony of slaughtering masses of indigenous peoples in Central and South America, in the name of Jesus. I fear that the political zealots in the midst of the Pagan community are equally bereft of perspective and are incapable of realising how intolerant and hateful they can become, in the name of the moral and political values that they claim to subscribe to.

This situation has become deplorable. Paganism is not one of the 'religions of the book', it has a multitude of forms, of Gods and Goddesses, practices and beliefs. Any moral code is somewhat nebulous as there are few universal values that can be applied to this particular set of paths. Clearly, certain standards of common decency should apply, but one must also remember that Paganism also includes a number of angry, destructive and morally ambiguous Gods and Goddesses, that have their devotees.

I wish to make no excuses for either the far-right or the far-left, both have become a scourge on the face of Paganism. However, that does not mean that one cannot ever speak out against perceived injustices within the Pagan community or wider world; that to many is not just preferable, but a sacred duty. Morality is clearly part of our spirituality, but that does not mean that politics should be allowed to establish itself within Paganism. I say this because of the tyrannical history of theocracy and the terrible struggle to establish truly secular government in many countries across the world.

I reserve the right to keep my political beliefs separate from my life within the Pagan community, and totally private if I so wish. I also do not want to be recruited, lectured or denigrated by members of the far-right or far-left, or disrespected, insulted or mistreated because I refuse to play the game. If I choose not to comply with the political expectations of others, I should be free to do so. As a Gnostic I follow my own path, I need no guru to tell me how to be Pagan. I also do not require a political guru to tell me what values I should have, who I should vote for and who I should or shouldn't associate with.

If we truly believe in freedom of religion and tolerance of a plethora of beliefs, then surely the same rules should be applied to other areas of life (criminality being an obvious exception). If we truly believe in tolerance then our tolerance should be universal and not reserved for our friends and colleagues — tolerance means tolerating opinions that we don't approve of. Our freedom as Pagans has been hard won, we are diverse and entitled to remain so, please let us retain independent thought, diversity, free speech and not give our freedom away to appease political extremists and bullies.

Should Paganism Become Democratic?

Previously unpublished

Recent decades have seen increasing domination of the worldwide Pagan community by extreme politics of both the far-right and the far-left, with the far-left gaining greatest traction and succeeding in taking over control of a large number of Pagan organisations. This is a rather worrying situation I fear, as it would appear that neither extreme is representative of the rump, the vast majority of ordinary Pagans, who remain mostly silent on political and social issues.

Unfortunately, very small but highly vocal extremists, on the fringes of the Pagan movement (from both extremes) have been able to gain an undeserved place at the table within the organisations of modern Paganism and thereby dictate many of the conversations that happen within the Pagan movement and also shut down debate where it does not serve their interests. From my observations, and my own experiences, it is to a small extent far-right/Fascists, but more so by the far-left, Marxists or crypto-Marxists, that have been most successful in infiltrating and taking control of formerly non-political organisations.

The net result of these moves has been a vast reduction in freedom of speech — with often those who are right-wing, centre or centre-left being ostracised, censored and shut down by these new guardians of morality. In right-wing Pagan organisations, it is the opposite — the left is de-platformed. Sadly, very few Pagan organisations are actually democratic in any way and therefore members generally have no say in the decisions of the leadership, political bias, or any capacity to vote out the current leadership if they are unhappy with the situation.

In most cases, the only options for those who are discontented are to silently put up with extremist and minority-oriented propaganda or just leave the organisation. If politics and social commentary is to be permitted within Pagan organisations, should it not be fair and balanced? Is it not fairer and more reasonable to either allow all sides free expression or to simply refrain from offering any platform at all?

Of course, with the non-democratic takeover situations, politically biased leaders are only too delighted if the objectors leave the organisation, as it strengthens their own position. I have heard several accounts of the social culture of Pagan organisations changing, with members powerless to have any input. I have also witnessed this sudden or gradual shift into social/political positions, where previously this was left to the individual. I myself have been faced with this decision on whether to remain silent or leave on several occasions. In more than one organisation, I have expressed my opinions and I have been unfairly hounded by senior members, censored (on social media) for no justifiable reason or, in one case, had my membership cancelled without the right to appeal and banned from any means of communication with other members.

Some of these such organisations are total theocracies, and worse still, spiritual dictatorships with one authoritarian, sometimes self-appointed, person calling all the shots. In some cases there is a 'committee' of sorts to keep errant leaders in check, but this is not often the case. On reflection, I realise that I do not want to be part of any Pagan organisation that is run by a dictatorial autocrat, but that does not change the fact that this is a deplorable situation, where members effectively have zero rights to complain, ask for a hearing, make suggestions and they are at the mercy of the whimsical nature of the current leader.

Further still, where there is some kind of multi-person leadership, the less senior roles are often appointed by the non-democratically or self-appointed leader and so in effect just become an echo chamber or body of 'henchmen' or 'enforcers' for the will of the leader. Such a situation is little better than the structure of the Roman Catholic Church, where the Popes had absolute authority, although at least no inquisition style torture or execution is permissible within modern Paganism!

I ask you, does Paganism need a 'Pagan Pope' or a body of enforcers or influencers dictating dogma and political correctness to the masses of the Pagan community? I would suggest that no, we do not need this, nor should we desire such an arrangement. In fact, we should be fearful of this — as it can only be of great detriment to the future of Paganism if our organisations are allowed to be dominated from within by dictators.

Furthermore, we currently have a situation where any dissenting voices can be effectively silenced by the leadership, before they have a chance to be heard, within many of these Pagan organisations. In most instances there is no right of appeal, no internal court, where grievances could be heard by an impartial panel — which gives free reign to the autocrats to dispose of any opponents or dissidents within their ranks.

Even the Roman Catholic Church, with all its many crimes against humanity, afforded the Heretic and the Witch a public show trial, even if it was a sham. They at least bothered to go through the motions of justice. The modern Pagan organisations, that one sees act in a shameful, biased and autocratic way, most often don't even offer any form of appeal, redress, trial or hearing — their decisions are absolute, with not even the vaguest nod towards real justice, fairness, equality and democracy or any proper procedures, or right of appeal.

It is quite ironic, I find, that many of the Pagan organisations that claim to prize justice and fairness and teach its virtues do not actually have established procedures to offer that same lauded justice and fairness to any of their members. It doesn't take a rocket scientist to figure out that this is a particularly toxic, hypocritical and unfair situation. This seems especially worrying for a newly re-established religion (neo-Paganism) that has barely 70 years under its belt, and cites unfair treatment by others as part of its history.

If we have come to this in only 70 odd years, what does this bode for the future of the Pagan movement? Surely it is time that our Pagan organisations became truly democratic, with leaders actually elected by their members? Surely every organisation should have a redress procedure, with impartial hearings and a right of appeal for supposed transgressors? Surely every organisation should have leaders that are culpable and responsible for their actions? Surely there should be a transparent procedure for these leaders to be held to account for their actions and be voted out and replaced where they are guilty of corruption, unfairness or other misdemeanours?

If ordinary Pagans do not stand up and express themselves and use their individual voices, to demand rights from Pagan organisations, then this toxic situation will persist. I think it's about time that the Pagan community grew up and established leadership for the future that is accountable, responsible and that represents the needs of the membership — instead of the needs and whims of the leaders, and their cronies. If we fail to demand this then I can only see a future of corruption, despotism, nepotism, which has plagued many religions in the past and does to this day. If a lack of accountability persists in neo-Paganism, then I predict there will be eventual decay and possible dissolution, as angered and disillusioned members gradually leave to follow a different path.

The current situation is dire, but it is not unsalvageable, perhaps it's time for real change, not just in our generally corrupt and overblown Western civilization, but within the spiritual organizations that profess to be aiming to create a better and more inclusive future? Sorry, this all seems rather negative, with no good news — but sometimes it is necessary to acknowledge that which we don't want to look at, in order to eventually arrive at a better place.

Transcending Division in Darkness

First published in Pagan Ireland *magazine,*
December 2021

So here we are, at the darkest time of the year (in the northern hemisphere), a time of cold, the time of lack, hibernation, stagnation and also of death. It is the time when the forces of destruction and negativity are at their strongest but also it is the beginnings of change, in preparation for the coming re-emergence in Spring.

This time of year is not an easy one — it is a necessary part of the year, a necessary part of life, where that which is no longer of use, value, that is dead, expired is swept away and re-cycled by the universe, either on a physical or meta-physical level. While it may be difficult to confront this, particularly given the hardships of the ongoing pandemic, lockdowns, illness, isolation and all the repercussions of that, there is value in looking at these things during this time of stillness and relative inactivity.

There are so many issues that can potentially divide us — age, religion, politics, class, gender, sexuality, lifestyle etc., that adding the issue of health on top of all that is rather unfortunate, to say the least. The issue of the pandemic and the rights and wrongs of the medical and governmental approach to this has caused massive arguments across society — between friends, work colleagues, within families and within the esoteric communities too.

Winter is a time for shedding, for letting go of things, and also for reflection, planning for the year ahead — when Spring finally begins, we will become active again and begin to manifest our hopes, dreams and intentions.

It is in the darkness that the seed germinates, putting down a root into the soil, before sending up a shoot into the light, to begin the process of growing and fulfilling its destiny. Although the Earth may appear to be dead, it is only dormant. Trees, bereft of leaves, and seemingly inactive are actually still active below ground. In winter the roots of trees and bushes continue to slowly grow and the stores of energy are consolidated from the autumn (especially in bulbs) for the eruption of new life when the sun's warmth and light begins to return.

It is in darkness that we are also born, from the womb of our mother, into a world of light that we have not experienced before. So, like the womb, or the soil under our feet, we can consider the winter as a time of preparation, consolidation and also healing, for the year of activity that lies ahead of us.

Winter time is the perfect time for the inner work of transformation and transcending of what may be holding us back or creating difficulties. That may be physical problems, psychological issues, relationship issues, or simply more mundane but still important problems such as work, money or lack of opportunity.

One thing that is for certain, there are some issues that we have no control over and can do little about, apart from make our peace with them. Other issues are within our own sphere of influence and perhaps those are what we are best placed to consider during the cold and dark months of winter. Whatever hardships we face, there is always something we can do, there is always hope while the spark of life remains. Difficulties can be overcome, solutions found, bonds broken, new bonds made, or old bonds re-established and positive ways found to manifest a better future. So let us embrace the darkness and find solace in its quiet potential.

Perspectives on Truth

First published in Pagan Ireland *magazine,*
December 2022

The Druid path has long regarded truth as being of prime importance — the Irish and Welsh triads that have come down to us cover many subjects, but a good many of them extol the virtues of truthfulness.

There are many such examples, but I am going to present you with just one, that I think is particularly powerful, and which comes from *Trecheng Breth Féne (A Triad of Judgments of the Irish)*, translated into English by Kuno Meyer and published in 1906.

Three candles that illumine every darkness: truth, nature, knowledge.

The trouble with the idea of truth is that everyone (well almost) would agree that truth is a virtue, but often people cannot agree on what the truth is. This seems to me to be the biggest stumbling block to consensus, harmony and peace in human society.

Over known history people have questioned what is truth and whether there is only subjective truth (true for me) or also objective truth (universally true). This is a bit of a conundrum, with possibilities that nothing can be proven to be true, multiple subjective truths are valid, both subjective and objective truth can exist or that subjective and objective truth is mutually exclusive.

Each of us has our own unique view of life, and each of us has our own singular sense of what is true and what is not. In many cases we can agree on things (e.g. the Earth is round) but while most would agree with that statement, there are others, perhaps in other countries and cultures outside of Ireland who would insist that the Earth is flat.

Such statements as "The Earth is round" may be considered objective truth by the majority of people on this planet, but this is not universal and would be not even a subjective truth to some, it would outright falsehood.

When it comes to objective truths, such as we find in science, it is generally accepted that there is some kind of proof to validate claims, but even in science, this is a moveable feast.

Up until 1777 with the work of Joseph Priestly and Antoine Lavoisier proving the existence of the element Oxygen, scientists believed in a non-existent substance called 'Phlogiston' for over 100 years. Their work dispelled the remains of alchemy and Aristotelian thought regarding Chemistry and Physics, leading to the modern age we are in now.

Of course, this and other examples, show that what we think is 'set in stone' is not always as believed, and that objective truth can become falsehood in time.

Subjective truth, where nuances of emotions, beliefs, experience and prior knowledge are factors, is worse again and two people will seldom agree on everything. In the current times there are great arguments socially, politically and philosophically, and theologically about what is true. People fall out over it, hate over it, cancel and even kill over it. Ultimately, we cannot know what it is to be someone else and to see through their eyes. Perhaps we should learn to accept non-agreement and just be ok with it? Perhaps we don't always need to be right or to chastise those who we perceive as wrong?

Interviews

Interview with Mabh Savage

First published on paganpages.org, May 2015

Luke is a musician, poet, painter, photographer and the author of *The Journey* and *A Druid's Primer*, as well as numerous articles on subjects ranging from politics to horticulture. He currently writes a blog for Moon Books on Druidry and Celtic belief. I caught up with Luke to quiz him on his many projects.

Mabh: What inspired your original interest in Celtic culture?
LE: It has been so much part of my life for so long that I can't remember where it started. My father sometimes enthused about Bonnie Prince Charlie and King Arthur, which left a deep impression; my Granny bought me fairy tales — I remember being read 'Peronique' (a Breton tale I still have) in a picture book version before I could read myself. I had a set of Ancient Briton and Roman soldiers about 1 inch high that often fought for hours on my bedroom floor, the Romans usually won as they had all the sexy weaponry!

MS: And how did this lead to your involvement with Paganism?
LE: I had been a Roman Catholic but found myself dissatisfied with it, although I did feel attracted to the teachings of both Jesus and St. Francis. I could see that the true roots of Christianity had become obliterated by the Romans and in looking through the dark history of the Church I discovered that much of R.C. ritualism is derived from European and Middle-Eastern Paganism. At this point in time, I had come to regard Jesus as a prophet, like Moses or Muhammad, so it was not much of a leap for me to abandon Christianity completely and become a Pagan. Being strongly connected to nature, Druidry/Druidism seemed the obvious best fit, although I did investigate Buddhism, Hindu pantheism, Hermeticism and Wicca on the way to choosing this path.

MS: I know from experience that studying Celtic history and mythology can be arduous and time-consuming, although always rewarding. What have been your finest resources, and what source do you return to again and again?

LE: Yes, it is extremely time-consuming but ultimately rewarding as you say. Apart from the many people I've learned from (often informally) I've found many books to be incredibly useful and/ or insightful. To name just three, I'd suggest — *The Religion of The Ancient Celts* by J.A. McCulloch, *Irish Trees: Myths, Legends & Folklore* by Niall MacCoitir and *The Celtic Heroic Age* by John T. Koch & John Carey. Books can be wonderful but book knowledge alone is useless in my opinion. Experience of living and working spiritually is far more important but at times the 'knowledge' accumulated suddenly elucidates an experience or gives some frame of reference that completes the picture. Without the living and breathing experiences, the sum of all I've read is just so many pages in a dusty old tome, as dead as the wood from which the pages came!

MS: You paint, write poetry, books and articles, make music and take some beautiful photos as well. Is there any particular medium in all this creativity that you connect to more than the others, and why?

LE: No, there isn't a preference I'm aware of. It has occurred to me that I've gone through several creative phases in my life, some overlapping slightly. In the last few years writing has been my main focus and it will probably continue to be so until my intuition draws me elsewhere. I am unable to work to order creatively for myself, I do only what feels right, so I'd be hopeless if I had to rely on it for an income. I suspect I'll return to playing music fairly soon, it's something that has always been part of my life in some form.

MS: What drew you to Druidry initially?

LE: I can't really explain it. I think it appealed on a subconscious level. I had great difficulty in finding out about it, most of the books I found were very shallow and uninformative, which lead me to explore other less obscured areas, such as Hindu Culture. However, I remember walking past a bookshop in Swiss Cottage, London in 1996 and seeing *The Book of Druidry* by Ross Nichols in the window. I rushed in and bought it, even though it was £20 or something ridiculous like that. This was the first book I'd come across that was written by a real Druid as opposed to some academic or historian.

MS: And now, what is the most vital part of being a Druid for you?
LE: For me, being able to go outside and watch the world happening seems more vital than anything. If I were unable to do that, I think I'd be incredibly unhappy.

MS: Was this part of what inspired you to write *The Druid's Primer*?
LE: I didn't feel that any one single Druid 101 book was sufficiently in-depth or comprehensive to provide a useful guide in one volume. I'm not sure that *The Druid's Primer* is either, but it is my attempt to compile all the basics from all of the Celtic traditions I could find. In particular I was keen to promote the Irish traditions and knowledge, which has been neglected, as well of that of the other Celtic/ex-Celtic nations.

MS: What advice would you give to someone with an interest in pursuing Druidry?
LE: Try to find the fine line between experiential, intuitive practice and academic, knowledge acquisition. Knowledge was always an important aspect of Druidry but so too was creative, empathic and intuitive skill. To be balanced I think we need to try to develop both sides of ourselves in a harmonious way so that what we do and what we know become integrated completely into who we are.

MS: Can someone be a Druid without worshiping any particular deity, or perhaps without honouring a deity at all?
LE: Not everyone would agree with me, but I would say yes to both. I would say that it is essential to have some understanding of the Celtic concept of deity and the mythology associated with it. However, many people have a nebulous sense of deity or even regard nature itself as the source of divinity or perhaps even just the source of life. I don't see why such theological differences would stop someone from being able to live a Druidic life; I'd say that sincerely walking the path is more important than points of dogma.

MS: Tell us a bit about your recently republished book, *The Journey*. What was the key message you wanted to convey?
LE: In truth the way that we live is more important than what we profess to believe. Our deepest beliefs and concerns are demonstrated and manifested by the choices we make in how we live in the world. Much of the truths about human experience and the universe (from a human perspective) seem to me to be independent of the religion from which they originated. It strikes me (using a crude analogy) that many religious people are obsessed with the colour of the car they are driving or that other people are driving, when what is really important is keeping your own car on the road!

MS: You play an astonishing range of musical instruments; do you think this talent ties back to Celtic ancestry at all?
LE: I really can't give a definite answer. I can say that my recent ancestors and relatives, including my father and grandfather have been very musical. I've been listening to music since I was born so it's almost part of me at this stage. My siblings and my daughter all play instruments too, I guess it's a minor compulsion in my family!

MS: And do you have a favourite instrument?
LE: I suppose guitar is my most played instrument but recently I've an urge to get back to playing the cello. I'm very rusty right now, but it has such a wonderful sound I really think I should make more time for it.

MS: Your bio says you are currently working on a novel; can you tell us a bit about that?
LE: It's a sci-fi with a spiritual element to it. I've projected some of the current concerns relating to secularism and religious strife into the future surrounding one particular character who experiences a momentous, life-changing event. That's about all I want to say, any more might reveal too much.

MS: What other projects do you have on the horizon?
LE: I'd very much like to write a book on sacred sites, cross referenced with some of the most ancient writings related to each of them. Although I love photography it might be interesting to work on this in conjunction with a photographer with a different view of such places.

MS: Do you still write poetry? What themes inspire you?
LE: Yes, I do, but only when I feel inspired. That might happen three times in one week or once in a year. I appear to have no control over when I write poems. Nature, love and modern society are three themes that seem to crop up over and over again; usually something that has happened or something I've seen will inspire me and the words will just come flooding out.

MS: You write on many socio-political themes. What currently has you fired up?
LE: Injustice is something that makes me very angry — injustice to the weak and impoverished of the world and also injustice to the natural world. I think that inequality is a perennial problem

and in some countries, it seems to be getting worse not better. As the human population grows the stresses on the planet and on human society are growing, I really think that we need to collectively find creative and fair solutions fast if there is going to be any kind of future worth having.

MS: Tell us a bit about Éigse Spiorad Cheilteach. [Gathering of Celtic Spirituality]
LE: I was very inspired by Féile Draoíchta (Festival of Magic & Spirituality) in Dublin, which is run by Barbara Lee and Lora O'Brien. Basically, I decided to copy their idea and move it outside into a rural setting, but focusing more specifically on the Celtic end of magic/spirituality. Both ladies have been very supportive with advice and Lora also gave us a talk in August just gone. 2014 was our 5th year and I'm delighted by how it has gradually grown since the first one. For me being outside is the main plank of my spiritual practice and I'm keen to provide others the opportunity to share that kind of experience with other like-minded people.

MS: You've had a very interesting spiritual journey it seems; from being raised Catholic to an interest in Buddhism, to studying Wicca and eventually becoming a Druid. Do you feel that where you are now is where you are meant to be, or is there still a further journey ahead for you?
LE: Yes, I suppose it is a bit strange, I guess I've wandered like a stray dog until I found a comfortable spot to rest! I've learned a great deal from exploring these different paths and I'd be a different person than I am today if I had not done so. I do feel that I am where I am meant to be right now but, of course, there is still more to come. We are always learning every day, there is always something new to learn. I think that the day that I feel I have nothing further to learn from life is the time for me to shuffle off this mortal coil.

Interview with NF Reads

First published on nfreads.com, 2016

Please introduce yourself and your book(s)!

My name is Luke, I live in county Kerry, Ireland although I've moved around a lot during my lifetime. I've done many jobs — my first job after university was as a car-park attendant, which was mind-bogglingly boring. I've been an artist, professional musician, journalist, sub-editor, graphic designer and more recently a horticulturist. I have also had a longstanding interest in spirituality and that is a subject I've written about extensively. *The Journey* is perhaps my favourite book, but I am quite excited about my new ecology book *How to Save The Planet* which will be out soon.

What is/are the real-life story(ies) behind your book(s)?

There aren't really any specific stories but much of what I write about is inspired by personal experience. I first discovered Buddhism when I was 15 thanks to a very eccentric uncle. I was Catholic at the time and my interest in other paths was not approved of, however, the seed was sown — I went to India in search of answers, I explored psychedelic substances and I read voraciously and looked for a teacher. Eventually I concluded that you really have to be your own teacher, although I've learned a lot from the kindness and insights of others.

What inspires/inspired your creativity?

That's hard to say, creativity kinda descends on me from an unknown source. I might see or hear something interesting and sometime later an idea will pop into my head that demands to be expressed. I have no real control over it, I just go with it when I feel inspired. From a Druidic point of view this is described as *Awen* or *Imbas* — it is the creative spirit or energy that comes from a divine source and manifests through humans when we connect with deity our higher selves or whatever you might want to call it.

How do you deal with creative block?
Fortunately, I don't usually suffer from this. However, I did suffer from a total creative shutdown for two years as a result of poor physical and mental health brought on by chronic insomnia. Yoga and other spiritual and physical practices helped me get better and then the creativity just came back by itself.

What are the biggest mistakes you can make in a book?
These days you cannot rely on publishers to edit your book properly in many cases. I've discovered that it's best to go through your MS with a fine-tooth comb and get two or three competent friends or colleagues to read it first, before submitting the final draft. Things do slip through unfortunately but nowadays many publishers cut corners on proof reading and editing in order to reduce costs.

How do bad reviews and negative feedback affect you and how do you deal with them?
I've been really lucky in that there has been no negative feedback from either readers or reviewers. However, I have been rejected by countless publishers, which is always hard to deal with. If you know that your work is good you really just have to press on regardless and not let negativity put you off from writing and promoting your work.

Do you tend towards personal satisfaction or aim to serve your readers? Do you balance the two and how?
First and foremost, I write for my own pleasure and to express what I want to say about life, society and what is important

to me. I do though hope to say something worthwhile and of benefit and interest to other people and provoke people to look at the world in different ways. If I thought what I had to say was boring or irrelevant then I would not bother to do it but I try not to be arrogant or egotistical about my writing. I realize that I am not that important and my opinion is no more valuable than anyone else's. It's for that reason that I don't generally do blogging or lots of social media posts — I'm not so interesting that anyone would want to read my daily thoughts!

What role do emotions play in creativity?

For me emotions come into play particularly with poetry — I can't write to order, poetry comes as an emotional response to something, pretty much at random moments. This can be annoying when it happens in the middle of the night or somewhere where you don't have a pen and paper handy. Generally, my prose is less emotional, far more pragmatic, although emotions definitely play their part in that too.

What are your plans for future books?

Right now, *Kerry Folk Tales* is just out so I am promoting that. I've a new book completed called *How to Save The Planet,* which is pretty self-explanatory — it's a short book and done on recycled paper. The plan is to give half the profits from this to Greenpeace. They are a wonderful organization and I think they have done so much to make the world a better place, I urge everyone to support them! I've also nearly completed a follow up to *The Druid's Primer,* which is somewhat different but still very much connected with Druidry — I'll not say much about that until it's in the bag, but I'm very pleased with how it's turning out.

Tell us some quirky facts about yourself

I have almost been killed many times — as an infant in Scotland I ended up in hospital after a severe allergic reaction but recovered miraculously. In England a friend shot me in the back with a rifle when I was a kid, I also fell in quicksand and barely escaped. I got severe dysentery in India but I was fortunately near the only hospital for 100 miles which saved me from certain death. I fell down a well near Dublin narrowly missing an iron spike, I've had several serious bicycle crashes in England. I fell off a roof in Wexford (Ireland). Someone nailed my hand to a door just missing a vein and I was in a car crash, both in USA. I accidentally slit my wrist working in a deli in England and was rushed to hospital. In London I got a bad electric shock and on two other occasions almost got crushed by a bus and a JCB. I also fell asleep on the motorway but somehow woke up just before I went off the road. In France I split my head open on a low road sign and almost knocked myself out. I'm so accident prone that actually when I think about it, it's amazing that I'm still here!

Interview with Rachel Patterson

First published on rachelpatterson.co.uk,
May 2020

What or who inspires you the most and why?

I find creativity and positivity very inspiring, both in humans and in the natural world outside of humanity. On the other hand, negative events can spur you on to do something about them and react in a proactive way. I'd say stimulating events, opinion and ideas leads to your own creative and inspired response, hopefully at least!

Do you have any set daily spiritual practices?

Yes. The first thing I do when I wake up is look out of the window and say a prayer of gratitude. I also do Reiki every morning. I also regularly do a Druidic energy exercise or chi gong and I try to do yoga most days. I'll also do meditations or journeys as I see fit, but this is less frequent.

What is your favourite subject to write about and why?

I enjoy writing about social issues that relate to our time — I think it's very needed as humanity is generally a bit lost. We're beginning to realise that our modern way of life is rotten, but have yet to discover a unified way forward. It feels like we are in the process of doing that — humanity is having a collective teenage identity crisis.

Do you have a sacred or spiritual place/area (anywhere in the world) that you feel connected to?

I feel very connected to Ireland where I live, but also feel connected to Taoist, Buddhist and Vedic practices from China,

Japan and India. I have visited India, which was a life-changing experience, but not China or Japan, hopefully one day.

Where do you work your magic/practice your faith? Do you have a special room or area set aside?

I always work outside, regardless of the weather. Often, I work outside the house but also often at specific sites on the Dingle peninsula or around Kerry. I do have a space in the house that I share with my partner but I use it more for meditation than ritual. It would have to be a severe storm or super freezing before I would abandon working outside.

What book/talk/article of yours are you most proud of and why?

My favourite book of mine is *The Journey*, which is my shortest book. It's not a Pagan book, more general Gnosticism and eclectic spirituality, I guess. It covers environmentalism, tolerance and open-mindedness — areas that I think are sadly lacking at the moment in human consciousness. I think it's the best thing I've ever written.

Luke Eastwood, the Druid Gardener

First published on ninunina.com, April 2021

Luke, you have such a fascinating background, please tell us about yourself.

I was born in Scotland but we moved to south-east England, and had a pretty pedestrian childhood. After a falling out with my folks I ran off to London and became a Casino Croupier at 19. I almost joined the RAF as a trainee jet navigator, but I went to university instead, which was useless apart from one class. I worked in journalism, sub-editing, and graphic design while working on my music career and developing my interest in photography, world religions and other cultures.

I later traveled to India and learned Dolakha and Bansuri, while there almost dying from dysentery. Four dance/ambient albums later I decided to pack in the music and move to Ireland, with my then wife and infant daughter. I continued with graphic design and photography and after my marriage ended, I began to pursue old interests in spirituality, yoga and music. I began training as a Druid, retrained as a horticulturist, began to record music again and began writing — both articles and books. I have always been interested in activism (Greenpeace, McLibel in London) and set up an Extinction Rebellion group in Ireland. A small book: *How to Save The Planet* was published last autumn and I just released a new album of electronica in March called *5th Element*, by Children of Dub.

Greatest inspirations or influences?

I do remember one pivotal moment when my school French teacher did not answer my question about whether to drop French or German. Paraphrasing, he said — don't worry about what other people think, learn to be your own man. That really stuck in my head, and I've always tried to do what really interests me, regardless of how strange or foolish it seemed to others.

Tell us a little about your new book and what it means to have a more spiritual approach to gardening?

Despite all its advantages, it's pretty clear to me that we've gone down a dead end with technological approaches to life, not least in our interaction with nature. I don't want to live in chastened and sterile world, bereft of wild beauty, being forced to eat soulless GMO food. I think a great many people feel the same way, but maybe lack the knowledge of how to change that and make a real connection to nature in their everyday lives. *The Druid Garden* is all about that, but it is 100% practical as well.

How do you feel about the changes we are all experiencing these days and how you see things are going to unfold?

This crisis is a moment to reflect and re-evaluate where we are, the culmination of the industrial mode of living. I think that the next phase of human existence is going to be one of two things:

- A spiritual awakening and reconnection with the natural world and each other, leading to a more benevolent and altruistic society.
- A new era of oppression, technological oligarchy and removal of freedoms, increased reliance on industrial living, but with automation, robotics and AI being at the fore.

I think it is very much up to every one of us to ensure that corrupt and elitist powers do not use this crisis to force entire nations down a bad road. We have strength together and in unity we can triumph over the greatest of difficulties.

What do you feel most inspired to talk about when it comes to social issues and your involvement with extinction rebellion?

I've been interested in history since I was a boy. What has occurred to me is that many of the same challenges have repeated throughout our known history, in different civilizations. Our biggest challenge is denial — the failure to learn from our mistakes and the misguided belief that somehow 'it will be different this time'. The repeated mistakes have taken a huge toll on both humanity and the natural world, over many millennia and now we are finally seeing the full extent of our collective stupidity as a species. I think that we have to take better care of the planet, but we also need to take better care of each other.

Social justice means redistribution of wealth, fairness and protection of the most vulnerable. XR is about more than 'being green', people need to wake up to the fact that the system is broken at a fundamental level.

Favourite websites, or social media handles?
Here's a few that interest me.

- I love a good laugh, this Irish news parody (waterfordwhispers.com) is hilarious.
- Jiddu Krishnamurti had a big influence on my thinking.
- I did most of my Druid training with OBOD.
- William Orbit has made a lot of inspirational music, his art is amazing too.
- I really love Goldfrapp, their music is never dull.
- Still doing great work, Greenpeace rock!

Anything else you'd like to share?
I realized a long time ago that we only have one shot at this life (at least in this body). It's ok to make mistakes and I'd

rather make a mess of things trying to do something good, fun, interesting and hopefully of value to the world. Forget about making your fortune or being judged — do something worthwhile, while you have the opportunities, before it's too late to try something different.

Interview with Damh the Bard (extract)

First published on Druidry.org,
October 2021

Luke Eastwood: I had a real big interest in Vedic culture. You're probably aware, yourself, that a lot of people have suggested there's a big link between India and the Celtic culture?

Damh the Bard: Yes.

LE: The idea migrated across into Europe. And there may be some truth in that. It's so far back, it's quite hard to prove, really.

LE: So, I kind of stumbled towards it, towards the Druidry. And then I really got interested in the whole eco movement. When I was about 16, I joined a conservation group at college. And we'd gone round removing rhododendrons to make room for other species because they'd invaded so much of the college; there was very little else, really. And then I got involved in Greenpeace as well, when I went to London.

LE: And then, as this was happening, I kind of came more across Celtic stuff, and the Neo-Druidism. At that time I didn't really know anyone, I wasn't involved in any groups or anything. Just, sort of, reading and stuff, myself. And I thought, well, this really fits, because I'm really into the whole eco thing. And then, so you've got this religion that very much revolves around nature, in the same way that Daoism does. In fact, probably, I would have ended up being a Daoist if I lived in China or somewhere, because there's so many parallels between the two, in their approach.

DTB: Mm-hmm (affirmative).

LE: So, it just seemed to make sense; that my kind of ideas about how to live in the world in terms of ecology, fitted very well with modern Druidism. So, I thought, well, yeah, I think this is probably what I want to do. But I had a great difficulty in making any connections.

LE: It was kind of later on, I suppose ... Yeah, I think it was in, something about 1996, I think, I stumbled across *The Book of Druidry*, Ross Nichol's book, in a shop window. I'd never seen a real book on Druidry. And it's all been history books that I ... Like, this is what the Druids did, whatever. There's loads of books like that, but I'd never found a book that actually told you what being a Druid is, or how it works.

DTB: There weren't many around, at the time, were there? There weren't many books around, in the mid-90s, like that.

LE: No, not at all.
DTB: Yeah. Yeah.

LE: So, when I saw this in the shop window, I rushed in there. I think it was quite expensive, actually, at the time. But I came back at lunchtime, from work, and bought it. I think they only had the one in there, actually. But it was in the window, which was lucky for me.

LE: I found that really difficult, at the time, because some of it was over my head. I didn't really kind of get some of it. But I came back to it again, later, read it again, when I think I started the OBOD course, for, you know, the Bardic Grade. I returned to it, then.

DTB: And that's where you do it.

DTB: So, it's amazing isn't it, I think, a lot of people, probably their first kind of explorations of these kinds of things, they were films like *Excalibur*. And for me, it was *Robin of Sherwood*, back in the 80s.

LE: Oh, I remember that.

DTB: You remember? With Michael Praed? And that was the first time I'd ever seen a figure of Herne, an antlered god, in the forest. And I was young at the time, and it was the same thing for me: there's something going on here, that's way beyond everything I've been taught. I've been taught that horns on a figure is the Devil. But that is just fantastic!

LE: Yeah, it was great. And the music as well, Clannad.

DTB: That's right.

LE: They'd been massive in Ireland, for a long time. But they weren't really, really known, at all. But that soundtrack kind of propelled them into the limelight, a bit.

DTB Yeah, very much.

LE: In fact, I bought the soundtrack album of that series. Actually, no, it must have been not that long ago, probably maybe ten years ago, or something like that?

DTB Yeah.

LE: I saw a copy of it in a shop, and I thought, "Yes! Great."

DTB: Great. I've just got to hear that theme, "Robin, the hooded man," and I'm back, sitting down, Saturday night, with my mum and dad, eating our tea in front of the TV.

DTB: But it's the mysticism that draws people. It's the sense that, inside, many of us know that there's more to life than just the three dimensional: get up, go to work, come home, go to sleep, life, that many of us seem to ... That there is more to this. That life is such a miracle, that there must be more to it. These programs, I think, just, go, "Yes, there is," and they allow us to become more in touch with that kind of mystical side of us.

DTB: And you use the word "religion" a lot, in your search for Druidry, which is not what everybody says. A lot of people would say that it would be a "spirituality", or something like that. But I know, for many people, it is a religious path. Would you say it was, for yourself? I mean, for instance, would you say that you were animistic? Or polytheistic? Or is there a labelistic that can describe your view of that kind of stuff?

LE: I came from a religious dogma, and then, sort of, dropped that idea. Religion, it means different things to different people. It can be a dogmatic, hierarchical system, but it doesn't necessarily have to be that way. I mean, Quakerism is a religion, but as far as I know, people just sit around in a circle, in equality, and then, when they feel moved by the spirit, they just speak. So that's a kind of religion that isn't dogmatic. But as a general rule, yeah, throughout history, it has tended to be hierarchical and a bit dogmatic. So, I'd say it's whatever you want it to be. It can be a spiritual path, it's a spirituality, but it also can be a religion, if you want it to be that. As you know, there's a massive diversity of different types of Druids.

LE: Going back to what you said about, there's more to life than the house and the car and the job, that's one of the reasons why I wouldn't be an atheist. Because I just thought, well, for me, atheism is absence of meaning, that I feel like there's no point in existing, particularly. If life has no meaning, because it doesn't mean anything, there's no consequences, nothing is important. There's no need for morality, or any sense of value, if nothing has any point at all. So, I felt I really needed some sense of meaning.

DTB: Yeah.

LE: So that kind of brought me towards ... I sort of figured out, what I really believe in is animism. I suppose I'd be a kind of Pantheist, or a Polytheist, in that I do kind of ultimately think there's one godhead, if you like. But I'm kind of, like, I suppose, Henotheist, in that I believe that all these different gods and goddesses or whatever, they're all aspects of the one, because they're just anthropomorphisations of whatever spirit is. I think spirit is beyond human definition, myself.

LE: We're like little goldfish in a bowl, looking at the world through this sort of distorted bowl. But the reality of the world is so much bigger than that. We've got very limited faculties, we're only human, and so we have to describe spirit in some way that we can understand.

DTB: Yeah. Yeah. I've only got to go for a walk with my dog, every day, and just watch him as he explores the world through him. And he will read the newspaper, as far as he's concerned. I call it the "P Mail." So, he will just go with me, and we'll go for a walk, and he'll read his P Mail as he walks along." Now, I can't see the world through that. I look at my dog, and I'm just in a sense of wonder at the different way that a dog will see the world. And sometimes I think we're so tight with how we see the world as it being all there is, but, actually, you've just got to look at another creature to know that there are many ways of experiencing life, you know?

DTB: And I love what you said about meaning. I think it was Rupert Sheldrake, I think, is the name of the writer that brings to mind, he says something that really struck me, a long time ago, as being like a truth with a capital "T". And that is that the constant drive and search for happiness is a mistake. Happiness is elusive, and can literally fall through your fingers. What will keep that is a search for meaning. Meaning is what makes life powerful. It's what gives you direction in life. It's not just about happiness, it's about meaning. So yeah, I absolutely agree with that. It's about finding the meaning in your life. And I think spirituality, myth, for instance, can give meaning to our lives, and direction, as well. So yeah, yeah, absolutely.

DTB: You've just released a new book. I know you've got a few books out, haven't you? You've got some under your belt, already, to be honest with you. But you've just released a new book that is all about *Samhain*, which is why I've asked you onto Druidcast this particular month. A book dedicated to the festival. So, what I probably need to ask you is, what inspired you to write one book about one festival? What led you to make that decision to write that book?

LE: Obviously, I've become interested in Celtic cosmology, over the time, through my studies with OBOD, and various other people and organizations, mostly here in Ireland. So, one thing that struck me is, that it seems to be quite a common theme, not just in Druidism, but in other Pagan parts, that the Celtic

New Year, the beginning of the year, is *Samhain*. So, I often wondered, why is that? Wouldn't it make more sense if it was the Winter Solstice? Because that literally the cusp of the shift between light and dark; that's that point where the light starts to return. So, I kind of thought, that's a bit odd. What's that all about? Why is that happening?

LE: So, I would have thought, myself, you've got the year end, with *Samhain*, and maybe the year kind of sleeps and starts again when the Solstice comes. And you talk about it with people, and it's this idea of incubation, this whole thing, for the winter. But then I thought, well, there must be something that substantiates all this, where does it come from? So, a bit of digging, you start to find, there it is, hidden in the mythology, and you've got the practices which are folk practices which survived, plus, some of which have been recorded in history, as well.

LE: So, really, strong evidence to show it was a very significant time. And literally, is the beginning of the old Pagan year in Britain and Ireland. And also in Gaul, which, the Coligny calendar has a particular reference to *Samhain* on it, with the three days marked very clearly. Obviously, the whole thing was in pieces, but I think there's about two-thirds of the thing, of the big plate as it originally was, that they'd put it back together and managed to translate a lot of it. So that's going back into the pre-Christian era, that discovery of the calendar in Gaul. So, it's definitely ... You could say that proves it's that old, at least.

LE: But in my kind of researches, I came across a book by John Gilroy, called *Tlachtga: Celtic Fire Festival*, which he wrote late last century... And it was published in 1999, I think. Anyway, that's out of print, sadly, and it's really difficult to get it. The only place I've managed to get a copy is going to the library and taking it out, repeatedly, so I could read it, or get it out again, if I wanted to look stuff up. I actually spoke to him, and he didn't even have any copies himself!

DTB: Wow!

LE: So, I couldn't buy a copy anywhere. It was like gold dust. But that book was really good. But things have moved on a lot, since, in the last 20 years, in terms of research. And a lot of archeology has happened, as well, particularly at this place in County Meath called the Hill of Ward, outside a little village called Athboy. The hill was formerly called Tlachtga, which, if you trace it back, goes back to this Druidess or goddess called Tlachtga. There's a lot of stories about her, and also her father, Mug Ruith. And it's all a bit confused. So, one of the things I've done in the book, is trying to unpick the stories.

LE: Because one of things that happened, very much in … Particularly in the Norman conquest onwards, you had a Christian Church, but it was very Gaelicized. And then after the Norman Conquest, they replaced all of the Irish bishops, a more sort of egalitarian clergy, with a lot more hierarchical Roman church. So, they were very keen to eradicate all of these Pagan survivors. And one of the things, of course, was Halloween; they wanted to get rid of *Samhain*, as it was called. *Samhain*, actually, is still a word that you'll find in modern Irish, it's the name for the month of November. So, it has survived.

DTB: Yeah.

LE: But the actual festival, they're trying to stamp all these practices out, all this Festival of the Dead. That's why you have

All Souls Day. All Hallows Day, as well. These two days were brought in, to try and stamp it out. And then, you've also got St. Martin's Day, a little bit after the beginning of November, which has got associated with *Samhain*.

DTB: Yeah. Yeah. *Samhain* and Beltaine are definitely the two most popular, I think, Pagan rituals, of the wheel of the year. And, of course, when you look at the Earth, they are part of an axis that goes through the Earth. So, when it's *Samhain*, for us, it's Beltaine of the southern hemisphere. And when it's *Samhain* for the southern hemisphere, it's Beltaine for us.

DTB: One of the things that I love about *Samhain* is, it's said that the veil between the worlds is thin. I love that kind of part-mythology that is centered around *Samhain*. Where you can utter the name of a friend or relative into the air, and they will hear your words, and they will know that they are remembered, and what is remembered lives. And I love that part about the *Samhain* ritual, that thinning of the veil.

DTB: A couple of years ago, we were in Australia. And we were down there for May, for their *Samhain*. So, I had two *Samhain*s that year, and no Beltaine. I was interested to send out our little spidey senses, to see and feel whether or not that veil is thin there too, in May. And it really is. I mean, we did a *Samhain* ceremony under the stars, the stars were above us. Orion was upside down to me, because we were in the southern hemisphere, but that was the only star constellation I could recognize. The moon was waxing and waning, backwards. It was very alien. But even in that time of May, you could still feel the influence of the Otherworld, in Australia. And that, to me, is one of the great things about *Samhain*.

DTB: I don't know if you've had experiences of *Samhain* that you can share with us, like that? Practical stuff that's happened, with you?

LE: Before I tell you that, you reminded me of something, actually. As you mentioned, about May, *Bealtaine* is one of the three times when the veil is supposed to be very thin. So, as you mentioned, they're right opposite each other. Yeah, *Samhain*, the summer solstice, and also *Bealtaine*, are times when the *Sídhe*, and the faeries, and the ancestors, are more accessible. So, it's no accident, really, you mentioning May; that is a special time, as far as the veil.

LE: This ceremony, or ritual, or a few days, even, it can be, has been historically a day, three days, even, some peoples say, a whole month. It was very much a time for connecting with the ancestors, and either connecting with the *Sídhe*, or trying to avoid them, as is also the case for some people who may have been a bit frightened of them. That's why people wore an iron pin in their lapel, or something, or in their tunic, or whatever they had, to try and keep them away. Because they could be considered, both benign or malevolent, depending on your relationship with them.

LE: One particular thing, for many years I celebrated *Samhain*, and nothing really happened. I might have left a plate of food for ancestors, prayed for ... Tried to communicate with, say, my grandmother, or something like that, and not really got anywhere with things and just been a bit disappointed. One particular year, we did a Druid ritual out in a woodland, in Wexford. And as it happened there was, for some strange reason, just two of us. Because we had quite a decent sized grove, but I think we had 12 or 13 members. And on this particular occasion, there was just two.

LE: So, we went and did our ritual. We'd sat down and started our meditation, and then there was this flood of the souls of the dead that just sort of hit us, washed over us, like hundreds of them. It was almost like getting slapped in the face, really, it was quite shocking. But then, after this had happened, I felt a bit sick actually, from the experience, temporarily. And then we realized we'd actually been sat down in the middle of a crossroads.

DTB: Yeah. Yeah.

LE: And you're just like, "Duh!" That was really, really stupid, to have done that. Because, as you know, yourself, on a spiritual level, it functions the same; it's a place where traffic converges. In a more sinister sense, you probably know about Robert Johnson, the crossroads, the Devil; that they'd taken that idea, and then just have turned it on its head. Where, instead of being a spiritual meeting place, it's a sinister place where you meet the Devil at the crossroads.

DTB: It's a liminal space. It's like the seashore, or somewhere else. There's a liminal space where two areas meet, and that's it, really, isn't it?

LE: Yeah. Well, I don't think there's much point in being terrified of spirits and the dead. But, at the same time, I think they do deserve a certain level of respect; they're not to be trifled with.

LE: Years and years ago, a friend of mine, he knew I was studying to be a Druid, and he says, "Right, let's go down to the graveyard and see if we can raise a dead person or something." I said, "Well, okay, when we get there, and we call up some spirit of a dead person, what are you going to do, when they show up?" He says, "Oh, I don't know." Well, when they say, "Why have you called me here? What do you want me for? What's going on?" And you're, like, "Oh, no reason. I just thought I'd just do it because I felt like. And see what would happen."

LE: And I said, "That's not really a very good reason to do this, is it?" So, "No, we're not doing it." And once I explained it to him, like that, he was like, "Oh, yeah. You're right, actually. That's really stupid and disrespectful."

DTB: Yes, absolutely.

LE: I think, a lot of people, maybe because the modern celebrations have got very blasé about this stuff and think it's just a bit of fun, "Oh, it's a bit of *craic*. Let's go off and do silly stuff." It is, primarily, a festival of the dead. And it's interesting how foreign concepts, like the Mexican Festival of The Dead, have begun to merge. And that's at a similar time of year. But they take it very seriously in places like Mexico; reverence of the ancestors, and paying respects to them. Whereas that's been lost, to some extent, in Europe. Well, in North America, you know, it's all fun and tricks and pumpkins, and it's got very detached from it.

LE: People should have a respect, not just for the fact that their ancestors, they've gone, but also, they have a certain, I suppose, power, in themselves, as spirits. So, you don't want to be messing with them and really annoying them. Do that at your peril, really. And the same applies to the *Sídhe*; otherworldly creatures do have the ability to punish you, if you're going to just mess around with them, in some sort of trivial manner.

DTB: We're very protected from death, these days, I think. When people pass away, they're taken away from us, now. They're dealt with by someone else. I think that *Samhain* is a beautiful opportunity to acknowledge our own mortality as well, and also to reconnect with our loved ones. And they don't have to be human, either. I mean, I always think of my pets, at *Samhain*, as well. I don't think that it's only a place filled with human souls. I just feel that connection too; of all those people that I've loved, and things that I've loved, over the years.

DTB: When we hold our open rituals for *Samhain*, it's the one where I just say, "It's okay to cry." I mean, it's okay to cry at any ceremony. But the likelihood is that if you connect with that feeling, and you visualize your father, mother, sister, brother, or dog, or whatever, cat, and you want to step into the circle and call their name out into the wind, the air, to let them know they're remembered; that can create a deep emotion in people. That is important too, at *Samhain*, is to just not push that down, but just say, "Yes, let it go. Let it out." It's the one time of year it's totally and utterly right to feel those things. And they can feel those things as well, they can feel that emotion. Emotion is energy in motion, isn't it? And so, it goes into the other world and they feel that as well. It truly is a beautiful time of year.

LE: Yeah. I totally agree with you. And I think it's really healthy.

LE: I suppose that kind of distancing from death, maybe that began in the Victorian era. And it's got to the point where people might be buried, a month after they've passed, which is a very bizarre situation. And certainly, from Ireland, for instance, really, you're normally buried in three days, a week, at the maximum. And it's all very compressed. It's very, very intense. You have the removal of the body. It's prepared. It's often brought back to the house. You have people come to the house, paying their respects. And then you have the funeral, and you have the wake. And it's very emotional. There will be laughing and crying.

LE: If this is terribly tragic, like a little baby or something, you won't have the wake the same, with all the music and celebration of a life, because obviously it's so tragic. But in a normal sense of things, it runs the whole gamut of emotions in a very short time; it's very cathartic.

LE: And I think, as you say, *Samhain* is a brilliant time for this catharticism, or dealing with death, dealing with your own mortality. Some of us have unsaid stuff, that we never got to say to the people who've passed, et cetera. Burying all this stuff, as you said, pushing it down, that's really bad for your mental health, bad for your spirit, your soul. And it is, really, the perfect time to address all this kind of thing, I think.

LE: I think, you come out of it, feeling more complete, enriched, happier, more at peace with yourself, if you've made peace with those who've gone before you. And, also, learning to be prepared for your own death, and the fact we're not going to live forever. No matter how much plastic surgery you have, or you want to go and be put in a cryogenic freezer in L.A. or something; that's not the reality of life. We are all going to leave this mortal coil, eventually. If we learn to accept that, maybe the leaving won't be as painful and traumatic, I think.

DTB: That's what I love about the wheel of the year, because, of course, after *Samhain* comes the Winter Solstice, rebirth. We see it in nature, with the cycles, we see it in the Sun and the Moon, with the seasons; that, after death, there is still more. And I love that about the wheel of the year. And I love that about that little bit of *Samhain*, to the Winter Solstice, and then, of course, to *Imbolc*, first; the first stirrings of spring. Those three festivals fill me with hope, to be honest with you. I don't see them as dark. Even though they're the dark part of the year, they are like the gestation part of the year, for new life, and new hope, and everything that comes after it.

DTB: Well, I think we've talking for nearly 45 minutes. I mean, it's flown by.

LE: Yeah. It's been great. I've really enjoyed chatting with you, you know?

DTB: Yeah. No, it's been really lovely, Luke. Thanks for that.

Interview with Ev0ke Publication

First published in Ev0ke Publication, April 2021

ev0ke: How do you define your personal spiritual practice? Does it have a name, or is it more intuitive and eclectic?
Luke Eastwood: I am a Druid, but I also have an interest in other spiritual paths such as Buddhism, Hinduism, Zoroastrianism, and Taoism. I would not describe my practice as eclectic, really, as it is quite specific. I am not a huge fan of syncretism, but I understand its wide appeal. I enjoy looking at other paths and noting the similarities, but I prefer not to make a hodge-podge in what I do. I do yoga and reiki, but not as part of my Druid path. I regard them both as separate additional practices that I find beneficial. I tend to stick within the Irish traditions as that is where I live, where some of my ancestry is from, and it's also the path I know and understand best. Within that, a lot of ritual is intuitive and ad hoc as I don't like following scripts; I prefer a more 'Quaker' like process where one can be inspired by spirit, imbas, awen, or whatever you might call it.

ev0ke: Which Deities, powers, or other spirits are honored in your tradition?
LE: In neo-Druidism that encompasses the Irish gods, British and Gaulish gods, and Arthurian archetypes. I tend to work with the Irish deities mostly as its local and familiar. I have a particular penchant for Brigid, Áine, and Lugh. I am very solar-oriented generally, but I also have worked with 'an Cailleach' as needed, especially during the winter.

Nature itself is very much revered in Druidry/Druidism, whether anthropomorphised or not, which is similar to Taoism in some respects and the Taoist viewpoint is something

I very much enjoy. Holy wells, trees, and sacred sites are still important in modern Druidism, just as they would have been in the original practice, although methods have undoubtedly changed considerably from those of pre-Christian times.

ev0ke: You just released *The Druid Garden: Gardening for a Better Future, Inspired by the Ancients* through Moon Books. First, congratulations! Second, how did this book come about? Why a book about gardening from a Druidic perspective?
LE: I felt there is a gap between thought and action, in Paganism (as is also true elsewhere). Many people who profess to 'love the Earth' don't do a whole lot on a practical level and rather than go around lecturing everyone I thought that a practical book, that anyone could use, would be of greater benefit. It might also serve as a way of introducing spiritual ideas to gardeners who might be inclined that way, but have not made the connections in a concrete way. There is a mixture of folklore, history, spirituality, and practical instruction — primarily I wrote it to be useful and something people could use as a reference guide.

ev0ke: The Druid Garden treats the practical and the sacred, the mundane and the spiritual, as two halves of a whole. Composting is just as important as making offerings to the land. How long did it take you to create your own garden? What was the most difficult, but ultimately rewarding, aspect of the process?
LE: I have had several gardens. As a six-/seven-year-old, my parents gave me a tiny vegetable plot, which was disastrous. I forgot to water the plants during the worst drought in decades! My dad took it back after some time which stung a bit, but I was not keen on the digging, shelling peas, et cetera anyway.

After university I rediscovered gardening at an old Georgian house that I shared — the walled garden was abandoned and I enjoyed fixing it up. Later on, I planted a small grove of trees in Wexford (east coast Ireland) and then a larger one, with many ornamental areas, too, at my next house (also in Wexford). Right now, I have a tiny north facing back garden (in Kerry, west coast Ireland) so I grow most things in containers at the moment in front of the house. I have plans to plant another larger grove of trees and re-wild areas, but that may be a few years away into the future.

Ev0ke: *The Druid Garden* **also includes Land Blessings. Can you give us an example of one of these blessings? And how did you go about writing them?**
LE: The simplest one and most used one I have is a planting blessing, when I re-pot or plant permanently — "May you be blessed by earth and rain and wind and sun, may you grow straight/wide, strong, and true." I say this during or after, to the plant directly, which may seem daft to some, but I believe it has a positive effect. I just make up blessings as feels right. There is no rule about it. Personally, I think it is more effective to write one yourself that has meaning and power for you, than to use someone else's words. Of course, that does not suit everyone, so whatever is going to be helpful and beneficial for the plants and your own inner connection to them and to nature generally is fine.

ev0ke: How much research went into *The Druid Garden***? Long hours online? Long walks in your own garden? Stacks of books?**
LE: It took me three years to get the manuscript finished. The research and regurgitation of factual information was really boring for me and I hated that part of the book, but I just forced myself to do at least one plant a day until it was done. The other sections were a lot easier and fun, as personal experience came into play a lot more. The history section did take a lot of reading

different books and articles and was a good learning process for myself. Much of it was stuff I already knew to some extent, but I did also find out a lot of details that I had previously not known about. I did spend a lot of time thinking either outside or just fiddling around — I tend to write in my head or at least get the bulk of the material together there. When I sit down and I start writing it all comes pouring out at speed, almost as if my hands know what to write already and only minor adjustments happen as I go. I'll usually write a whole section or even a whole chapter in one sitting.

ev0ke: You also co-wrote *Kerry Folk Tales* with Gary Branigan. Which story did you absolutely have to include in the collection, and why?
LE: It's a bit of an odd one: "A Strange Tale of Oliver Cromwell," which the publisher wanted to leave out. It's actually a fantasy told by a child in the 1930's (received from a grandparent) in which Cromwell is killed in Ireland. It's such an oddity that I felt compelled to include it and I also detailed the even more strange true story of what actually happened to Cromwell's remains, which most people would not know about. From an Irish perspective, I think this story is very satisfying as he is probably the most reviled and hated figure in Irish history, and rightly so!

ev0ke: You have also released a solo poetry collection, *Through the Cracks in the Concrete the Wilderness Grows*, and some of your work appears in *Where the Hazel Falls*. What advice might you offer to those who are considering the publication of their own poetry collections? Things they must do? Mistakes to avoid?
LE: Poetry is a difficult one. It does not generally sell that well, apart from the big famous names, and it's a very subjective

thing anyway. It's hard to find a publisher for poetry as it tends to be a low profit venture and something that many people do simply for the love of it. I would recommend that any poet get several objective and honest opinions before committing to self-publishing. Scotsman William McGonagall (late 1800s) published his work through the support of friends and even in his own lifetime was widely acknowledged as terrible, but he kept going regardless of the lampooning and constant ridicule. He is renowned today as 'the worst poet ever,' but he is actually now very popular, simply because his work was so shockingly bad and it's quite hilarious as a result. One would want to avoid gaining a similar reputation, but unfortunately many 'vanity publishers' will tell you that your work is excellent simply to deprive you of large amounts of money for design and printing — beware of these charlatans!

ev0ke: Where can readers find your work?
LE: You can buy all of my books (signed) at my website or from the usual retailers. You can also read most of my articles and some poems for free on my website, too.

ev0ke: What other projects are you working on?
LE: I am working on a children's book with author/illustrator Elena Danaan at the moment. I also keep my hand in with music (such as Children of Dub and Kopyright Assassins) and I do bits of photography when I can. I tend to go in cycles of being really into one particular art form for a while and then switching back to something else. If find that it's really difficult to juggle them all at the same time without doing a poor job of all of it, so I tend to focus on one thing at a time generally!

Interview with Pagan Nation

First published on pagannation.com, April 2022

Q: What interests you about tales from Ireland? Does this relate to your background in Druidry?
A: It's not essential to modern Druidry, however, the bardic arts would be a major component of the Druidic path both in ancient times and in the neo-Druidic movement. Genealogy, wisdom tales, songs, poems and histories would all be part of the cannon in the past, with a massive amount of memorization required. Today the learning by heart is not a requirement, which suits me as that is not one of my strengths.

Nonetheless, the creative arts are vitally important in Druidism and story-telling is significant part of that, especially in Ireland. The *Seanchaí* (bearer of old lore), *Seanchaidh* in Scotland, is a role that still exists in a less formal way within society — with people telling stories in houses, at funerals etc. to this day. In the modern Druid movement, it is a distinct role as a story-teller of lore, the mythology, most commonly told from memory.

I've always loved stories, reading and mythology, I grew up hearing and reading stories of the British Isles, Rome, Gaul, Greece and the Vikings and I accidentally stumbled across Egyptian mythology in a library and loved it immediately. Sadly, I am not the best at remembering all the elements or names in a story, I have to sometimes use a flashcard or Post-it to remind myself! If I can remember where I am and all the key names, I can usually manage a decent tale, but I find they are always slightly different as I will *ad lib* around the main story.

Q: Which are your favourites from your book, and why?

A: I found the *Ryan's Daughter* story a lot of fun, not least of all the scandalous goings-on of Robert Mitchum during the filming around Dingle, some of which was very amusing indeed. I also loved the story *The Leprechaun and The Old Couple*, which is another very funny, although very short story. A more serious one is *Inis Tuaisceart*, about the most northerly Blasket isle, which serves as somewhat of an environmental horror story, a warning if you will, of what happens when people are stupidly greedy and destroy their own means of living.

Q: What do you feel is the importance of storytelling in general, and folk tales in particular?

A: Real physical culture is more important than ever in this age of virtual communication. There's nothing like sitting under the stars by a campfire and sharing stories, poems and songs. It's very direct and real and can often be quite touching, sad or joyful and emotional. It feels to me like we are losing the ancient culture and connection with the past to an armada of technology. Personally, I don't think it's a good road for humanity, although on the flip side it can connect people who are in faraway places or people who are isolated by disability, lack of money etc., so that they can also join in or watch. I guess it's how you use the tech that's the key here and if it can be used to keep traditions and knowledge alive then I guess that's a good thing.

Q: How did you go about collecting and editing the tales for publication?

A: It took me two or three years to collect all that's in this book. I had to stop somewhere as there were so many possibilities, otherwise this book could have ended up 1,000 pages and taken over a decade! I was lucky to meet many people who were either directly involved in some of the more modern stories or who had connections with the places or people in the older stories. I also had access to some old books as well as the *Dúchas* Schools Collection from the 1930s. I tried to get a good mixture of the ancient mythology, stories from the past few hundred years and also modern stuff — such as Fungie the dolphin.

Q: What advice would you give to people who wanted to explore the folk tales of their own area?

A: I guess the most obvious places to start are seeking out old people and visiting your local library. Often librarians will prove to be useful (they were for me) and many older people may either remember interesting stories or know an older person who has an interest in history and/or mythology. A lot can also be gleaned from mythology books if you don't have anyone to physically ask for stories.

Q: Are you working on any more anthologies or other writing?

A: I'm working on an illustrated children's book (with Elena Danaan) and also a photographic book on sacred sites in Ireland. That's also a collaboration with a photographer, which will hopefully result in a large format book, with some historical lore/info to accompany the images. These are both long finger (put-off) projects that I'd like to complete this or next year, but I am trying to avoid starting anything completely new for a while.

Q: Is there anything else you would like to say?

A: Recently I've come across quite a few artistic people who are now doing okay or very well despite a slew of rejections and disheartening events in the past. Being artistic is not easy and you really need to have confidence in your abilities if you're ever going to succeed. Of course, you need to be realistic about your potential but, at the same time, not be deterred by all the nay-sayers. At the end of the day, most of these people who judge you harshly or hold power over you have money and profit as their primary motivation and are often the least qualified to judge authenticity, passion and talent. If you can remember that and not let the industrial/corporate paymasters undermine and dishearten you, then you have some chance. Even if you do fail, artistic endeavours are worth doing for their own sake anyway!

You may also like

Foreword by Philip Carr-Gomm
Chief of the Order of Bards, Ovates & Druids

THE DRUID'S PRIMER

LUKE EASTWOOD

The Druid's Primer
by Luke Eastwood

*A comprehensive guide to genuine druidic knowledge and practice
based on ancient texts and surviving Celtic lore and customs*

978-1-84694-764-3 (Paperback)
978-1-84694-765-0 (e-book)

MOON BOOKS
PAGANISM & SHAMANISM

What is Paganism? A religion, a spirituality, an alternative belief system, nature worship? You can fi nd support for all these definitions (and many more) in dictionaries, encyclopaedias, and text books of religion, but subscribe to any one and the truth will evade you. Above all Paganism is a creative pursuit, an encounter with reality, an exploration of meaning and an expression of the soul. Druids, Heathens, Wiccans and others, all contribute their insights and literary riches to the Pagan tradition. Moon Books invites you to begin or to deepen your own encounter, right here, right now.

If you have enjoyed this book, why not tell other readers by posting a review on your preferred book site.

Readers of ebooks can buy or view any of these bestsellers by clicking on the live link in the title. Most titles are published in paperback and as an ebook. Paperbacks are available in traditional bookshops. Both print and ebook formats are available online.

Find more titles and sign up to our readers' newsletter
http://www.johnhuntpublishing.com/paganism

For video content, author interviews and more, please subscribe to our YouTube channel.

MoonBooksPublishing

Follow us on social media for book news, promotions and more:

Facebook: Moon Books Publishing

Instagram: @moonbooksjhp

Twitter: @MoonBooksJHP

Tik Tok: @moonbooksjhp